THE RAINY SEASON

THE
RAINY SEASON

Three Lives in the New South Africa

MAGGIE MESSITT

University of Iowa Press, Iowa City

University of Iowa Press, Iowa City 52242
Copyright © 2015 by the University of Iowa Press
www.uiowapress.org
Printed in the United States of America

Design by Ashley Muehlbauer

The University of Iowa Press is a member of Green Press Initiative
and is committed to preserving natural resources.

Printed on acid-free paper

Library of Congress Cataloging-in-Publication Data
Messitt, Maggie, author.
The rainy season : three lives in the new South Africa / Maggie Messitt.
pages cm
ISBN 978-1-60938-327-5 (pbk : alk. paper), ISBN 978-1-60938-332-9 (ebk)
1. South Africa—Social conditions—21st century.   2. South Africa—Economic
conditions—21st century.   3. Post-apartheid era—Social aspects—South
Africa.   4. Post-apartheid era—Economic aspects—South Africa.   I. Title.
HN801.A8M47 2015   306.0968—dc23   2014034885

For Mom and Dad,
and the women of Amazwi.

CONTENTS

PROLOGUE

My first memory of this place is on a Saturday morning. It was springtime, October 2003, and although the rainy season had started, it was hot and sunny that day. I can picture the taxi rank below the fig tree at the T-junction of the R40 and the main road into Acornhoek's shopping strip (deemed "main town"). Men were piling out of or waiting inside the dozen or so minibus taxis, luggage had been tied to the rooftops, and women were waiting, wearing their best, often with children in tow. Men were returning home from work in the north, south, and west for their monthly weekend visit.

I was twenty-four years old, and it was the first time I'd driven into Acornhoek, South Africa—a village just over the imaginary line that once legally separated white and black, a place about which I was more interested than the historically white community of Hoedspruit where I had just claimed a tent as my home. I saw a world unlike anything I had ever experienced, unlike the urban townships and informal settlements that graced postcards and most foreign tourist itineraries, unlike any community where I'd lived or reported before. This was post-apartheid, rural South Africa.

I was in the passenger seat of a car with my window down, taking in the month-end bustle, paychecks being spent, children being treated, and long lines outside the fishery. It was a place where an outdoor butchery occupied an old petrol station and a funeral parlor was situated in the attached garage. A village where an AIDS education center sat across the street from a West African doctor selling cures for the pandemic that is predicted to kill nearly 40 percent of the local youth population in the next decade. It's where BMWs parked outside of crumbling cement homes and the availability of water changed with the day of the week. Flyers screaming "Jesus Saves and Heals!" wallpapered cell phone towers, and a sign to the province's largest hospital had been hand-painted on corrugated tin. And one day, it's where I would have a newsroom tucked between the chicken shack and the railroad tracks, a gathering place for story.

I had been in South Africa for only a few months. No more than three. And I was green. A journalist. A teacher. A creative writing grad-school dropout. A young American woman (girl, really) with an eighteen-month visa, enough money to survive six months without a paycheck, and a newly purchased third-hand car. And, most importantly, I was keenly aware of the regressions that came with my move from the Northern Hemisphere to the Southern Hemisphere, from urban to deeply rural, from first world to a third-first hybrid, from an independent explorer, researcher, and writer to an outsider who knew nothing. Language. Resources. Politics. Culture. Community structure. To the smallest knowledge we need to complete daily tasks. In many ways, it felt like starting over.

What I did know, however, was where and how I wanted to start, where I wanted to invest myself. And the beautifully complicated village of Acornhoek was it.

I moved to South Africa with a one-way ticket in 2003, less than a decade after the end of apartheid and South Africa's first democratic election. The next one-way ticket wouldn't come for eight years.

During that time, I did a lot of porch sitting. I did a lot of hanging around and tagging along. I listened. I read. I researched. I interviewed. I learned how to work within the system as a resident and a journalist. Enough so, I was awarded a grant by South Africa's Media Development and Diversity Agency to develop curriculum for rural media education, specifically to train female print journalists to cover rural issues, culture, and communities. Eventually, that curriculum and grants from the Lonely Planet Foundation and the International Academy of Film and Television allowed me to open a school and newspaper.

By mid-2005, I was reporting for South African and North American publications, telling the stories of rural communities and human rights issues. I was embedded—as much as any white person could be—in a community that was once politically dictated as the Shangaan and Sotho homelands.

Between my first introduction to Acornhoek and typing the first few chapters of this book, I had prepared myself, and the community (as best one can), for me to invest in this way. I was no longer of immediate interest to most people I encountered. I was the newspaper editor and was always around. Easily identifiable, a white speck in a black sea, I was as close to old news as I was ever going to get inside a historically black African village and its surrounding communities. I'd reached the point where I knew people would generally ignore me when I was simply walking down the street with community members that grace the following pages. I knew that their relatives and neighbors weren't likely to shift their actions or dialogue because a *malungu* was in the room, and I knew they understood what it meant to write stories and have their community's stories on the locally printed page. In short, I knew that I had what I needed: a strong social, cultural, and historical foundation; the reputation required to gain (almost) unfettered access; and the confidence that my presence would have little effect on the story I set out to document.

In the community of Rooiboklaagte (locally referred to as Rooibok), one of nearly a dozen that make up the larger village of Acornhoek, three residents agreed to let me tell their stories: Thoko Makwakwa, a middle-aged *sangoma* (traditional healer) and *shebeen* queen (owner of a backdoor illegal pub); Dankie Mathebula, one of "Mandela's children," educated entirely under democratic governance; and Regina Hlabane, an elderly tapestry weaver in her sixties and devout Catholic.

For the next year, 2005 to 2006, as the land went from dusty winter blond to lush summer green and back again, I spent the large majority of my waking hours inside their small Sotho, Shangaan, and Mozambican Tsonga community of, at the time, no more than two hundred families. Rooiboklaagte is one of the older communities in the village, split by the Nwandlamare River into two parts, A and B. It is unique in its blend of tribal cultures but average in its challenges and lifestyle. I spent my evenings in shebeens and over fires cooking dinner; my weekends in church services, funerals, and cultural ceremonies. I spent my days fetching water, attending school, standing in government grant lines, and working beside Thoko's, Regina's, and Dankie's friends and family members. While I eventually chose to frame their stories within a single rainy season, my research and reporting spans more than six years.

What you will find in the following pages is the story of a community, a time in history, and three interconnected lives.

NOTE ON LANGUAGE

Reporting and fieldwork in South Africa, specifically within rural villages and communities, poses the greatest language challenges that I've ever come across. In the village of Acornhoek and the community of Rooiboklaagte, conversations could include English, Afrikaans, Shangaan, Northern Sotho, and Pedi. More often than not, conversations are a mosaic of languages, borrowing words from this language and that language, often feeling like a new language altogether. In order to stay true to the language shifts that go on in conversation and to maintain complete transparency, I have noted any dialogue translations in italics.

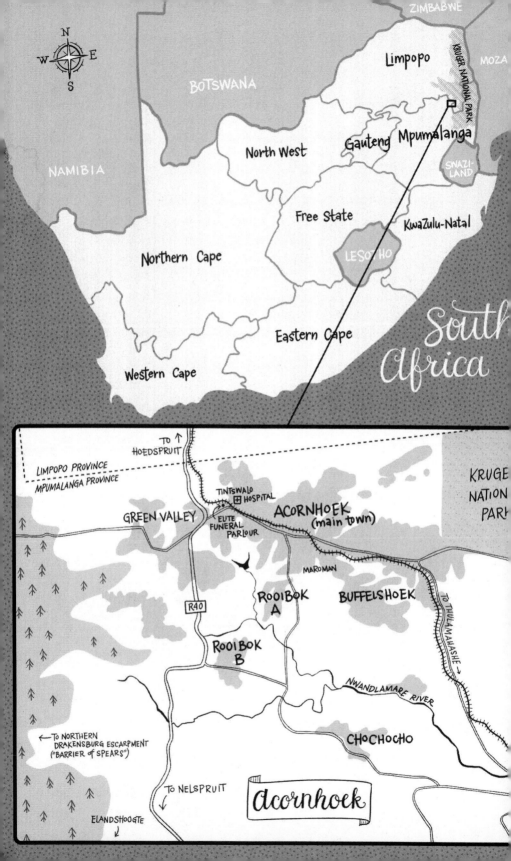

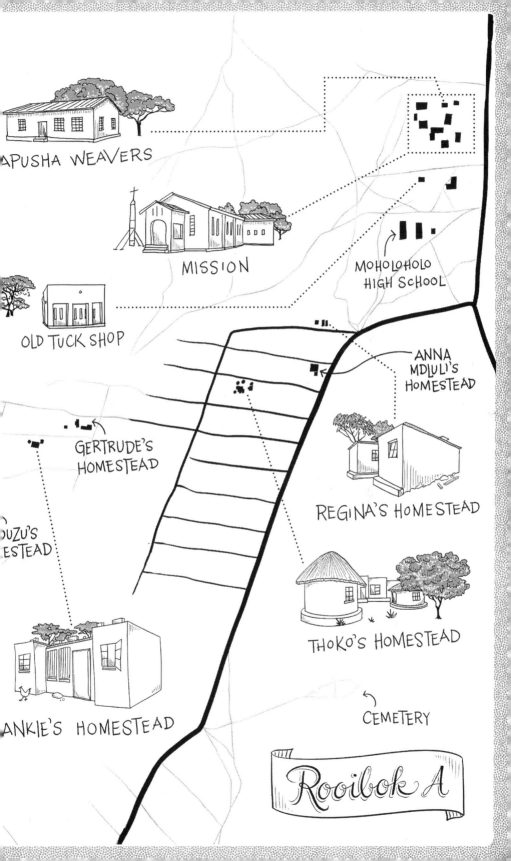

||||||||||||||||||||||||||||||||||||

SPRING

||||||||||||||||||||||||||||||||||||

THOKO

Thoko Makwakwa was always open for business.

Balancing beside her open back door, the totem of two speakers and red Coca-Cola crates throbbed Kwaito music, a South African fusion of hip-hop, house music, and jazz. Had you passed through this crooked door two years earlier, you would have found Thoko's pots and pans, her chipped mugs and mismatched silverware, her kitchen table and chairs, her tabletop baker and hot plates, her electric oven and stove top, bins of maize meal and baggies of dried mopani worms, and possibly a few barrels of water. But the kitchen had been moved to a small sitting room, and inside now stood a warped snooker table and a bright-red jukebox. Thoko—a forty-two-year-old, long-limbed, rawboned woman with two missing front teeth—had converted her kitchen into a shebeen, a backdoor, off-the-books pub.

Men sat on the stoop of Thoko's nine-room house with bottles of Black Label, "America's Lusty Lively Beer," and yellow plastic buckets of traditional brew. Young boys and their older brothers or fathers, who only appear at the end of each month, were playing snooker in the shebeen while music rumbled and the tin roof rattled. Single-rand coins were slipped into the jukebox, barred and bolted against the crumbling, handmade wall, and voices of Zulu, Sotho, English, and Xhosa jumped from the speakers. Music swirled around customers, riding on the backs of springtime winds, down the hill toward the river's reed-filled edge, or up toward the cemetery that borders the open bush.

Men just off the bus or taxi from the north, south, and west—where they work in the trees, city, factory, or fields—fed one-rand coins into the billiard table and five-rand coins into the hands of Thoko's children for a bucket of xikhapaka (traditional beer). The older men—retired, on medical disability, or simply out of work—sat with it in their hands, cheaper than the bottles of beer and a preferred taste for the more traditional tongue, not to mention more effective in making the world spin.

Buckets with the grainy residue of xikhapaka, consumed over time or in long purposeful gulps, lay on the ground and in stacks. The crack of a snooker break or the start of a new song rang like a till through the bodies and buildings in Thoko's yard. As the sun went down and the moon crawled into the endless sky, customers multiplied. The sweet smell of sweat, pouring down gyrating bodies, was the fragrance of Thoko making money.

It was payday.

Thoko's homestead was a collection of four plots, rented from the local tribal authority. A chain-link fence lined its perimeter, supported by a collection of mismatched, waist-high iron poles, and tree branches collected from the surrounding bush. A large, rectangular, Western-style cement house, two cement rondavels, and three mud-packed single rooms had been built on two plots, while the other two dust- and weed-filled plots sat empty.

At month-end, there are two kinds of pockets. Some are quiet, filled with crisp bills of blue buffalo, pink lions, brown elephant, green rhino, and maybe even a few leopards. Others are filled with noisy proteas and lilies, springbok and kudu, and hopefully a few black wildebeest in the herd. The men who have returned for their few days of month-end holiday arrive with cash-filled envelopes or crisp bills, just pulled from the mouth of an ATM. Their pockets are mute, at least before they enter Thoko's gates. Those who cross the threshold already jingling have generally been around all month, looking forward to the sight of more men, the arrival of friends, fathers, sons, and brothers. The noisy ones count five cents, ten cents, proteas and lilies, until there is enough to fill a garden, enough to exchange for a single springbok to play a song. Those who put their hands in their pockets to prevent the click and clank of their savings pull a collection of sweaty antelope for a bucket to drink around the corner—out of sight. Once empty, it's quickly replaced with a bottle of Black Label to hold while the traditional buzz crawls through their bodies.

Two single-room thatched buildings sit just inside Thoko's gates. The one on the right is for her mother's ancestors. The one to the left is for her father's ancestors. The second is Thoko's ndumba, where she consults with clients. While many men and the occasional woman play games, drink, sing, dance—inside and around the shebeen—Thoko sits inside her ndumba as a sangoma, connecting with her ancestors, answering questions about health, wealth, fidelity, foes.

During the first weekend after payday, Thoko's businesses were equally busy. Lines would form outside her ndumba with people sitting around the tree and on the ledge of the opposite rondavel. Bodies would fill her old kitchen, and the ledge around her Western-style house resembled the Saturday-night quarters of an urban shebeen queen.

During the last week of September, when the early winter chills had passed and spring gusts were dancing like children in the street, Thoko sat in her ndumba with a worried mother and deteriorating daughter. The three women sat on traditionally woven grass mats laid across the cement floor: two on the left, overlapping like the letter V, skewed by the curve of the wall. A third *sangu* crossed the center of the room, parallel with three white sheets strung on a laundry line and fastened with plastic clothespins, partitioning the far third of the room from view.

An emaciated young woman, Lindiwe, sat against the wall beside her mother and opposite Thoko, who knelt on her knees in the center of the room, preparing to connect with her father's ancestors. She pulled on her red, blue, and white beaded necklace and bracelets as a Western physician dresses in a lab coat and hangs a stethoscope around her neck. It was symbolic of credentials, symbolic of status and profession. And with the final fasten of her bracelet's lanyard-like loop, she pulled the far edge of her sangu toward her, revealing the floor beneath. As she reached for an arm-length spear from the edge of the white curtain, Lindiwe's mother placed her one-hundred-rand payment on the cold cement floor.

Thoko used the wooden handle of her spear to cover, but not touch, the crinkled note. She flipped the edge of the sangu to hide the staring blue buffalo, placed there by the apprehensive mother, cognizant of the ancestor's power, edgy for what could be. The glittery golden ink on the bill's lower-right corner popping the numbers one-zero-zero sat at the edge of the blue buffalo's chin and opposite the signature of South African Governor Mboweni, an amount the mother had collected over weeks and topped off by month-end payday. About fourteen dollars, or one hundred rand—roughly one-half of a monthly child grant, forty loaves of bread, fourteen liters of cool drink, just over half the initial cost of a tribal housing plot, or one student's annual school fees— one hundred rand to answer the questions that plagued her daughter. One hundred rand to reveal the reasons for her daughter's paralysis and pain, to offer what she saw as a propitious treatment for her child's deterioration.

Inside her ndumba, Thoko pulled a small burlap bag from behind the curtain, revealing, for just a moment, hundreds of bottles. After opening its top and rolling down its sides, Thoko held the bag with both hands like an offering. She reached beneath the neckline of her shirt, skimming the beaded necklace and its two acorn-shaped pendants, digging around the confines of her bra's right cup. She pulled out a plastic, disk-shaped container with a yellow cap. Removing the top, she pinched three fingers like a claw, extracted dark brown snuff, and dusted the contents of her bag. Lowering her head and arching her body toward the left, Thoko lifted a dash of snuff to each nostril and sniffed. *Kudzaha*. Sniff. *Kudzaha*. Sniff.

Thoko's *muthi* ingredients were hidden behind the stained white curtain. Her collection had grown from 170 (when she first trained in 1997) to 240 bottles, jars, tins, paper bags, and sheets of newspaper filled with shaven, diced, sliced, grated, ground, and whole portions of flora and fauna from in and around the region. Years of dust covered the caps, and dirt caked each crevice—from beer and whisky bottles to hair cream canisters and shoe polish tins, baby food and jam jars, pharmacy vials and vitamin bottles. A cross between a pharmaceutical cabinet and a hoarder's treasure hid behind the curtain—half a dozen matchboxes; nearly a dozen dung beetle balls; three spears, only one of which had a metal tip; porcupine quills; crumpled pieces of paper; several brown paper bags rolled closed; a stack of plate-sized cardboard squares; used razors; a few roots in whole form; two pieces of wood.

Speaking softly, with a voice deeper and raspier than outside of her ndumba, Thoko lifted the bag and tilted it to the right, shaking in a circular motion, filling the grass mat before her with the contents of the bag: dominoes and currency; bones from the lion, elephant, zebra, bush pig, steenbok, and baboon; one small water level; marula and futsu seeds; an odd collection of shells including one large blotched cowrie; and several other objects with origins in the bush. As the last item hit the mat, she dropped the empty bag and picked up the plastic canister of snuff once more. With her right pointer finger, Thoko lifted a dash of snuff up to each nostril and sniffed, just as she had done minutes before. *Kudzaha*. Sniff. *Kudzaha*. Sniff.

With this second inhalation, Thoko's voice began to dig deeper and deeper, raspier and raspier, chanting in question, seeking the ancestors for help. Repeating two words over and over again, connected by the tap of her wooden spear on the cement floor.

xa vuma,
    tap,

        xa vuma,
           tap,

                xa vuma,
                    tap . . .

Matching the rhythm with her body motion, Thoko rocked forward and back, forward and back, forward and back.

xa vuma,

tap,

xa vuma,

tap,

xa vuma,

tap.

With each lean backward, she sought the ancestors to join her in identifying why this girl had come, why she was sitting before her, and what problems she had for her to solve. "Xa vuma," she repeated, "xa vuma." *Speak,* she encouraged the ancestors, *speak.*

Thoko began to tell Lindiwe that she was sick. The wooden spear moved forward pointing out objects on the mat that identified her symptoms.

"Milenge ya wena," she said, pointing to an object on her sangu. *Your legs.*

"Voko ya wena," she said, pointing toward another. *Your arms.*

Pain in your arms and legs, she elaborated, never looking up, always pointing toward or inspecting the objects strewn across the grass mat.

Silence filled the stale, confined air of the ndumba as she looked for something within the objects spread across its center.

Thoko began to sweep the *bones* from the grass mat into a mound before her, leaning across the sangu, reaching as far as her arms would take her. From these objects she pulled a blotched cowrie shell the size of her fist and began to encircle the mound like the moon orbits the earth . . . one, two, three. Its open base never left the mat while she drew the revolving pattern, not until the third circle was complete, after which she placed the shell on the mound of bones and picked them up in the scoop of her hands, just barely large enough to hold the collection.

She began to move her hands upward and then let them drop to hit the mat, causing the rattle of each object—a motion she repeated three times before the final lift and release of the bones: across the mat, off the sides, onto the floor.

And there it was.

The ancestors were revealing the truth. The large cowrie shell had flipped. Sitting on the ground amongst a constellation of bones paranormally arranged was the white underbelly of the cowrie shell and its jagged-toothed opening. The young woman was ill because the ancestors were calling her to fulfill her predestined mission in life; they were calling her to train. She had been chosen to become a sangoma.

DANKIE

As the storm moved over the mountains and toward the western side of Rooiboklaagte—more commonly known as Rooibok—the corrugated tin roof covering Dankie Mathebula's house vibrated like a stack of dishes in an earthquake. The wind repeatedly lifted the ridged roof away from its wooden beams, away from the cement block walls, and upward, until the sheets unanimously slammed into the heads of the iron nails holding them all together. As quickly as they went up, they returned back down, again. Eighteen sheets bounced together, filling the five-room house with wind and noise.

Storms in the lowveld come from three directions: over the rocky escarpment to the west; from Mozambique, over the bushveld of Kruger National Park in the east; and from the south, pushing their way up the lowveld highway. Rooibok, one of many communities that make up the larger village of Acornhoek, sits in a pocket where a triangle of storms often collides. When the pressure systems line up just right, maize reaches for the sky, the arms of acacia trees trace the horizon, marula trees produce copious amounts of fruit, and cattle grow fat and in numbers. When rain comes early and steady, the lowveld's color palette seems to change as quickly as a tree frog's skin. But, more often than not, the storms come together and dance, a fusion of the romantic tango and an ongoing feud for dominance and power.

Dankie stood from his chair in the center of the household and opened a wooden door with chipped blue paint. An extension cord—running across the ceiling, over the gum pole beams, and through a hole in the wall—ended with a naked, burnt bulb, dangling from his bedroom ceiling. Dankie climbed over his peach, duvet-covered bed; ignored the drops of rain running through the roof's nail holes, widened by the force of the wind; and reached for a pair of plastic-coated earmuffs hanging on a sheet of fencing nailed above his bed like a headboard.

Dankie's brother, Jack, gave the pair of industrial ear protectors to his baby brother, just after leaving home to work as a security guard, just after Dankie was left to fend for himself while keeping up his high school studies. Jack would bring things home for Dankie as often as he could, and Dankie, with only one brother and a father that left before he was born, cherished every item: a faux-leather briefcase, a collection of used magazines, two sample upholstery cubes, a television through which people can be heard but never seen, and a radio that had lost its voice. The earmuffs, however, were most important.

The storm started to gain courage. The tin roof's acoustics amplified its speed and strength, until it sounded as if the ancestors were throwing baobab seeds from the skies or God was throwing down buckets to bring new life to dull winter foliage. As the pounding of rain grew, the water increasingly seeped through the roof. Dankie ignored the drips and pulled the tight pair of protectors over his ears. They were something you might find a construction foreman wearing to lessen the sounds of drills and blasts, or possibly something a hunter or policeman would wear at a firing range. For Dankie, though, they helped him focus. They deadened the sound of the rain and allowed him to concentrate on his studies. But, secretly, they were more than that. Late at night, when the big storms hit, he would pull them over his ears to keep the sound of thunder from getting inside his head, to protect him from the rolling rumbles that sent shivers of fear through his twenty-one-year-old body.

He took a seat at the round, laminate kitchen table, each night, under the beams of a naked light bulb. While the chickens and goats and people slept, he sat in the center room of the house and pored over his schoolwork. It was quiet, and there was no one to bother him, no music to distract him, no chores to be done. The water couldn't be fetched until first light; his sisters' children were dreaming, so they didn't need to be fed, or bathed, or watched; and his mother, if she wasn't asleep, was at least in her room with the door closed and the light switched off.

That night, Dankie was studying for the year's first exam, the first of eight matriculation exams that would determine whether he graduated or repeated the twelfth grade. Furthermore, if he graduated, they would determine if he passed with average scores or passed with exemption and the possibility of university bursaries. Economics and Business Accounting were his best classes, although languages like English, Afrikaans, and his mother tongue of Xitsonga came to him with greater ease than Mathematics and Biology. Dankie's first exam was Afrikaans.

During apartheid and for a few years into the new democracy, Afrikaans was a required course, but in the late 1990s, it was removed from the required list and offered as one of many second-language choices. Despite the end to a national fight against Afrikaans as the instructing medium, residents of Dankie's community, Rooiboklaagte, and parents of his schoolmates insisted that Moholoholo High School require Afrikaans, again. Fearful that their children would be unable to find and keep jobs without knowing the first language of most farm and business owners in the region, they insisted that the Dutch, German, and French colonial amalgamation be required once again.

Dankie sifted through his notebook and several answer keys from tests taken throughout the year. He was a hardworking student, not the best or the most intelligent, but certainly a strong-willed and dedicated learner. School was a priority over everything else in his life, and he dreamed of the places school would take him, the people school would allow him to meet, and the life doing well in school would allow him to have.

REGINA

In the northeastern corner of Rooibok, Regina Hlabane watched three generations through the warp wall of her upright loom. Grandmothers, sisters, mothers, and daughters were in the mission that morning, a union of past and present, challenges and hope. A second-generation weaver rushed back and forth between the storage room inside the cooperative's studio, and the trunk of a champagne-colored, decade-old BMW outside. She carried rugs and tapestries, bags and tablecloths, products of wool and cotton. Regina's granddaughter, who was waiting for her mother to arrive, ran along like the young weaver's shadow, watching each pile of reds, oranges, greens, blues, browns, and purples. The colors of the sun as it sets over the rocky escarpment and the undulating hills of the lowveld on a misty morning—all crammed together in the trunk of a car.

As the BMW was filled to the brim, Regina sat at her loom weaving. She was plaiting a tapestry that resembled the landscape around her, the gradual impala flats of the lowveld. Her hands worked together pushing and pulling bundles of wool in and out, and her feet followed suit, pulling the warp open and closed with the teeter of her right foot on the floor pedal. Not wanting to miss a moment of weaving, she watched the girls prepare the car for departure.

Earlier that morning, several homesteads northeast of Dankie and a block or so from Thoko, Regina stood over an open fire in her small outdoor kitchen made of gum poles and a sheet metal roof. She was preparing dinner as the sun started to rise over the dry bushveld and Rooibok's cemetery hill in the east. Just edging into her sixties, Regina had curves like the Lebombo Mountains and tight-spiraled hair, usually hidden by a scarf or beret.

Despite the orange horizon line, as bright as the daisies of Namaqualand, it was still dark outside, and Regina was navigating her homestead by memory and habit and the light of a small fire fueled by twigs and trash. She'd boiled water in an electric kettle before pouring it in a *poto* and placing the cast-iron pot over flames. Every morning, Regina prepared her breakfast, lunch, and dinner before the chickens emerged from their roost and the goats wandered her dusty yard. It was her quiet time. It was when she could think about the day, prepare for what was to come, and ponder the worries she kept hidden behind her heart and away from anyone who asked.

She was preparing *pap*, a stiff white maize meal porridge, and *marojo*, a thick sauce made of pumpkin leaves, tomato, ground peanuts, and vegetable oil. Pap—the staple in most families for most meals—has dozens of renditions, but Regina was partial to *crimmel pap* (typically Afrikaans) and *vuswa* (stiff and sliceable, easily stored and better for scooping). Regina arched over the steam of the boiling water and the heat of the fire. She poured cups of finely ground mealie meal (white corn meal) into the water and stirred, scraping the sides of the pot with force. Over and over again, pulling and thickening the porridge until it was too difficult to pull with her *nkombe*, a long wooden handle with two crescent-shaped metal wires.

As Emerencia was noisily packing for her trip, Regina was mentally counting her savings (hidden inside the house and often in her bra) and numbering her worries. Other than her daughter's rustling, the air was silent. She couldn't hear any movement in the distance, particularly from Anna Mdluli's house across the way. Anna hadn't left her house in days, possibly weeks. Her already frail frame was thinning, and her energy was nearly nonexistent. She lived one street over and two homesteads to the south, on the same street and block as the noisy shebeen where husbands and sons go to drink their salaries away. She was as close as a sister might be, but Regina and the others weren't talking about her ailing health.

"Tama," called a figure from outside the gate. Regina recognized the voice as Lizbeth, a young weaver.

Emerencia's reply could hardly be heard, muffled by the cement walls of their three-room house. "Ahee," she replied, in chorus with her mother.

"Ahee," called Regina, symbolically opening her homestead door for the young woman to enter. She hadn't looked up from her pap or slowed her stir. Nor did she pay much attention to Lizbeth, who was arriving to help Regina's youngest daughter. Her thoughts were still floating above Anna's house. Emerencia was packing for a trip to Magoebaskloof, a densely forested valley a few hours northwest, where the tea plantations run like patchwork across rippling hills and valleys. Regina had known Lizbeth well, had watched her grow up and helped raise her in Mapusha's studio. Like many of the elder weavers to the young, Regina was her mother, not by blood, but by yarn and rosary.

Emerencia wasn't more than a twinkle in her mother's eye the day Regina and several other women in the Catholic parish started Mapusha, a weaving cooperative. Now, more than thirty years later, she was preparing to travel to the Magoebaskloof Spring Festival in hopes to sell and market the hand woven products that the twelve women of Mapusha, two generations, make inside their humble grey studio, each day. The spring festival is held each year to honor new life, to honor the cherry and azalea blossoms, to honor crafters in the region. And this was the first time Mapusha would attend.

Lizbeth, one of Mapusha's second-generation members, is the youngest sister of Lindy Molemi, the first trained weaver of Mapusha from 1973. She was neatly dressed and perfectly pressed in wide, white cargo pants and a rosary hanging around her neck. Her chocolate brown hair with fine threads of silver had just been released from a night of sleeping in curlers. Arguably Mapusha's most promising young weaver, Lizbeth was joining Emerencia on the trip so that she could sit and weave on an upright loom, surrounded by their work and potential customers.

She'd brought her friend a thin plastic-fabric tote—the kind that are piled on top of long-distance taxis to form mountains, tied down by rope. Emerencia and her daughter Simphiwe were already outside filling a wheelbarrow with several plastic bags filled with groceries for the next three days and her Shangaan bag—stuffed too full to close its zipper. Lizbeth had a small duffel and plastic bag of solidly filled Tupperware; they were sitting at the mission. As quickly as she arrived, Lizbeth started her return to Mapusha's studio: out Regina's homestead, down the dirt road past Anna Mbetse's house, and along the northern path into the mission pushing Emerencia's wheelbarrow the whole way.

Simphiwe, who should have been at school by this time of the morning, was skipping at Lizbeth's heels, holding a plastic grocery bag in her left hand. Alternating between skips, high-kicks and knee-highs, Simphiwe could barely keep her pink flip-flops between the two toes that held them in place. After she recently insisted on cutting her dreadlocks, only to be filled with tears when she saw the result, her pink and grey hoodie offset her little boy's haircut.

Behind Simphiwe, Anna Mbetse—a senior weaver—joined them along the road, carrying a twenty-liter bucket of water in either hand. The three of them walked in a line like schoolchildren toward the entrance of the mission and into the studio.

By the time they arrived, their single-file line had spread its gaps due to age, energy, and cargo-load. Gertrude, Regina's cousin by marriage and her best friend, had already arrived. She was sitting on her sangu in the only shady patch of the chapel's stoop, hand-rolling several bundles of recently dyed wool.

"Cock a doodle doooo . . . ," cried a rooster that was pecking near the locked entrance into the compound of buildings that originally housed more than twenty priests and brothers. The compound had been fenced within the already fenced mission grounds. Its two-meter-tall chain-link and steel-pole perimeter was extended in height by the circular barbed wire, spinning its way around and around. The interior fence line closed off two-thirds of the mission from the public, leaving the northern third free to pass through. Its entryway remains bolted throughout each day.

The sounds of a garrulous springtime filled the grounds with birds in the trees, on top of the church steeple, and near the mission's closed-in gardens.

"Cock a doodle dooooooo . . ."

The sun was already strong enough to start burning skin, despite the hour. These are the days, or the start of them after a few long winter months, that many walk the roads of Acornhoek with open umbrellas, shielding them from the harsh rays beating down.

At the time of Mapusha's inception, the gates of the mission were not locked, and the gardens were open to the community. The women of Mapusha began inside the gates. In a small building within the walls of the mission, the four original members and several additions gathered each day to weave handbags. Unemployed, Regina joined the project early on. She'd previously taught at the mission school and was the secretary of a lay religious group called the Women of Saint Anne.

Like most rural women, Regina struggled to feed her family and could rely little on the money being earned in the city by her husband, Winfred. The women of Mapusha were left to fend for themselves and support their children: Gertrude Mbetse, whose husband was living and working in a sugar mill to the south; Anna Mdluli, whose husband owned taxis and worked at a mine to the north; Anna Mbetse, who was widowed only a few years after marriage; and Anna Ndzukula, whose husband cut trees in the south.

With heightened interest in Mapusha, the missionaries gathered materials and local unemployed women to build a studio and storeroom across from the chapel to house the cooperative. And there they have remained.

Quickly the project grew, and a German volunteer donated new looms and trained the women in various methods of weaving. Mapusha's products expanded from woven wool handbags to curtains, tablecloths, blankets, tapestries, and rugs. For a short time in the eighties, they also wove small tapestries depicting scenes of African women working the fields, collecting firewood, balancing jugs and bundles of wood atop their heads, and carrying children on their backs. The tapestries sold successfully at first, but their popularity soon dropped off.

Regina focused on tapestries, although she was no longer weaving depictions of African life. She evolved into a master weaver, plaiting magical patterns on her loom. For a long time, she was one of at least twenty-eight weavers, spinners, and dyers earning a living for her family and supporting herself through her own hard work. But one day, as fast as the weather turns, that all changed.

The women were told that the mission was no longer planning to work with them and that they were on their own. And for the next twelve years, they were. The interior gates were locked. They were outside. Twenty-eight turned into six, and income turned into nothing. Regina arrived each morning with her rosary across her heart to sit at the tapestry loom, weaving small masterpieces inspired by the world around her and the colorful designs she created in her mind. Her visions are painted before her from rolls of wool and a pair of skillful hands. Perched high on her bench, Regina was guarded throughout her days. To the left, she taped a prayer card to her loom with an illustration of Jesus and his crown of thorns, his sacred heart. To the right, she secured a photograph of Simphiwe.

Each day, Regina sat in this seat. She sat there when her husband told her he wanted a divorce and while he told her to leave his home. She sat there after building her two-room home from packed mud, secondhand doors, and secondhand window frames. She sat there brooding the breakdown of her eldest son, hospitalized for a mental collapse. And she continued to sit there, every day, in an effort to support the family her husband abandoned and she held strong.

But there was never a guarantee that her presence and her production would provide for her family. The women had never personally sold their work, only designed and produced it. They had wholly relied on the missionaries for marketing and sales. They had no phones. They had no cars. They had no money to hire someone to sell for them. All they could do was gather their things, hitch a ride, and find the closest tar road to sit on. And *thandaza*, to pray.

That was until an American woman in her forties arrived on their doorstep in 2001. Her name was Judy Miller. She had been in and out of South Africa on missionary trips and had recently completed chemotherapy for breast cancer. Judy was looking for them as much as they were looking for her. She had learned about Mapusha after seeing a tapestry of theirs sitting in a Hoedspruit consignment shop, just to the north of Acornhoek. A white juice shop owner, who frequently passed the women on the side of the road, had placed it there. Judy had academic experience as a textile designer but made a living as a yoga instructor and counselor. Excited to sit side by side with the women each day weaving, she committed herself to helping market the women's work and increase their numbers.

Because of Judy and the donors she rounded up, each of the six women remaining—Regina, Gertrude, Lindy, and the three Annas—were able to choose one daughter, sister, or close friend to train as an apprentice. The women and Judy were both concerned that their skills would eventually die out and the only memory of Mapusha would be the studio sitting on the mission grounds and the stories from the children who were raised inside those walls by their mothers who crossed cultural and blood lines. Judy was able to secure enough money to run an apprentice program for twelve months during which six women in their twenties and thirties were able to learn every stage of weaving, from dying and spinning to weaving and finishing. Emerencia, Regina's youngest, was one of the apprentices.

Regina knew that Emerencia wasn't like her or, in many ways, like any of the younger women. She loved to weave, but she didn't have the potential to become a master weaver, and sitting day in and day out in front of a loom or behind a spinning wheel would never fulfill her. She was pained inside watching her daughter yearn for more, a better life for Simphiwe, and a life to be excited about. Despite this, she knew Emerencia would do anything to help her mother and Mapusha succeed. She had helped weave cotton rag rugs when orders needed to be filled, and spun wool when a spinner was missing, but, more recently, Emerencia was tackling Mapusha's business management: working to keep inventory; documenting how long each product took from start to finish and how much wool was required to make it; guiding tours through Mapusha, ending in their small stockroom-turned-shop; and marketing their products at shows and festivals in the region. But Emerencia was realizing, firsthand, how difficult things can be running a business with no landline, no computer, no transportation, no experience, and very little money to do anything.

Regina eventually left Emerencia at the house and walked with a hum and skip in her step, balancing a blue duffel bag on the crown of her head. In one hand, she held a closed umbrella with which she would later shield herself from the sun. The other arched toward the balancing duffel, not quite touching the bag, but there just in case it started to slide. Regina had walked this path for just over three decades by herself, with friends, and alongside her children as they grew up into the adults whom, today, she doesn't always understand.

As she rounded the corner into the Catholic mission, a pair of German shepherds behind the locked compound started to bark, running up and down between the screened-in veranda of the priests' bedrooms and the northern fence line. Six-year-old Simphiwe, looking out the studio doors to see at whom the dogs were barking, saw her grandmother and ran toward her. She grabbed Regina's free hand, pulling it down from its precautionary position, and the two walked the rest of the way together.

Regina was late that morning, and she had missed Father Miguel's morning mass. She'd been helping her girls get ready. When she and Simphiwe entered the studio, she almost immediately sat at her loom, scooting her granddaughter to help Lizbeth and Judy pack the car.

When Emerencia arrived with the remainder of her and Simphiwe's things, Judy's champagne-colored BMW was waiting outside, and Lizbeth was already filling the car with cotton rag rugs, wool rugs, and wool tapestries of single colors, zigzags, blended palettes, and more.

Regina had been watching from behind her tapestry and through its warp. She left her loom for only the time it took to say goodbye and steal hugs from her granddaughter that would have to last her a week. Simphiwe was standing tall with excitement. As Regina returned to her bench and settled at her loom for the day, the quiet of the studio was deafening. There was someone missing, other than the girls who had just left.

In the far corner of the studio, one of the electric spinning wheels was silent, unplugged.

DANKIE

"I don't have a father," Dankie would say when his mother referred to the man she'd once married. Fathers are a scarce commodity in Rooibok. Some leave for employment and visit only at month-end for a few days, returning to work by Monday. Others leave for jobs and build new families closer to where they live—divorcing their rural wives or adopting a polygamous lifestyle, bringing their second wives home to the first and leaving, once again. Those that do work locally are often married with mistresses or one divorce on their records.

Dankie's mother, Maggie, was married at fifteen and divorced by thirty-four. After nineteen years of marriage, Lyson Mdunwazi Mathebula ran away with a younger woman, leaving his wife and four children behind. However, he didn't run far, marrying a woman from inside the community. Maggie was better off than most women, for she was already working. Maggie, like her father, was a sangoma.

Dankie was born two years after their divorce. Maggie had been working in Johannesburg, the City of Gold, as a sangoma and tuck shop owner, since her divorce, leaving her eldest daughter in charge of the family. When she returned from the city at month-end, alongside working men, her ex-husband visited her. Mdunwazi had remarried, and his new wife had already given birth to a child. Maggie loved Mdunwazi, though, and blinded herself for a short while, enjoying the company and companionship. Eventually, Maggie realized that she was pregnant, and the blindfold she had allowed herself to wear was torn free. Maggie had the final word, when she left him behind, instructed him to leave, and insisted that they would never be together again. Maggie gave birth to a son, and, despite the circumstances, she named him Dankie, which means "thank you" in Afrikaans.

Just before Dankie turned two, Maggie returned to the city. She left him behind under the care of her eldest daughter, who, at that time, had given birth to her own children. Dankie grew up around women. His brother, Jack, was only a few years older, and Dankie never knew his father as anything other than a man in the distance. His cousin Maduzu, nearly thirty years his senior, was the closest thing to a father that Dankie had ever encountered. Maduzu was openly critical of Dankie's father, angry that he'd deserted his children. And, in many ways, Maduzu's actions and reactions were much closer to Dankie's definition of father than anyone he's encountered. But their relationship truly solidified the years Dankie lived alone.

For just under two years, Dankie was left to fend for himself. He cooked and cleaned on his own—disciplined himself to study, get enough sleep, and stay on the right track. He would fetch water, feed the goats and chickens, and make sure he got to school on time and finished all his homework. Dankie was his own keeper. Maduzu watched from afar, living in the homestead just south of his young cousin, offering advice when he saw it was needed and security when the times were hard.

In Dankie's eyes, a father is someone who teaches you how to live, guides you in the right direction, paves the way to a better future, and loves you. Dankie will speak of his father only after he's emptied a liter of Black Label or Castle, referring to the man who impregnated his mother, who left his siblings behind, as Mdunwazi.

THOKO

Thoko married a man who filled milk pints at Dairy World just after she turned sixteen. The two were wed long before her days of connecting with the ancestors and selling traditional beer to customers; in between her first and second stint in the banana fields; before the crinkles snuck in beside the corners of her eyes; and before her long legs and torso met in the middle with maternal hips. Thoko was stunning. She had the height of a giraffe, the structure of wispy summer grass, and eyes as wide as ripe marulas. Thoko had her father's figure and her mother's beauty.

After her marriage, she lived in a two-room, mud-packed house in Rooi-bok with her infant son Patrick. She would see her husband only at the end of each month for a few days, and, even then, he would come and go as fast as a summer storm. Sometimes he wouldn't come at all. In the month Thoko received the note that changed her life, he hadn't come to visit. What did arrive, though, was a belated letter. Thoko doesn't remember the contents of the letter very well. All she was willing to store in her memory was that he no longer wanted to be her husband. He no longer wanted Thoko to be Mrs. Makwakwa. And he was preparing to marry someone else.

Thoko looked at the letter only once, tore it apart, and gathered her things. She moved herself and Patrick into her parents' home and started to plan. She devised how she might survive on her own and provide Patrick everything she had originally hoped for.

Thoko was born in Magwogwaza, a community where the land was open and people were less crowded. Her grandparents had lived there for many years, and their home consisted of several clusters of buildings. Her father worked as a security guard for the mountainside forestry mill, just north of what would later become the homelands border. In the year Thoko was born, 1959, the Promotion of Bantu Self-Government Act was passed. This classified black Africans into eight ethnic groups. Each group had a commissioner-general who was tasked to develop a homeland for each, which would be allowed to govern itself independently without white intervention, without the apartheid government's rule. In that same year, the government put an end to blacks, Coloureds, and Indians attending white universities. Each homeland had its own government departments, officials, and tribal system. The lines took years to draw, and the recognition of those lines and the systems within them were often questioned or ignored entirely.

In 1964, families living in Magwogwaza were called to a meeting by homeland government officials and informed of their need to move. Thoko was
only five at the time. She remembers being told that the family had to leave,
picking up right away and relocating to Rooiboklaagte A. Her oldest sister,
married at the time, remembers differently. Once they were told to move,
they were given the chance to visit with the *nduna* (local tribal chief) of Rooibok and choose a housing plot, and then given the time to build their new
home. That drastic transition from their established home to a two-room
tin *mazenge* for nine people had been seared in Thoko's memory. Once their
home was finished, they moved, but the day her family moved from their
shack into a new four-room, cement house built on the same plot seemed
to leave little mark.

The reasons behind their move are confusing. Everyone has an answer,
but very few can actually agree upon what that reason is. In 1950, before
Thoko was born, the South African government passed the Group Areas Act.
This legislation declared that there must be a physical separation between
the races. This eventually led to forced removals of people living in "wrong"
areas. The effects were seen more clearly in and around cities, eventually
trickling down to rural villages on a smaller scale. The following year brought
the Suppression of Communism Act (making any call for radical change
illegal), the Separate Representation of Voters Act (leading to the removal
of Coloureds from the voter's roll), the Prevention of Illegal Squatting Act
(allowing the removal of blacks from public or privately owned land and the
establishment of resettlement camps), and the Bantu Authorities Act (setting
a fire in the belly of the apartheid government to establish black homelands,
dividing South Africa's tribal population). It is most likely that the move from
Magwogwaza to Rooibok was a forced removal from private or public land, a
very late enforcement of the Illegal Squatting Act. And, by the time the move
actually happened, the Natives Act, denying any court appeals against forced
removals, had already been passed.

As a little girl in Rooibok, Thoko started to gather traits and qualities
from her mother and father that would later help her become *MaSociatie*.
Her mother was an entrepreneur. Her father had power, wealth, traditional
clout, and Western respect. Her mother would sell traditional beer from their
home, while her father worked as a security guard (often referred to as a small
policeman) and a sangoma. Thoko's mother would make the traditional brew

herself in large three-legged potos and sell buckets to customers who would come to drink and sit in their yard. Thoko and her siblings would help their mother serve customers and collect one-rand coins in exchange for traditional beer. But what she loved, what made her the most money, was her small pottery business. She made mud bowls from the soil around her, fired in an underground kiln. Thoko's father was rarely home.

When Thoko was thirteen, she left school. She says that there just wasn't money for her school fees. Others say spending money to educate a girl just wasn't considered a good investment. In any case, she left home and moved to the banana fields of Farm Zulban, several hours south.

In that same year, the homelands of Lebowa and Gazankulu were officially recognized and released from South African rule. They were declared self-governing states. Although the rest of the world did not recognize each homeland as its own country, the South African government did, eventually encouraging people to give up their South African citizenship for citizenship within their ethnic homeland, whether or not they actually lived within its borders. Once the imaginary lines were drawn, and the homeland borders were legally designated, the shifting of families within rural villages became evident. But, this time, people weren't moved and placed in new areas based on the color of their skin; they were moved based on their surnames. They were divided into ethnic groups. And within the lowveld they were divided into Shangaan and Northern Sotho (specifically Mapulaneng).

Thoko's father had always worked long hours. When he left his job on the mountainside and started as a small policeman within the homeland borders, his time at home was further reduced. He would spend his day checking on people's papers, making sure that they were in the right place, and he would see clients who located him during business hours for consultation. He was a well-respected sangoma, known for curing snakebites that no one else could touch.

After Thoko's husband left her, she didn't stay with her family long. She gave Patrick to her mother and sister for care and returned to the same fields she worked in her early teens. She would send money home at the end of each month and return as often as she could. Providing for Patrick was her top priority. Eventually, Farm Zulban hired an older woman to operate day care, allowing mothers to work and still live with their children, bringing Thoko and her son—her one love—back together.

It was in the fields that Thoko met David Mondlovu, a Mozambican Tsonga man. David looked at Thoko one day and said, *"You should be with me."*

Thoko responded, *"I don't need someone to play with me. I don't need someone to lay in bed with me. I need someone who is willing to build a house with me."*

David agreed. From that day forward they were together, and Thoko moved back to Rooibok. After several years of cleaning and harvesting banana fields, she and David were given their own plot by the tribal authority on which they built a mazenge, where the three lived. With David working, returning at month-end only, Thoko began to sell traditional beer, like her mother had, to earn a living. She also sold cool drinks like Coca-Cola and Sprite, and liter bottles of Black Label from a small, square shack made of thin timber waste from the mill her father used to guard. As she earned more money, she poured it right back into buying more stock. She would purchase drinks and snacks in town and bring them back to sell with a markup for profit.

In the late nineties, Thoko woke up one day paralyzed in both her feet and one finger. She was afraid. And the local sangomas were not helping her. She was praying at the Catholic church, where her mother had attended her whole life, but that was not working.

Seeking answers from her ancestors, she decided to travel to Giyani, the capital of what was then part of the Gazankulu homelands, to find a sangoma by the name of Malungu. Malungu was a female sangoma of note. The name Malungu, meaning "white man," was bestowed upon her after she was trained as a traditional healer. Thoko explained that the spirit of the ancestors within Malungu required her to do Western things, like Western things, and, in many ways, live a Western lifestyle. This meant big houses, Western clothing, Western travel, and Western food. Malungu's spirit had turned her on to the white man's ways.

Thoko went to Malungu for her to throw the bones, to ask the ancestors what was wrong with her; if she was ever going to walk again; what she must do to heal her paralyzed limbs and digit. Malungu threw the bones and threw the bones and threw the bones. The ancestors revealed through these bones the truth: they had been talking to Thoko through her illness, paralyzing her as a signal of what she was to become. It was time for Thoko to be trained, for she was born to be a sangoma.

Thoko stayed with Malungu for the next year as a student, borrowing money from her son Patrick, leaving her and David's children in Rooiboklaagte. She learned how to read the bones once they were thrown. She was taught how to communicate with the ancestors to discover hidden ailments and taught how to explain the reasons behind each problem presented by clients. She was trained to locate medicinal plants and trees in the bush and, eventually, how to mix muthi (herbal medication) from hundreds of ingredients. But, before Thoko could leave Malungu, she had one final task to complete. A test.

The sun had yet to rise when Malungu woke to prepare. This coming-out event, or graduation, is held when the instructing sangoma feels that the apprentice is proficient. She had to slaughter a goat, announcing to the ancestors that a ceremony was to begin. She had to drain its blood and pull its inyongwa (the gall bladder) from inside its belly. Malungu left her homestead and walked beneath the stars until she located a place to hide the inyongwa from Thoko. She returned to concoct a powerful muthi and mix it with the blood of the goat. When she was ready, she woke Thoko, holding out a jar, instructing her to drink. Inside was a mixture of muthi and goat's blood. By drinking this, Thoko would be able to communicate with the ancestors who would assist her in identifying her task and guide her in completing it. The time in which an apprentice returns signifies the strength of ties he or she has with the ancestors. Only if Thoko could return with the goat's inyongwa could she become the sangoma her ancestors wished her to be.

Each time Thoko sits inside her ndumba, slipping on her necklace with acorn-shaped pendants and her two bracelets, she remembers the moment she found the inyongwa, deep in the bushveld. After Thoko's successful retrieval, Malungu placed a portion of the inyongwa and a sampling of the muthi blood inside a small plastic container, the size of a marble. She sealed it shut and tightly wove grass and beads around it. With this, she created a necklace. And with two small bones from the sacrificial goat, she created bracelets. Each color within the necklaces and bracelets signifies the ancestors of the Shangaan and Sotho people. The red represents mungoni, a Shangaan ancestor. The white represents mundawu, also a Shangaan ancestor. And the blue represents masotho, the ancestor of the Sotho people.

After returning home, Thoko's reputation as a sangoma spread, and her sales grew too large for the temporary shack, causing her to build a cement home and a single cement room with a tin roof, one door, and a sales window with bars. Eventually, the outdoor shebeen with indoor storage wasn't good enough, so she moved her kitchen to the sitting room and opened the single-room shebeen in the back of her house where people could come inside, listen to music, and play snooker. The snooker table and jukebox were a separate business in themselves, the profits shared with a man named Axon who provided the equipment.

With the empty storage room in the front of the house, Thoko stocked the shelves with Fatti's and Moni's Macaroni, long life full cream milk, Lucky Star Pilchards, Lion matchstick boxes, Gold Star Instant Yeast, Robertson's Bicarbonate of Soda, Royal Baking Powder, hand-packaged baggies of corn nuts and cheese curls, tins of Koo Baked Beans, Neolux 100-watt light bulbs, yellow bags of DL brown sugar, Swift fine salt, red boxes of Five Roses and Joko teas, plastic bottles of Golden Lite cooking oil, candles wrapped in blue paper and sold by the dozen, single toilet paper rolls covered in flowery plastic, a black crate of fresh white bread loaves, six old mayonnaise jars of sweeties (lollipops, taffy squares, and gum balls), a chest freezer full of one-liter bottles of cool drink (Coca-Cola, Orange Fanta, Lemon Twist, and Sprite), and a stash of cigarettes to sell one by one.

As the partial owner of a jukebox and snooker table, as the owner of a shebeen and tuck shop, and as a well-trusted sangoma, Thoko earned the nickname MaSociatie (many societies, many businesses).

When Thoko was working in the banana fields, she used to meet with people who gathered to confer about the African National Congress and most often talked about how they could work within the system set forth by the apartheid government to start businesses of their own. They would discuss issues like the expense of getting a permit and the rules of owning a business, but Thoko never had enough money to get a permit necessary to own a legal business, and in order to make money, you have to have already earned money. So she started at the bottom.

REGINA

Regina knew what she had to do. She'd been thinking about it all day. She had locked up the studio and walked home, but she knew that she needed to leave once again and take a walk to Anna Mdluli's house. It was only a short path around the homestead opposite her, across the road, and through the gate of Anna's yard. They were close enough that one could call from one's home and catch the attention of the other, provided her ears were perked and she was near a window or outside in the dusty yard. But Anna hadn't been sitting outside for many weeks. Anna's house was larger than many others in Rooibok, although, with changing times, people were catching up with the home her husband built her before he married a second wife. The sun was setting when Regina walked through the chain-link gate and toward the front stoop of Anna's home.

"Tama," called Regina from outside.

"Ahee," replied Anna from inside her dining room, inviting her friend indoors.

Regina walked inside, shutting the door behind her, and into the sitting and dining room. Anna was on the couch beside the window. She had moved from her bedroom into the front sitting-room-cum-dining-room, where she rested and visited with friends by day and slept at night, hoping to catch any cool breeze to cross through the large windows in the front of the house. She lay there all day sleeping on and off, and visiting with the occasional passerby and catching a word or two from her son Muzi as he passed in and out of the front door.

"Anna," Regina said, "*how do you feel today?*"

Anna looked up at Regina with her gaunt eyes and replied, "*I am still in pain.*"

And Regina released the words she had cooped up inside, "*Why can't you go to the hospital? They will take your blood and find out what is wrong with you.*"

She continued to tell Anna about a special clinic. She heard about people going there, but she didn't know much more. She just knew there was a place called Rixile beside Tintswalo Hospital. Rixile, meaning "rising of the sun" or "the dawn of day," is where they test the blood of people who are sick. And many of the people tested are getting better. Regina looked to her friend for an answer.

As if she had been waiting for someone to confront her, she replied, "*I will go.*"

Six months earlier, Anna started to feel weak with pains in her stomach and legs. Her husband had passed away in the late 1990s, leaving behind two widows and children from both. Anna didn't have much financially, although she did have more than most. Her monthly income from Mapusha wasn't enough to cover food and visits to private doctors, so Anna had decided to visit a sangoma in hopes that an answer could be found for the painful throbbing in her legs and her aching stomach. There were two sangomas in Rooibok and possibly hundreds in Acornhoek alone, but Anna chose to stay inside her community and visit a Sotho sangoma named Mahlasele.

She had been to a sangoma many times in her life. The most memorable were her visits seeking help from the ancestors in solving her fertility problems. Anna had miscarried, followed by trouble conceiving. Her last resort was to ask the ancestors for help, for answers, for a solution—something that would solve both medical and marital concerns.

This time, her sangoma threw the divining bones and spoke with the ancestors, revealing that Anna had been witched. The ancestors had explained via the sangoma that Anna was a victim of xigiso, black muthi put on Anna's food with the intention of a slow painful death. It all made sense; Anna had a constant feeling as if something was in her throat, stuck there. She had little interest in eating or drinking. It seemed logical that it would be xigiso because the poison must have been sitting there, and it needed to be taken out. It needed to be forced out. But Mahlasele had caught things early and said that she could help Anna in reversing its effects. She prepared a liquid muthi for her to drink. For several days, Anna drank half a cup of the mixture, three times a day, but things didn't seem to get better. In fact, Anna started feeling worse. She continued to drink the concoction, despite the continued and often worsening pain, until Mapusha offered to pay for specialist visits in town, a private doctor who might tell her what was wrong and provide her with medicine. But two specialists, 240 rand (one-third of Anna's monthly salary) out of Mapusha's meager pocket, and two different packets of pills later, Anna continued to worsen.

The next day, Regina sat in front of her loom, as she did every day. She saw—between each line of warp she slipped her fingers through—an empty space, a vacant place, a void in the composition of the day. While laughter and chatter would normally be muddled by the sound of the electric spinning wheel, the spinner had been unplugged for weeks. While its seat was usually filled, it sat empty. Regina couldn't help but see, feel, and hear the void of Anna Mdluli. She sat there knowing that Anna, with the help of her sister-in-law, was traveling to Tintswalo Hospital and the special clinic they had spoken of.

Regina's heart was small that day, shrunken by the sadness and pain of what could become of her dear friend. Anna's wheel hadn't really spun for six months, only used on the rare occasion she was feeling strong enough to come through and work for a few hours. And even then, her wheel usually remained silent while she pulled wool for Mapusha's second spinner.

Regina knew that unless Anna found herself real help, she might never return to the grey walls of the studio that for so many years she had worked inside. Anna's illness had crept up slowly. For over a year, Anna's body was constantly fighting illness. She'd catch a cold or flu that would linger for weeks. The winter months were particularly bad. Anna had always been a thin beanpole of a woman, but her body started to wither into nothingness, and the muscles that she'd gained—from the continuous motion of the spinning wheel pedal or from planting, weeding, and harvesting during the rainy season—had atrophied dramatically. Anna, a widow living on her own, still responsible for her youngest son, Muzi, was clearly not getting better. Anna grew up around illness. Her mother was mentally ill, requiring daily care and watch. As a result, Anna left school after standard one and was expected to cook, clean, and care for her mother. Her father worked for the railroad and was gone the majority of each month, sending food and extra money on the train to be dropped off for her family at the Acornhoek station.

Anna married the boy next door. She was fourteen and pregnant with her first child. He completed high school, which meant that he could provide for her, and she considered him to be a good, kind-hearted man. He worked in a copper mine north of Acornhoek in a town called Phalaborwa, driving a vehicle for the world's largest opencast mine, the widest man-made hole in Africa. Like most workingmen, he returned home at the end of each month for three nights.

Anna had three children before the trouble started. She miscarried several times, eventually giving birth to a fourth child after consulting a sangoma. It was that moment that Anna now describes as "when my husband became a bad man."

Anna's husband explained that he might have to find himself a second wife because she was too old to bring him more children. She told him that she didn't want a polygamous marriage; she did not wish to share a husband. Anna had listened to another Mapusha member's stories of a polygamous father in the land of the Rain Queen Modjaji, and she did not want that for her family. She did not want this for herself. Polygamy wasn't common in the Shangaan and Mapulaneng Sotho people like it was in other South African tribes (like the Zulu, Venda, and Pedi), but there was no convincing him. His mind was set. He arrived home at the end of one month to introduce Anna to a young girl, the daughter of a miner and his second wife. He had already paid lobola—the traditional bride price of a woman, given to her family as a symbol of engagement—and completed a wedding ceremony.

Life in a polygamous household was cramped and awkward. The second wife lived in limbo, sleeping in the dining room. She was responsible for the cooking, which meant that Anna was essentially kicked out of her kitchen. Until a second house could be built, Anna shared everything with the second wife. She was up close and personal with a girl who was closer in age to Anna's children than her husband. Eventually, the second house was built, and, soon after, babies were born. As first and second wives, the two never really got along. At the end of each month, Anna's husband returned home to spend Friday night and Sunday morning with Anna and Saturday with his second wife. Years later, when their husband was dying, they took turns caring for him in their homes.

When he passed away, the women were left with the minibus taxi he had as a side business and a Bronco bakkie that sits in Anna's backyard, unused, unable to start, infiltrated with weeds. Although a house and vehicle was left to each woman, Anna had to find herself a job. She no longer had the income of a wealthy husband, and Mapusha was in dire straits. Working on a farm was her only option. She moved away from Rooibok for several years, returning only on weekends and holidays. She has since battled to stay healthy.

Only a few kilometers from the studio, as the sparrow flies, Anna sat inside a private room of Rixile, a special HIV and AIDS clinic. A nurse counseled her. She explained to Anna that she was going to take a sample of her blood and test for HIV. The woman held a long, rectangular, plastic plate in her hand and pointed to two parts. "This is where I will put your blood," she said, pointing to a small conical entrance leading to what looked like a soft sponge. "This is what we are looking for," she said, pointing to a space further down the plate. "If two lines appear, you are HIV positive." Anna looked at the disk and watched the woman mix her blood with a solution and then drop it into a small hole labeled "sample."

The nurse had spoken with Anna about accepting the results, however they turned out, in a positive way. She reminded her that there was treatment for HIV and that people were getting better on the treatment. As the nurse dropped the solution into its designated space, Anna's eyes followed the channel through which her blood would speak the truth. Anna watched the liquid saturate down the path as the first line—the line that always appears—revealed itself. If she was positive, the second line would appear, further away from the sample's entrance. Anna watched intently and, as she would later recall, it happened so fast. It was as if the results were instantaneous: the second line appeared.

For as little or as much as the nurse told Anna about this thing called HIV, she didn't really understand what it was, exactly, that was wrong with her. But she did know that it was inside of her blood and that there was treatment. She was told that she needed to return for blood tests every month and that she would have to take medicine for the rest of her life. Pummeled with counseling, tests, and classes in one day, Anna returned home remembering three things: eat lots of fruit and vegetables; the warning that having sex with anyone could kill her; and the number fifty-three. She wasn't sure what they were counting, but she knew that low numbers were bad and high numbers were good. And fifty-three was not good.

*   *   *

Several years earlier, a Zulu truck driver by the name of Zeblon Gwala was visited by his deceased grandfather in a series of dreams. In each of those dreams, the former sangoma would speak to his grandson and identify trees and plants, teaching him one by one. After each dream, Zeblon would wake up and write down the name of the flora his grandfather identified, unsure as to what they meant. Eventually, after the number of trees and plants equaled eighty-nine, his grandfather came to him one last time and gave him a task. *Take these, he said, and mix the ingredients I have given you. This is the cure of the disease everyone is dying from. This is the cure for AIDS.* Zeblon followed his grandfather's instructions and created a muthi with ingredients from South Africa, Swaziland, Zimbabwe, Namibia, and African countries as far north as the Democratic Republic of Congo, eventually testing the concoction on his sister who was deteriorating from HIV/AIDS.

Zeblon's muthi is now called uBhejane, the Zulu word for black rhino, a mammal that was near extinction and is currently being revived. It's sold near the southeastern coastal city of Durban. The waiting room of the Nebza AIDS Clinic, one of two locations where uBhejane is sold, is filled with clients who choose uBhejane over AZT and seek a traditional cure over Western medicine's promise of merely delaying the progression of HIV. This muthi—a dark brown, bitter, and smoky-tasting liquid—is bottled and sold in reused two-liter plastic milk containers for 342 rand and, if taken according to instructions, should last forty days. Patients—who are told to stop smoking and drinking and to abstain from sex or use condoms—are given two bottles. The white-capped bottle is said to increase the T-cell (or CD4) count in the blood, increasing the "soldiers" available per cubic millimeter to fight infections within the body. The blue-capped bottle is said to decrease the viral load of the human immunodeficiency virus, and Zeblon claims to have lowered the viral load in some patients below its detectable number of fifty.

While rumors and myth of uBhejane creep across the country in both urban and rural communities, nurses have been reported as telling patients that uBhejane would soon be rolled out across the country like ARVs (antiretroviral drugs); the health minister—who has been nicknamed Dr. Beetroot by the media for pushing nutrition over ARVs and who initially opposed their rollout—has publicly supported its testing and privately encouraged a Durban hospice owner (the deputy president's mother) to provide uBhejane for all of her positive patients; and the mayor of Durban has sponsored its rollout for patients of a rural clinic just outside of the city.

Juxtaposed against conflicting messages about ARVs and AIDS, in general, patients have expressed a greater trust and faith in uBhejane and other traditional remedies for their familiarity and the promises of being cured.

*　*　*

Regina's hands and feet moved without thought, in and out of the loom, heel to toe, toe to heel, on the pedal below. She moved through the motions in attempt to disguise the confusion, the sadness, and the hurt inside. Regina feared for the worst; she was worried that her prayers were not working. Inside, behind the façade of hope, behind the protective covering she had wrapped around her emotions, Regina was afraid that Anna was dying. And with several dozen thin lines of warp and a partially complete tapestry with which to mask herself, Regina moved closer in and let go of everything she had trapped inside. Regina allowed herself to cry.

She hadn't told anyone. She knew that Anna would be tested for the sickness called HIV. She didn't know much about it. What she did know came from tidbits of people talking here and there. Some people say that the white man made this disease in a laboratory, and it was a last attempt to control the population of South Africa's black majority. Some people are afraid to get flu shots each year, thinking that doctors are injecting people with the virus. Many elders say that the big bags of eighty-kilogram mealie meal have been contaminated, while others won't use condoms because they think the lubricant inside carries the virus. And many people, young and old, believe that HIV is just a traditional punishment for having sex during funeral days.

Regina left the studio immediately after final prayer and walked directly to Anna's house, hoping that she had returned with information from the doctors.

"Tama," she called from the stoop of her old friend's home.

"Ahee," came softly through the cracks in the windows and doors.

Anna was waiting inside to tell the story of what she learned.

DANKIE

Dankie was sound asleep inside his room. It was dark, darker than any other room in the house. The walls were layered with the past and the present, with the old and the new, and the old that seemed new. His walls were bespeckled with white paper grains and dried glue, left over from the soccer pictures his young cousin had pasted to the cement and later removed. The dull walls were brightened and the spots were partially hidden by three fabric sample books from Jack; the long mirror his sister found him (on which he hung the clear plastic rosary given to him by a church member); two "I am special" cartoon posters; two rectangular hanging grass mats; and a white photocopy posted at eye level beside the door that reads, "You can say no to sex. Be faithful to your partner."

In one corner, Dankie's desk was wedged between the wall and his bed, displaying an open briefcase filled with magazines and his newly purchased

Bible. The briefcase was a gift from his brother. And the Bible that cost him fifty rand was opened when the preachers on Christian radio shows quoted verse. Above the desk, Dankie had made a small shelf, slightly crooked, held by two nails on which to balance his schoolbooks.

Lying above his peach duvet—next to the television that talks, but shows no pictures, and the stereo Dankie swears will never cry again—he took his midday nap. He usually slept in the afternoon so that he could stay up late and study into the night. It was quieter then, and everyone else was usually asleep by eight, a habit created by years of no electricity and a tight budget. He was sound asleep when suddenly light streamed into his room.

His mother had swung the door ajar, accompanied by Maduzu's wife. She wasn't really his wife. They weren't actually married. He hadn't paid lobola, nor had they experienced a proper wedding ceremony, but they shared a child and had lived together for several years. Like many couples living similarly, Maduzu considers her his wife, and everyone referred to her as such. She had gone to Dankie's mother for help. She was leaving Maduzu that very moment and had walked from his home with no intention of returning. Dankie woke quickly and was told in short terms that his cousin was threatening to "commit himself out of society." His cousin had warned his departing wife that he would take his life if she left. Her speed didn't falter, although she did stop to ask for Maggie and Dankie's help. Maggie told Dankie that, as the only male family member close by, he needed to go and check on his cousin, to comfort him. And so Dankie set out to do just that.

He ran down the dirt road and cut across the unoccupied plots, along a thin walking path to his cousin's home, a path he has taken many times over many years. Inside, Dankie found his cousin. Maduzu had prepared a rope, fastened it firmly around one of the tin roof's wooden support beams in his bedroom, and hanged himself. His body was floating limp in the center of the bedroom, lifeless, just a short distance from the floor. Running to the bedroom door, Dankie saw the rope that was pulling the life from his cousin's body. He turned and ripped through the kitchen drawers in search of a knife, the serrated bread knife he knew he could find somewhere, the only chance to pull his cousin from the grips of the noose.

Dankie dragged a chair from the kitchen to the side of his cousin's body, climbed on top, and began to saw away at the braided rope pulled taut by the weight of Maduzu's body. Sawing the bread knife over and over, incising each thread of the braid, weakening its strength, and eventually dropping the body of his cousin onto the cement floor beside his bed, Dankie could only react. Pulling the noose from around his cousin's thick neck—Maduzu was a much taller and larger man than him—Dankie looked into the oxygen-deprived face and saw the possibility of life. He saw hope through a cloud of confusion. Maduzu was alive. He couldn't talk, but Dankie could see that he was still alive. After looking at his cousin's large eyes and round features, Dankie pulled himself from the ground and ran out the door, screaming for help.

Dankie ran to his mother, a choice he would later not recollect. Maggie ran to Maduzu's side as Dankie ran to a neighboring homestead, to a family he didn't know, and cried for someone, anyone, to help. They followed him, ran with him, into his cousin's homestead and inside the house. He was too afraid to return on his own. His mind was muddled, his understanding confused. Time seemed to slow, speed up, and go missing in places. They helped him pull Maduzu's body from the cold bedroom floor onto the kitchen table. But Dankie was unsure as to what he should do, or could do. One of his neighbors told him that he must call the police and an ambulance. But when Dankie pulled his cell phone from his pants, he remembered that he'd run dry of prepaid time, which meant he couldn't dial out. Dankie started to dial a number he recalled seeing on a billboard advertising emergency calls. An operator answered, and he started to talk about Maduzu, the rope, the knife. The operator connected him to the local police department, who then called the ambulance service and directed them to Maduzu's home.

The afternoon was fading, and the night sky was falling quickly. When the ambulance carrying Maduzu drove away, one of Dankie's older relatives, a member of his father's family, rode along inside with Maduzu.

Dankie spent the evening inside his house with tears that would not stop. His mother watched him from afar and, when he allowed, with her arms around him. Dankie cried for many reasons. Sadness, death, fear. And a crack in the ladder of power and respect. Dankie had seen Maduzu at the moment of his greatest weakness. He'd prevented his cousin from finishing something he'd clearly wanted to be done. He'd pulled the weak body of a man, his protector, from a death that he now feared. The thought of losing him forever nearly equaled the pain he thought he might have if he had to bear Maduzu looking back at him again—afraid if Maduzu did live that their relationship would be broken forever.

A family elder returned from the hospital just after nine that night with news of his cousin's death.

THOKO

Along the tar road of Acornhoek, the dirt roads of its surrounding communities, and the dusty paths of remote homesteads, people are counting their money in the yard. They are watching the fruits of progress. They are recognizing the rebirth of hope. In front of most houses, growing faster than anything they could plant, are stacks of bricks.

One brick represents one step closer to a better life. A collection of bricks in someone's yard means that a decision has been made to begin building a new house. It could take one, two, or four years to gather everything a family needs in order to start building, but the sight of bricks in someone's yard is like standing outside screaming to everyone that you are doing well, that you are moving up on the ladder of life.

Instead of putting money in the bank to save for the day you can hire a builder or purchase all of your supplies at once, spare change accumulates over time. When there is enough left at month-end to buy a bag of cement and building sand, it is purchased and immediately turned into bricks. If someone is trying to save money, he or she will purchase only the bag of cement and send children down the road to collect wheelbarrows of sand from its center, where it accumulates into a small hill between the cars going opposite directions.

The ladder of progress looks something like this: sheet metal shacks; rooms made of thin forestry offcuts; mud-packed houses and rondavels; followed by cement and clay brick houses. Cement bricks are ideal because they are larger than clay bricks, and you can make them at home. Clay bricks must be purchased from a local factory, and the cost of your house increases tremendously, but they are far more attractive and last much longer.

Thoko's street represents all rungs of the ladder. One family lives in a small collection of sheet metal shacks and a room made of wooden offcuts. Another family has built a five-bedroom clay brick home with clay roof tiles and a cast-iron gate to drive through. They share the same fence line, and their children go to the same schools.

Thoko's eldest son Patrick and his younger brother worked between two barrels of water and a sheet of corrugated metal roofing. Patrick stood and supervised as his brother mixed an inconsistent recipe of water, cement powder, and road sand on the metal sheet. Like a chef leaning over his apprentice, Patrick instructed his brother to add a little of this and a little of that, until they had just the right consistency. Beside them were two homemade brick molds, modeled after the ones sold in town at the builder's store, resembling the shape and size of a car battery. To lessen costs, each mold had two holes running through, forming a figure eight instead of the more expensive solid block. When the rectangular metal mold was full, a plaster-finishing trowel was swept across the top, removing excess cement, and was slapped back onto the wet pile; the mold was lifted, shaken, and dropped; lifted, shaken, and dropped; then, finally, flipped over, removed from the mold, and left to dry alongside the others.

Hundreds of handmade cement bricks separated Thoko's two developed plots from the two recently cleared, but undeveloped, plots. As Patrick and his younger brother filled each brick mold and laid wet cinder blocks out to dry, Thoko would walk back and forth from the open tap near the marula tree (just a few blocks over and down the hill) to fetch water. When the borehole system in Rooibok worked, she could access water behind the house from the single black hose appearing, as if from nowhere, out of the ground. But since it had been broken for over a year, she had to fetch water for cooking, cleaning, drinking, and now construction, each day. In the morning, she would walk down with a wheelbarrow and a few empty twenty-liter containers to fill and trudge back. But as the sun centered and moved closer to the mountains, she would walk with only a single canister, returning with it balanced on the plateau of her head.

The stacks of bricks dividing the yard showed days of work, and the gradient of color, from dark grey to a light dirty sand, illustrated to what extent the bricks were actually dry. Like piles of ten-rand bills in a shoebox under the bed, a wad of rubber-banded cash between the mattresses, or money neatly sorted, counted, and organized in a bank vault, each brick piling tall for everyone who passed to see represented money, a deposit down on the construction at hand, a small step toward amelioration. And a pile that starts with fifty bricks grows over time, until hundreds of bricks have been banked to build.

Thoko had too many to count.

Laid across the coffee table inside the house were plans purchased from a man on the side of the road in town. They were draftsman's drawings of Thoko's dream: a tavern. Several storerooms, a kitchen, a dining room, and an entertainment area were sketched in detail. Each window with exact measurements, each doorframe with exact positioning, and every last angle, nail, and tile was accounted for. Five wide floor-to-ceiling windows would line the main dining and entertainment room to bring light inside where people would sit, drink, listen to music, play snooker, and eat—the room where money would come in and stay. A hallway in the back, closed off to customers, would lead to rooms where stock could be accounted for, meals could be cooked, and an office would be set up. The plans even showed an outdoor patio where tables and chairs would be placed for people to sit outside facing the Drakensberg escarpment, uKhahlamba, "the barrier of spears." Thoko had purchased plans to transform her shebeen into a legalized tavern, nearly double the size of her home and quadruple the size of her current establishment.

Long before bricks started to collect, Thoko's plan was set in motion. She doubled her land, taking on two more plots to the west. She took a tavern management course in Pretoria and a computer course at the Women's Development Bank offices in Acornhoek. And, eventually, she counted her money—enough to start but not enough to complete—and called her son Patrick, who was working in Pretoria. She instructed him to come home. Reluctantly, he came and brought his girlfriend, Lizzy. Thoko needed to purchase building plans, hire a lawyer to apply for a liquor license, take courses required to obtain the license, negotiate distribution with the breweries and bottling companies, and build the tavern. She had hired her sister's brother-in-law to take care of the tavern construction. He and a younger relative showed up one blistering October morning, during the gap of time when winter turns into summer like a slap in the face and boils until the rains eventually come to cool the land and settle the winter dust. They started digging.

DANKIE

Students started to pour in with ten minutes to spare. A group of girls in recently curled, braided, and dreaded hair walked in and sat on three desktops in the far corner of the classroom, chatting with high-pitched laughter. Two boys walked in, passed the girls, and found their place leaning against the thin, chipped chalkboard. Above their heads read: *Lost and Found*. Although they both looked equally lost. The bodies kept coming. Some faces were filled with nerves. Stressed eyes and crinkled foreheads. Others seemed to mask their stress with utter disregard for the importance of the day. And a few looked as if they prepared to write their names down on the exams and walk right back out.

Dankie fixed his collar and took his seat. The increase in bodies filling the room wasn't helping his efforts to cool down. The sweat kept pouring. Down his neck, down his back, and across his chest. His neatly pressed white collared shirt started to stick against his body where his undershirt didn't cover. His hairline, nose, and chin glistened with perspiration. He pulled his collar like a napkin to wipe the accumulated sweat over his mouth and kept it there. As if he were using his shirt like a brown paper bag to prevent himself from hyperventilating, he breathed in and out. He was fidgety. The classroom was loud. It was difficult to think. The noise of those who stayed up through the night to study and those who were well rested filled the four walls. Classmates screamed out the eastern windows as students passed through the schoolyard gate. And heads popped out of the western windows to yell at the tardy ones still on walking paths. A blue bakkie entered the school grounds with more in its bed. A twelfth-grade student leapt from the back of the low-riding vehicle, as it parked in the center of the horseshoe shaped buildings, below the tree where a teacher had just been sitting.

Inside, students started to take their seats, placing calculators, pens, and rulers on each desk. Dankie looked around and saw the calculators. He looked down on his desk and looked back up in horror. He had forgotten his ruler. He hadn't brought a calculator.

The chairs started filling in around him. In front of Dankie, a thick girl, younger looking than the others, took her seat. Her stiff hair formed a helmet, and her ponytail stood erect, pointing outward like a knobkerrie on the back of her head. A tall, slender young man sat down behind Dankie. He pulled his calculator from his pocket and started rubbing his face. He kept rubbing and rubbing as if he wished to wipe away his worry or wipe away the scene before him. Dankie glanced over his shoulder and saw the calculator.

37

"We will start the examination at nine, and we will stop at twelve," explained the chief invigilator. "It's a three-hour paper." He unsealed the packets of blue exam booklets and started to pass them up and down the rows, starting at the doorway and working his way to Dankie in the fourth row.

"If you look on the back of your timetable, there are certain rules and regulation for your examination." The noise outside was overwhelming. The sound of desks moving next door, dragging on the cement floor, filled the room. Yelling from the tenth graders in the schoolyard made the voice of the barefoot invigilator difficult to hear. "Do not open the examination paper until I instruct you to do so," he said, sliding up and down the narrow aisles handing out the booklets. A girl in the first row with the front half of her desk in the doorway pulled open the front cover of the booklet halfway. He looked at her and repeated his instructions, "Do not open the examination paper until I instruct you to do so."

He stepped out of the room, and the students burst into conversation, many opening the covers of their booklets. The desks and chairs were packed so tightly that moving just to turn around and talk to the boy or girl behind or to the side or even fidgeting in your seat created a ruckus of noise in the room.

Dankie didn't talk to anyone. He was distracted, as he had been throughout each day, thinking of the previous Friday over and over again. He couldn't help but see Maduzu's face. See the rope. See the body of his cousin on the cement floor. And his mind was filled with feelings of fear and hours of tears waiting to hear if Maduzu were dead or alive. While he should have been studying for his Mathematics exam, he was digging a grave. He had left his books on the table and joined his cousins and other young men in the community to dig the grave of Maduzu for Saturday's burial.

The school's namesake, Moholoholo, dominated the skyline of craggy granitic mountains like Jo'burg's Hillbrow Tower. Homesteads dotted the scenery between the two ablution blocks. Mothers and young girls walked along the path running parallel with the school and the mountain, stopping here and there to rest. Umbrellas blocking the sun's intense rays were held up high by many on their way to town or the T-junction from which to catch a taxi. Even the women from the local weaving cooperative passed the school on their way to the studio.

Dankie's space to sit was so close to the chair in front and the desk behind him that the back of his chair butted up against the desk behind him and his stomach was pressed against his own desk. When he leaned forward to look at his booklet, that stiff ponytail of the girl in front just barely poked him in the head.

He tapped her shoulder and asked to borrow her calculator for just a moment, negotiating its use throughout the exam, if he needed some extra help. Luckily, she was willing to share.

End-of-year exams determine whether students repeat grades or advance to the next year. Dankie had taken exams each year, but this was different. This year was critical. Each exam taken in the twelfth grade determined his future, his chance to advance out of Moholoholo High School and into a classroom outside of Rooibok, outside of Acornhoek, and, potentially, outside of the bushveld, into an urban center filled with taxis, people to talk to, people to learn from, libraries to sift through, and experiences to be had.

Dankie had already taken his xiTsonga, English, and Accounting exams and part one of his Afrikaans exam. To pass matric, he would need to accumulate a score of at least 720, but to pass would not be enough. To pass does not necessarily mean to advance. Dankie didn't want to leave high school and find a job; he wanted to leap out of one classroom and into another. And, to do this, a student needs 950 to pass with Exemption. Exemption means that you are allowed to advance into university-level coursework.

Without a Certificate of Exemption, you are not allowed to register for university (without jumping through some impossible and expensive hoops) and will not qualify for a bursary.

A few days earlier, one of Dankie's neighbors visited the school principal and his instructors to explain the death of Maduzu and how it was affecting Dankie. It was a gesture that certainly illustrated love for the young man and respect for his continued diligence in school, but his effort was wasted before he even entered the schoolyard. Instructors and principals have no effect on the exam process and have nothing to do with the grading, which means they could do very little for Dankie, who was grieving the loss of his cousin and taking two exams between Maduzu's death and his burial.

Dankie arranged his papers. He took several and placed them in the far right corner of his desk over the masking tape on which his examination number was written. He took the question booklet, still stiff from the tight packaging, and flipped through the pages from back to front, landing on the open first page.

The principal walked in and instructed the students to tidy each row of desks. Dankie was punching numbers on a borrowed calculator while the principal directed his request once again. He looked up, straightened his desk, and looked back down, leaning over the calculator like a hunchbacked hyena.

The morning's fierce wind had died down, but the open windows seemed to catch a breeze every few minutes or so, cooling down the slowly boiling room. Dankie wiped his chin with his collar and rolled up his long-sleeved shirt. The boy to his left pulled his entire shirt over his head to wipe the summer sweat from his hair and face. And the girl in front of him, with whom he was sharing the calculator, had a blue cloth to wipe her face.

A few students to his left, a boy placed both hands on his head, as if he had never seen anything like the first question in the booklet he'd just opened. Several of the students stared into the wall, and the closer they were to the windows, the longer they stared out into the changing grass.

The breeze picked up again, causing Dankie to strategically situate himself so papers wouldn't fly off his desk. He wrote with his right hand and pointed to each question with his left. Dankie carefully focused on the words and details of each question, writing out every mathematical step. While the girl in front of him wrote in slow, calm loops, he was scribbling quickly with his black pen. There was intensity in his movement. He didn't want a second to go by without numbers in his head for fear that Maduzu's face would replace that space and then his test would be over.

REGINA

Regina leaned lower and lower until her cheek was flush against the cold cement floor. Biting her lower lip, she examined beneath the treadle, the platform that allows her foot to pull the warp open and closed. The wooden pedal mimics the movement of a seesaw when pressure is applied with heel or toe. As she kneeled on the opposite side of her upright loom, Regina tried to figure out why the pulley system seemed off kilter. Two ropes ran through holes on either side of the treadle and were knotted beneath, resembling a homemade tree swing. She pulled the platform upward to look at the knot that keeps it in place.

After a closer look, Regina reached to her left, around the loom, to slide a small cardboard box closer. Inside were pieces of cotton sliced into long strips. She pulled a neatly folded batch and a pair of scissors from the box and then pushed it to the side. Unfolding the bundle in front of her, she pulled one from the group and snipped (just once, down the center), gripped each side, and tore the fabric into two. She returned her right cheek to the ground once more. Between the platform and the knot on which it should rest, Regina wrapped the cloth around and around, tying it off and examining how the platform rested against its new base, rocking it back and forth, several times.

Standing, Regina slid the box back into position, beside her basket of colorful wool bundles, and returned to her bench. Across the room, across from the spinning wheels, she could see her best friend Gertrude and another woman lifting a wooden table and placing it on another. Gertrude pulled a splintered ladder from the wall and slid it in position beside the stacked tables. Shaking the rickety ladder, making sure it was in lock position, she climbed up its six steps and crawled onto the top platform. As she stood and pulled her arms toward the roof, she could just reach the top wooden frame of the three-by-four meter rug loom. Gertrude slid her fingers through the heddle—the long, horizontal row of nails spaced millimeters from one another, around which the vertical warp is secured. She pulled the scraps of warp left behind from the cotton rug that two young weavers had removed from the frame the week before. Below, another woman knelt on the floor and did the same, pulling scraps from the bottom heddle.

Towering near the rafters, Gertrude cleared the spool of warp's loose end and fastened it around the first free nail in the top row. Tugging to be sure it was taut, Gertrude bent down and handed the string to the woman below, who followed suit. Up and down, back and forth, the two women slipped into a rhythm, smooth with a little creak because of age and arthritic knees—every motion had become instinct after decades.

"Ahhh, haaaa-haaaa!" Gertrude shouted and rolled into laughter, echoing through the cavities between the rafters and tin roof.

Regina looked up and around, when Gertrude belted again, "Ahhh, haaaa-haaaa ... Judy. . . . Ahhh, haaaa-haaaa!"

Turning her head away from her loom and toward the window, Regina saw the top of Judy's champagne-colored BMW roll past the church entrance and park under the shady tree.

"When is she going to America?" asked Regina as the door swung open.

"Helloooooo!" shouted Judy, wearing a green wrap-dress tied at her waist. "Kunjani, Regina. Kunjani, Gertrude," she said with barely a breath, continuing to greet each of the older women. "I have brought wool!"

"There was a mistake on my tickets. They called me Sunday just a few hours before I was leaving and said that there was no airplane booked for my second flight. A mistake. So I am leaving next Sunday. I am really leaving this time," said Judy in a slow and exaggerated tone.

Judy quickly kneeled beside Regina, changing her demeanor altogether. "How is Anna?" she asked.

"Good. The doctor is giving her medicine which should help," Regina replied. "I thought you were in America," she commented, halting the rhythm of her fingers and letting the wool drop below the heddle, swinging.

"I have brought many things," she said, spinning in a circle to speak to everyone. "Come help me bring the wool inside," said Judy to a few of the younger weavers, waving them in her direction as she walked away.

As they passed her loom and walked out the door, Regina continued to weave. The double doors were pulled open, bringing light into the grey studio's center and expanding Regina's view outside. She could see the girls pull the barrel-sized plastic bag from the trunk and plop it on the ground, causing a small plume of dust to lift from the dirt driveway. Judy pulled something from her back seat as Ambrocia and Emma dragged the twenty-five-kilogram bag of wool along the ground—to Mapusha's entrance, up the cement stoop, into the studio—and plopped it beside the silent spinning wheel.

Judy returned with several plastic bags and held them in the air. "I have prezzzzz-ants," she called, walking back to the younger women. Judy stopped one of the girls who was seven months pregnant.

"See if they fit," said Judy.

Regina could see her drop something down on the floor and explain to Ambrocia that they were a gift from someone who visited a few weeks back, emphasizing that they were given to her especially in thanks for doing something kind. Regina couldn't quite hear what they were saying over the chatter of the girls to her right. With her hands still in between a wall of warp, Regina tilted her head to the right to catch a warp-free glance of Ambrocia's surprise: a pair of black flip-flops with clear rhinestone-lined straps. Ambrocia bent down, blocking the flip-flops from view with her plaid, floppy hat, and slipped her bare feet into each glisteny strap. She straightened back up, and a rare, tooth-filled smile filled her face. Regina smiled, as well; she pulled her hands free from the warp, scooted to the left of her bench, and slowly stood facing the windows.

A long wooden counter held by three weaving benches sat below the two window frames facing the little yellow chapel, under which the women had stored four multisized three-legged iron pots used to dye wool on an open fire. On top sat an electric kettle; two tin pots used to cook pap, porridge, or beans; a stack of notebooks and papers; several chipped ceramic mugs; an open plastic bag of salt; a turquoise House of Coffee tin; and two twenty-liter white Buffalo Acrylic PVC buckets filled with recently fetched water. Regina picked up a striped ceramic mug and, peering into the left bucket, submerged the mug until it was full. Passing Ambrocia who was still examining her new flip-flops, Regina went to the two stacked tables on which Gertrude and another woman were warping the loom. She lifted the mug to the level of the top table and slid it on the platform for her best friend. Gertrude smiled and stopped for a moment to drink from the mug, eventually passing it to the woman below and then back to Regina.

"Girls," Judy said in a raised, but nonchalant, tone, "I have some books here from David and Neil about sex." Regina's ears perked as she returned to her loom, and the girls just looked at one another. Flapping two books in the air, Judy signaled for someone to come collect. "Everything you need to know about sex is in here."

As Regina resituated herself on her bench, Judy went to her right with a gift. Regina had started to refocus but was quickly distracted by the magazine Judy crossed between her eyes and the warp.

"You're famous," Judy said with delight. "The woman from Magoebaskloof who came to visit a few months ago wrote about you. Look," she said, flipping through the pages. "Look: you're famous."

Regina looked down and spotted herself in the center of the page. She remembered the day. She had been weaving a design that Judy had given her for an order. It was a tapestry of a baobab tree with a zigzag pattern framing each side. It was for a large company in the United States. Texas, something or other. Judy had brought a woman to visit and speak with Emerencia about the Magoebaskloof Spring Festival. She didn't remember having her picture taken, or whether she was weaving that consignment during the visit, but there it was, she thought, so it must have happened. Above her photograph in bold block lettering read, "Weaver Back on the Road to Success." Looking up from the page, Regina looked around, as if to check to see who might be looking, and stretched her arms outward, pushing the magazine further from her eyes to get a clear look at what exactly she was holding. On the left page, opposite her photograph, read, "Limpopo and Kruger Park." It was the first page within the magazine's section for the province. Just when Regina was curious to look further, Judy knelt down at her side, lowered her voice, and began to talk.

"How is Anna doing?" Judy asked, starting the earlier conversation over again.

"She seems to be getting better," replied Regina as she closed the magazine and placed it on her lap. "Are you going to see her?"

"Yes, I have brought some things. I have brought food, and I'll go down to see her, soon. Where is Emerencia?" Judy inquired.

Regina hesitated. "She is in town, working, helping out for a few days," Regina said, speaking in half-truths.

"Where is she?" Judy asked in confusion laced with irritation.

"She is helping out at Buzi."

"Where?" asked Judy, unsure if she was naming a person or a place.

"Buzi. B-U-ZED-I. Buzi. It is in town. Where she worked a while back. She is helping out," explained Regina.

Tension as thick as maize porridge grew around Judy's head and into Regina's space before she continued talking about Anna Mdluli. The discussion, like many that occur with Judy, was spotty. Regina understood much of what she was talking about, but Judy kept repeating words like "T-cell count" of which Regina had never heard. But she nodded her head and let Judy speak. She would never stop and explain that she didn't understand what Judy was saying; she'd just nod and nod some more.

"She needs to get strong," continued Judy. "The most important thing is that she eats. Things like aloe and cabbage juice. She needs protein, but no sugar."

Judy explained to Regina that Anna needed the aloe to heal her stomach. She had brought information to give to Anna's family about the types of food that were good for her and the types that were bad. It was all in English, and somewhat complicated, set up like a textbook, so Anna's son, Muzi, would have to translate for her, but all of the information Judy knew Anna needed was stacked away inside.

She walked outside the door while still talking about the food, seeming to have left Regina's understanding of all she was saying behind, and returned talking about a plant that was outside the door—the aloe plant that can be used to make juice.

"I was *going* to ask Emerencia to be in charge of her food. To be sure that she eats what she needs to," she explained to Regina, returning to her side. "But Emerrrrrenciaaaaa's not here," she said, drawing on her disappointing absence, once again.

"You can visit her," Regina said. "Buzi is behind the market in town, near the taxis. You will see her there at the door checking slips."

Regina paused.

"I think I will," replied Judy. "Do you think Emerencia is *even* interested in coming back to Mapusha?" asked Judy, then standing to Regina's left.

"I think she'll be back," said Regina, unsure herself as to whether her daughter would return.

Pulling the magazine from her lap, Regina examined the cover of *Discovering South Africa*, a magazine published and sold by a national petrol station. The round, zigzagged sticker reading "R9.95" was stuck over the cover article's title, "Whale Watching," and the photograph of a whale with barnacles along its back sliding out of the water. Regina's right hand touched the back of the whale, before flipping to the page of her photograph. Peering at it once more for just a second, she quickly closed the magazine, curled it in half, and slipped it behind the warp into a nook created by the canvas roll and completed portion of tapestry. Hidden from everyone's sight, except for Regina's, and in a safe place for her to keep and take home, or save for later.

Judy continued on with the younger women of Mapusha, flying around the room like the little white autumn butterflies that flutter around in packs, but Regina's eyes and ears were focused on the rhythm in front of her, until she could see Angie walking toward the unopened body-sized bag of raw wool, and Gertrude and Lindy who had just finished the first half of warping the large loom. Angie had a brown Lycra sleeveless dress slipped over the pink dress she was already wearing, but her swollen breasts and pregnant belly turned the short dress into an empire-waist shirt with brown ruffles to curtain her growing baby. As she turned, pointing her belly toward Regina, she smiled and placed her hands across her unborn child.

The girls were filled with laughter, and Judy broke in and explained, "The woman who owned this dress was fifty-four and living in LA. Lots of money!"

Regina—a handful of years older than the previous owner of Angie's new maternity shirt—widened her eyes and exuded a powerful, but silent, laughter. Suddenly, a screeching noise worth closing one's ears filled the studio, cutting the sound of laughter entirely. Gertrude had climbed down her ladder and was sliding the stack of tables to the right to finish warping the loom's second half.

Regina stopped to ask Judy if she needed someone to go with her to Anna's, since Anna Mdluli's English was quite limited other than basic greetings and directions to get from here to there. Emerencia would normally be the one to help translate.

"Yes. But Wonder will take me," Judy replied. "Don't worry, Reginaaaa. You don't need to come."

Judy and Wonder walked through the door, and Regina could hear them drive away.

She would have loved to go, but sitting before her loom she worried that her order of tapestries would not be done by the tenth of the month, as she had wished. "If I leave to go this place and that place, it will never get done, and I want to finish before I go to the Saint Anne conference next weekend."

Regina turned, with one hand still holding a ball of wool, to the bench behind her, up against a long horizontal loom used more for hanging things on than actual weaving. On the bench sat a pair of scissors, a pair of secondhand reading glasses, a copy of the Magoebaskloof Spring Festival itinerary, and a thin floral scarf. Regina reached for the scarf and wiped the beaded sweat from her face, along her neck and across her chest, undoing two of her buttons, fanning her shirt up and down, seeking relief with the movement of air through her blouse.

As she returned her scarf to the bench, Regina saw Angie weaving a tapestry of light brown, purple, blue, and pink. Regina heard a raspy cough followed by the jingle of keys outside the studio and voices inside the mission's open yard. With the doors still open from pulling the wool through, Regina could see a fellow Woman of Saint Anne walking through the yard and toward the mission door.

"Ngena," Regina called out the door.

Regina stood up and walked along the counter to a stack of papers through which she shuffled, locating a thin accounting notebook. She returned to her loom and flipped through the pages to the first blank space and started writing the visitor's name.

A tall, thin, elderly woman, with beads of sweat dripping down from the edge of her scarf-covered hair, pulled thirty rand from her pocket, handing Regina a green ten-rand bill, which she balanced on the left side of the loom's lower beam, and a brown twenty-rand bill, which she placed on the open notebook in Regina's lap. From inside the secret niche of her loom, Regina pulled a packet of envelopes and bills bound by a rubber band. She tucked the twenty-rand bill behind a blue envelope labeled "Diocese of Witbank."

Regina was collecting money from the Women of Saint Anne for the coming trip to a diocese-wide conference at a nearby parish. Ten rand each. Although many of the women could not afford the ten rand, those who were willing to spare an extra ten often paid the dues of those who could not participate.

Before leaving, the woman handed the pair of keys to Regina, who hung them on a nail on the inside of her loom and started to walk back outside. It was Thursday, so she sat down on the stoop of the studio, leaning against the wall outside, and waited. In just an hour or so, the women would come all together for their weekly prayers, Bible discussion, and meeting. Regina heard the sound of Judy's car approaching and continued to weave. "That was fast," she said.

Wonder entered with Judy behind her. Judy came back to Regina, knelt down once again, and explained much of what she had before. "She is looking better, but she cannot have any sugar and must eat a lot of apples."

Judy explained that she would make sure eight hundred rand were available each month for Anna's food and to keep paying for a doctor, for now, but three hundred rand or four hundred rand of Mapusha's money needed to be set aside for an emergency situation. Regina listened. Judy said that she was going to make an executive decision about the use of funds set aside. "Do you think everyone will be fine with that?" asked Judy. "Or won't they understand?"

Regina, in agreement with the use of funds to help Anna, hesitated. Then she said to Judy, "I think you should talk to another committee member. Talk to Lizbeth."

Judy often shifted from topic to topic with such speed and disconnect that Regina and the other women would take a few seconds to realize that she was talking about something different. Moving the conversation in another direction, Judy looked at Regina's tapestry and radiated praise for her "amazing" work. Judy further explained the order to Regina, allowing her finally to understand what exactly she was making: an order of two floor mats, to be placed on either side of a bed, consigned by someone in Jo'burg. They had given Judy the color scheme of each and asked for Regina's signature style of blending colors.

"But there mustn't be fringe on the end. No fringe," instructed Judy. "No fringe."

Regina had returned to her work, despite Judy still continuing the conversation. Her eyes and ears were locked in the rhythm of her weaving. Judy continued to talk of increasing stock for twenty-five Catholic Belgians coming in the new year, but the details were lost and the important information retained.

"We need to have a show, Regina," insisted Judy with a smile. "You are an artist. Even though there is no word for it in Shangaan, you are." Judy paused for a moment and surveyed the studio. "I will see you in January, and this time I am *really* leaving for America. What are you doing this weekend?" she asked before stepping out the door.

"I will visit the sick, go to a funeral, and attend a celebration, the removal of a woman's black clothing, Saturday," Regina said.

"Whose funeral?"

"There is this man who has hanged himself near Gertrude's house."

SUMMER

THOKO

"It is very bad to commit suicide," said a woman beside Thoko.

Six middle-aged women and one young man were packed tightly in the back of an enclosed short-wheel-base truck, a small square box with four pull-down seats and just enough room for knees to knock and heads to skim the ceiling. There were two small sliding windows that let in just enough air to breathe, resembling the holes children poke into tin cans with a fork when they've caught a butterfly or millipede. They filled the final vehicle in a procession of six for Mbangu Maduzu Mathebula's funeral.

Thoko, like the others, was wearing her finest: a long red dress that hung on her thin, curveless body; a generously sized zebra-print jacket draped over her shoulders; and a wide-brimmed straw hat with a plaid sash tied around its neck, covering her short, untidy hair. An elastic ribbon held her wide-brimmed hat in place, cutting a deep and distinct line across the back of her jaw and beneath her chin, preserving itself in her dark, sun-drenched complexion.

From the moment they climbed in, the women had spoken over one another, at one another, and to those who weren't even listening. They were yelling. It was different from the yelling they do at home when a young person has done something wrong, or to call someone to fetch something they would rather not get up and fetch themselves. It was the yelling that took place in casual conversation, a yelling used when you're talking to your neighbor across the road, when you're in a store and your friend is a few aisles over, and, in this case, when there are several of you talking about something very important. It was a conversation turned up to painful decibels.

Thoko had been riding in the final bakkie of the procession before spotting the empty truck that her nephews Dankie and Jack were climbing inside. Her body had been squeezed like the folds of an accordion into the back of a metallic-green lowrider with more than a dozen others. At the sight of an open space, she pulled her body, unfolded her limbs, and leapt from the open vehicle. With her followed four others.

The women continued their conversation as they scrambled to the new vehicle and, once inside, spoke as if Dankie and Jack were further than an earshot away.

"He should have killed his wife first, if he was going to commit suicide," said Thoko in a considered, yet uncomplicated, tone. *"You just can't commit suicide and leave a wife, stealing away the good life."*

"*He should have explained to someone, if he had a problem. Not deciding to take his own life,*" a second woman chimed in over Thoko.

"*She couldn't even attend the funeral,*" said another.

"*No. She can't come. She's still frightened,*" Thoko said. "*It'll take her some time to see other people, because she knows what she has done is wrong.*"

The women mulled over the idea of suicide and their recollections of suicide in the past. One woman remembered a man in the nearby village of Thulamahashe who had "*committed himself out of this world*" and into another, but—of course—the reason behind his death was debatable.

Thoko's nephew, the youngest of her eldest sister, was sitting in the passenger seat up front with his window rolled down and the wind in his face. He said nothing. His eyes were fastened to the dusty dashboard, and his mind was in another place. He was the one who had found Maduzu. He was the one who cut him free from the rope so many people were talking about.

He heard the women in the back seat *skinnering*, but he preferred not to listen, not to digest. He preferred to wish it all away. Wish it out the window and into the wind, to float out of the car, out of Rooibok, beyond Acornhoek, over the mountains, and into a place he would never have to see.

He turned to his right and all the way around to face his brother, his aunt, and the tangled bodies behind him, acknowledging their presence only once.

The commotion of voices bouncing back and forth, ricocheting off each surface and occasionally off one another, seemed to bother Dankie at first. The women's voices bled together, their conversation eventually blending into one great static over which his thoughts and non-thoughts meandered.

There are five turns between the Mathebula homestead and the funeral home: left, left, left, right, left. Eastward away from the mountains. Northwest past the roads to Thoko's shebeen. North away from Rooibok A, past the road to Moholoholo High School, past the mission's entrance, and parallel to the escarpment painting the skyline of the lowveld. Westward once the dirt road met the only tar road in Acornhoek on which you pass through town, past the open market butcher, past the Spar and Buzi Cash and Carry, past the Indian shop, and past the police station. North again toward a dead end, and then one final westward turn.

And with each turn, seven bodies shifted.

Thoko's back was up against the right side of the truck's interior, and she sat crammed between two women and Jack. The side window behind her was open as far as possible, but the rear window's inability even to crack created a simmer of suffocating heat, the breath of seven adults in such close proximity, and the warmth of seven bodies dressed in long sleeves, long skirts, wraps, and formal jackets.

Turning right off the main tar road and down a short, steep driveway, the caravan of cars slowly crept toward a dead end with the option to go straight over the railroad tracks into Tintswalo Hospital's emergency entrance or left into the parking lot of Elite Funeral Parlor. Elite, locally pronounced as "e-light" (as in the light of God), sat at the base of a hill and along the railroad tracks, invisible to those passing on the main road, but with higher foot traffic than the local market and government grants' line.

The procession turned left into the closed-in parking lot, and all but one vehicle were held in line like taxiing airplanes waiting for their number to be called. Other than the road signs directing vehicles to Elite—one of seven parlors within a three-kilometer stretch—there was no exterior sign to be seen.

The sound of voices suddenly burst above a grey cement brick wall at the edge of the parking lot and filled the air, permeating the vehicles and halting the constant conversation of those inside. The sounds of claps echoed like drums and kept a beat that jumped from ear to ear, and the rhythm of their voices was solemn but laced with life.

Suddenly, a green hearse pulled through the front gates, out of the confines of the grey walls and into the parking lot of grey gravel. Walking on either side of the vehicle were three people, six in total, only one of which was male. Each was dressed in a long white cotton gown, the uniform of the Nazareth Baptist Church. The six mourners left the side of the hearse and climbed onto an eight-wheel flatbed truck parked parallel to the wall. They sat on the back, as they would sit beneath a tree on a hot summer day, legs swept to the side, grass mats protecting their clean gowns. All of this without missing a beat, without slowing the pace, without lowering their harmony.

As they pulled from the parking lot and drove up the driveway toward the busy tar road, vehicles in waiting were being directed into positions along the wall and the remaining edges of the lot.

Thoko looked out the truck's open back door and reached for Jack. His right hand reached out from the sleeve of his thick leather jacket and helped her balance while she jumped from the tall vehicle and gained her footing below.

She landed with her left hand holding the top of her straw hat, straightened herself up, and began to brush her dress clean and straight.

Inside the entrance, there was a line of "cars that carry the coffin" parked along the right interior wall of the funeral parlor compound, a wall with an exterior lined by tall pine trees used by local farmers as natural fence lines protecting their crops from strong winds. Each vehicle's front windshield had "Elite Funeral Parlor" written in white script across its top quarter, and each rear window was filled entirely.

In the center of the cement-walled compound stood a sizeable, square, windowless building painted in smoky blue with a set of large double doors standing wide open. "Elite Funeral Parlor, Open 24 Hours" was painted in large purple lettering, above the entrance. Opposite and along the front wall of the compound were two large, blue, wall-less tents held up by thin metal poles. Underneath were several dozen green plastic chairs lined in tidy rows of twelve.

Each tent represented one viewing. Friends and family of Thoko's elder sister's husband's nephew Mbangu Maduzu Mathebula filled the first tent. Opposite the first tent, to the right of the building's open double doors, were two rows of green plastic chairs against the front wall of the building, facing the tent. Traditionally, these are for immediate family members only: brothers, sisters, mothers, fathers, children, and, sometimes, close cousins or in-laws. Several women and a few men filled the seats against the wall, dressed in secondhand tweed jackets, pressed button-down shirts, large draping scarves, and long ankle-length skirts. Thoko took a seat, third from the right, beside Maduzu's elderly mother and his sister, Joyce. Thoko's nephews filled two seats beneath the tent.

The second tent stood empty, but a few people began filtering in to occupy its seats, gain refuge from the summer sun, and wait their turn. The row of family chairs sitting opposite the tent were nearly filled, and those sitting there were being served ice-cold water by two women with trays of plastic cups.

Maduzu's sister and brother silently signaled to Dankie to join them against the building, but he remained beside his brother and beneath the protection of the tent above and to the right of the Muchongolo people. At the end of the row, a thin gangly man wore a red, green, and yellow beaded necklace of multiple strands, nearly a fistful in width. He had a large, knee-high silver drum, like those used in a marching band. Its strap was slightly torn and weathered, and the bulbous end of his white drumstick looked worn down from use.

Mbangu Mathebula, known more commonly as Maduzu, wasn't Christian like most of his family members. He didn't go to church, and only a few people recall ever seeing him read the Bible. He was what some might call a traditionalist, or others might have just described him as a Muchongolo dancer. Directly translated from Tsonga, *muchongolo* simply means "dance session." It is held on Sundays, which means, if you are a Muchongolo dancer, you don't attend church. It isn't a religion per se, but it is definitely associated with strong spiritual and moral beliefs, and its people follow the old generation's traditional ways of dancing, sharing of traditional beer, and choices in daily lifestyle.

Suddenly, the sound of singing burst from the left side of the building, an area Dankie couldn't see. Led by a man singing in Northern Sotho, the voices of several women followed his lead.

We thank you. We thank you.
There is no one to which we can compare.
There is no one to which we can compare.
There is no one to which we can compare.
You're so amazing.

Painful cries of women, more like lingering wails, broke the flow of each line, and the vocals' tone and mood reflected the somber moment. But only their voices could be heard. Their bodies were still to follow, although, with each beat, the voices grew closer and closer, creeping closer until they rounded left and along the front of the building. Crowds of people were walking alongside the green vehicle transporting the coffin of the deceased. So many, it seemed as if they could be carrying the vehicle themselves out the gate's entrance and back to their home. As they exited the grey walls and climbed back into their vehicles, the sound of several others pulling away was replaced with equally as many pulling in. Through the open double doors, a man in black dress pants and a collared uniform shirt appeared. Forming his right hand like an arrow and curving his arm to the right, he cleared his throat and called in a clear loudspeaker voice, "Mathebula. Rooibok."

DANKIE

Everyone stood but Dankie. He hesitated and slowly lifted himself from his seat. The strong posture that normally framed his back was missing. His shoulders curved forward, following his eyes, trailing his toes. Dankie could hear the echoing cries of Maduzu's sister and mother.

He shuffled around the left of the building, along the tall grey wall, around a car parked outside the only open door, and behind a crowd of community members waiting to enter the viewing parlor.

Nearly everyone had passed through the room, and his brother, Jack, exited just as he contemplated entering. Pushed into position by the brother of Maduzu, Dankie fell third to last in line.

The room was dark. And very small. In the center on a metal stand with wheels sat a long coffin made of grey-and-white-grained, plastic-coated wood. It was thin and narrow—so narrow, it's hard to imagine a man of Maduzu's size could lie to rest in such confines—and shaped with sharp abrupt points at the shoulder, much like those constructed of raw wood with as little number of pieces as possible.

People were already standing in every open space to the left and right of the anthropoidal-shaped coffin, allowing just enough room for those still viewing to walk the pathway from left to right, around Maduzu. What space remained was filled by the slow lyrics lapping like waves in the Indian Ocean. Led by one woman, "*Alleluiaaaaaaaaa, Alleluiaaaaaaaaa . . .*"

God appeaaaaared
God has just appeared
Deeeescendinggggg
Descending through the clouds

Dankie shuffled his feet behind a woman with his eyes running along the edge of the coffin from the bottom upward past the waist and to the shoulders, where his eyes looked away from the grey-and-white exterior and into its only window inside. A triangular opening revealed the face of an older man with round, yet strong, features. A small stream of light let in by the open doors ran across his face, unveiling his lifeless Necco-colored skin. It looked almost like putty or clay, shined, then powdered—a process that caused each line in his face and the crow's-feet along his eyes to pop.

Maduzu's body lay inside, but Dankie could see only his round face. He couldn't see whether Maduzu was wearing traditional Muchongolo clothing or a suit and tie, as his Christian relatives would have preferred. He couldn't see if there was a Bible inside, something Dankie believed all people should be buried with. He couldn't even see Maduzu's neck or shoulders. A sheet of thin, white butcher paper was secured to the walls of the coffin's open hatch. Dankie couldn't see his ears, the top of his head, or his neck through the narrow oval-shaped opening, only his strong chin and facial features. Like the portals in a carnival or fair that allow you to place your head through and take on the body of another person or animal. Only Maduzu's face could be seen.

The flow of the line moved like the music around him, but Dankie slowed as much as he could. As he curved around the top half of his cousin's coffin, he stood between Maduzu and a podium on which a Bible lay. Peering down, looking at Maduzu from above, looking at Maduzu upside down and slowly becoming right side up, he continued to walk behind the woman in front of him, widening the gap with each step. As he reached Maduzu's left shoulder, Dankie turned his body to stop, but didn't. He continued walking, having decided to circle around once again. And he almost did. But his mother pulled him out the door and into the light, before he could pass the small, flat foot panel at the base of the coffin.

Maduzu's male relatives and several men of Muchongolo were already unfolding a king-size, soft wool blanket with a red, yellow, black, and green pattern on the left side of the room. The line had passed, and they were preparing to take Maduzu home.

Dankie stood outside with his back to the viewing room. Facing the grey wall and line of tall trees, Dankie let go. His shoulders shook. His face was buried in his hands. Dankie's tears poured through his fingers and down his right wrist.

He stood alone. Several feet away, circling around the green hatchback hearse, everyone sang and waited for the preacher to speak. An oddly choreographed orchestra of sounds blended slow lyrics about God's followers, the lung-filled cries of Joyce and her mother, the frequent birdcall "pit-may-fro," and the repeating beep of the vehicle's open door.

When Dankie turned around, he watched the blanket-covered coffin being carried from the viewing room and onto the bed of the vehicle.

"Thank you very much for giving me this chance to speak to you, and I thank you all for coming to Maduzu's funeral. I am going to read to you from the Bible," announced the preacher, standing beside the open hearse door. Dankie wiped his hands across his tear-stained face to sweep away the sadness and dry away his tears. He rubbed with such force and so repetitively that it seemed as if he wished to wipe away his face altogether.

"Thank you, God," the preacher continued, "for giving us this chance to speak to you. Now we have to take our friend to the cemetery. Please be with us through to the cemetery. Amen."

"Amen," the crowd replied.

As quickly as their tongues released the last syllable of "amen," one of the women began to lead with Zulu lyrics to carry Maduzu through the compound of Elite and to the procession on the road.

Follow
Follow him wherever he goes.
Wherever he is
We will follow him.

Dankie watched the coffin. The car door shut. He stood in the rear until the engine started and the vehicle began to creep slowly along the side of the building. He started walking, following the hearse. It wasn't long before the sweet melody of those around him was suffocated by the harsh Muchongolo drum.

dong, dong dong, dong
dong, dong dong, dong

The vibration of the drum leaked through the pores of each mourner as if their skins had turned to sieves allowing the sound waves to force their way into the blood and shake the beat of each heart. Although the singers surrounded the car, walking Maduzu along the side of the building and between the rows of mourners waiting their turn, only the sight of their song could be seen—as if they were moving their lips, but nothing came forth. Even they could hardly hear the sound of their own voices. The vibration of their collective vocal cords could not break through the force of the Muchongolo drum.

As Dankie passed through the gateway, trailing several meters behind the rear of the vehicle, he stopped. His heels stood heavily on the line between the cement of the compound's floor and the worn gravel of its parking lot. He looked around, scanning his eyes from the parked cars on the far end of the lot, past those in line being directed to wait for spaces to free up, to the tar driveway leading to the hospital. "Welcome to Tintswalo Hospital" read the large white billboard painting the small patch of sky uncovered by the hospital building.

The hospital and funeral home sit at the base of a slope just on the edge of Acornhoek's main street, almost hidden. It was a place Dankie had avoided with great effort. A road, a driveway really, on which he had intentionally chosen to never turn.

Less than ten minutes after the man announced their turn to view Maduzu for the final time, Dankie climbed into the vehicle, his aunt and the five women climbed into the rear of the truck, and Jack squeezed himself between the supple hips of one woman and the hard metal of the closed back door.

Dankie's aunt—whose tall, bony frame reached the ceiling—sat behind the driver's seat with her chin resting on top of the headrest. She stared out the window the whole way home.

While driving through town, the sounds of Friday afternoon filled the vehicle. The sounds that blended well with the chatter of the women, on the first drive through, now felt heavy. A long container, like those loaded with cargo onto semitrucks, had been offloaded on the northern side of the main shopping strip, brought in by a regional radio station. Its sides were imbedded with speakers so as to fill Acornhoek's busy drag with the sounds of their disc jockeys and pop dance music. One end sat wide open with people standing about in traditional dress. A shirtless man with rings of faux leopard tails around his neck and a short cloth of leopard skin around his waist stood barefoot near the edge of the road, watching the slow procession pass. It was one of many that had already crept through town.

The women who first chattered on about getting cool drinks when passing through, the women who waved to friends as they passed through the two stop signs just twenty minutes before, now sat and stared past the shoulders of those across from them, out into the crowds of the market, and outside the large shops.

Dankie sat in silence. His eyes were closed.

The slow tortoise crawl of cars held traffic from speeding along the stretch between the main area of Acornhoek and the turnoff to MaRoman. The two-lane tar road was filled with trucks barreling in the opposite direction, but an impatient bakkie driver shifted his gears, slid to the right, and attempted to speed past several cars in the convoy while driving uphill. The sight of a semi heading his direction only weighed his foot down further on the diesel and faster toward the front. With four cars to overtake, he ditched his efforts at the last second, shifted down his gears, and slid into the convoy, nearly driving a bakkie full of mourners off the tar, through the gravel shoulder, and onto the red soil.

The lead vehicle—a bakkie filled with Muchongolo men and women, one of whom still maintained the beat of the drum—slowed to turn onto the dirt road into MaRoman and eventually Rooiboklaagte. The impatient bakkie sped past, overtaking the last of the procession.

The sun was falling. The children who filled the roads as Maduzu's mourners first passed were now inside homes, sitting under trees in small number, or walking along the roadside meandering with no place to go. Just a few children were left on the soccer field, no longer playing against one another, but lazily lying on the dusty field, propped up by their stringy arms or leaning back with their heads on the ground.

The escarpment that paints the sky like a city in the distance radiated. A deep line of bright pink laced the edges of the rocky, defined features and the tabletop of the mountains. Splashed like watercolors haloing from its perimeter bled a palate of African oranges and pinks across the sky.

The shadow of this great backdrop losing the light of day slowly covered the speckles of homes seen across the lowlands, moving its way across the lowveld eastwardly up and down each gradation, stretching its way to the impala flats of Rooiboklaagte.

As the procession creaked along the eroded roads leading past Dankie's home and to Maduzu's homestead, Dankie began to rock his head—not enough for most to notice, but a small nervous beat slowly tapped forward. Maduzu's home was located on the slow slope of Rooibok's west side, leading toward the river and just a short walk from the natural spring where cattle drank, gardens were grown, and community members collected water when the taps ran dry.

Maduzu's home, identical to Dankie's, faced the mountains with a view unobstructed by any other homesteads. Located on the lower end of Rooibok's slope, the home had no direct neighbors with which to share a fence line like the homesteads further east, closer to the main road of Rooibok. The property was larger than others and looked like a collection of three or possibly four plots appointed to Maduzu and rented from the tribal authority. A link fence, wooden poles, and the occasional sheet metal or collection of sticks bordered the outline of his homestead. Unlike most, the entrance was wide enough to drive through.

As the vehicles rode the curve of the road to the left, just after passing Dankie's home, a large blue-and-white tent towering in the rear of Maduzu's homestead came into sight. Cars in the front of the line had already begun to park and unload, entering the homestead on foot, while the green hearse slid in, maneuvering through the crowds of neighbors and community members surrounding the house and filling the tent's interior.

The rear door of the hearse opened, and the men of Muchongolo reached in with the help of two Elite drivers to pull the coffin of their friend from its interior. Hidden beneath the soft drape of the wool blanket, the coffin was lifted to shoulder height and carried around the left side of the hearse, up the single step, onto the cement stoop, and through the front door of Maduzu's home. Immediate family and a few Muchongolo men followed behind closely.

Dankie, still separating himself from the crowd, just a few body lengths behind, heard the ululation of Joyce, Maduzu's sister, leaping from her body into the air like a call for help to the ancestors. Turning to the left, he saw Joyce throw her body flat against the ground, tipping like a signpost. She didn't even buckle. Gripping the sandy soil, her body, covered in black cloth, quivered as she cried. Two women, Joyce's friends from her home village, ran to her side and pulled her up by the arms, carrying her around Maduzu's home to the rear, where she could sit alone, away from the crowds.

"Come," said Jack.

"No," Dankie replied.

"Come," Jack insisted, holding his brother's arm.

Dankie stepped around the crowds, past the hearse, and through the closed-in stoop to enter Maduzu's home for the first time in seven days. Inside, every curtain was drawn, and dark shadows painted everyone and everything. A step behind his brother, his left shoulder against Jack's right, Dankie stopped in the center of the kitchen, beside the Muchongolo man holding the oversized, silver drum.

Each side of the main room—a kitchen and living room—had two wooden doors leading to small rooms. The doors were closed with the exception of the first room to the right. Inside, Maduzu was carried and placed on his bed to rest. Family members followed, filling the three remaining walls of the room with bodies, leaving little space for movement or light to break through.

Dankie turned around to look at the kitchen. At the table. The drum began to bang. It filled the small room—a room in which Dankie wished to never walk again—with violent force. An older man, the brother of Maduzu, left the bedroom door's entrance and signaled to the drummer, pushing his hands downward as if waving away the chords of Muchongolo. Stop, he was trying to say. Stop. Another elderly man joined him in motioning away the beat. The drum eventually quieted, and the drummer walked out.

Dankie took a few steps closer to Maduzu's room to hear the preacher speaking, but, as his view of the room's interior became clearer, he turned around and walked away. Inside the room, above the heads of too many people, hung the rope from which his cousin had hanged himself. Serrated in the effort to save, the rope attached to the roof's wooden beams hadn't been pulled down. It was a candid way of telling the tale; the remnants of the rope that pulled the breath of life from Maduzu's body showed mourners the real story.

REGINA

"*A dead man is not blamed.*" Mahlampfu, salani!

Some Shangaan and Sotho proverbs say that goodness is recognized only after death—that one never praises the living, only the dead. But then, again, it is also said, "*The good man dies in the bush.*" He dies alone, in grief, away from his family and his people. He lived a good life, a life that is forgettable. "*The evil one dies in his village.*" He dies amongst his people. He dies with family, friends, and foe side by side, talking of him long after he is buried. Long after he is gone.

Regina was not a member of Maduzu's family, extended or otherwise. Maduzu was one of many men and women who drank beer from the traditional clay pot called a *jomela*. They would gather together and pass around traditional brew of fermented local fruit and maize in honor of, and celebration for, the ancestors and traditional ways. In Regina's mind, they were what some called "drunkards." They danced on Sunday, while Catholics were in church and the local Zionists were singing underneath the fig tree and inside the kraal. They sang on Sunday of betrayals, anger, and war. They sang songs of the past and present tugging war, while gospel could be heard from blocks away, pouring out of the born-again's grey cement church, and the Nazarenes jumped up and down in circles, clapping.

While Regina accepted God's blood from the chalice, Maduzu drank a symbol of his culture from a jomela. And it was that which confused her. The more she thought about it, the "goodness" that God looks for in his children was not exemplified as she and other Catholic parishioners lined up to drink his blood. After they drank, the cup was sure to be wiped clean, as not to pass along the germs of others. Preventing the lips of each parishioner from indirectly touching. It was Maduzu who was filled with more goodness than her, she thought. It was the men and women who passed their beer amongst themselves, back and forth, with no worry about with whom they were drinking.

"The drunkards that we condemn share with one another, are not afraid of one another," Regina pondered. "Good people go to the Kingdom of Heaven whether they are Catholics or not; it does not matter if they go to church."

While Regina was not a friend, close or distant, she knew Maduzu as well as any Shangaan woman could know a man to whom she was not married. Maduzu was the subject of both gossip and rumors—the words of women skinnering and men telling tales. But she knew of him best through the words of his wife, the younger sister of Gertrude and a cousin by marriage.

Maduzu's reputation wasn't clear. Some said he hit his wife. Others said he stole in the night. And many agreed that when he was drunk, his fists were strong and his words were sharp.

The day Maduzu died, his wife had sought refuge in her sister's home, hiding from what she described as abuse and dominance. Rumor and gossip became indistinguishable against the testimony of his wife, but the story went something like this: Maduzu discovered his wife's adultery. He grew angry waiting for her to return home, planning, contemplating, wondering what he should do. Some say she had already left him. Some say she was moving out because of a job she'd found at a bakery. Others say there was no job. It was just an excuse to escape, to run away, or to be with her new man. And a few say that she hadn't planned on leaving at all.

When she returned home, he was angry. He had rope and something sharp. Maduzu's wife told of being tied down and held captive. Some say it was just hours. Those closest to her say it lasted for more than a day. Most say it didn't happen at all.

Maduzu's wife secretly revealed her truth. A recounting of the days uncovered a punishment so great that she refused to ever go back. She told her sister of Maduzu cutting her. Like many men, he blamed her adultery on womanhood. There is one thing that causes a woman to betray—a part of her that every man wants, a part of her that every husband owns. And Maduzu, according to the mother of his child, chose to destroy the cause of her betrayal, to destroy any chance for her to cheat again, to destroy her physically in hopes to keep her.

★   ★   ★

Regina's pace picked up the closer she got to the cemetery, and as she entered, she spotted Dankie, not much younger than her youngest son. She passed him on the left, put her hand on his shoulder, and said, "Hello, Dankie," in a soft maternal voice. She continued walking through the open gates, weaving her way through the tombstones of the friends, family, and neighbors she had buried in the past few years: Gertrude's daughter, Anna's husband, and her own. The cemetery—one of eight within a mile radius—was at the highest point in the community. Perched between the primary school and a soccer field, the cemetery rode the ridge of the hill, long and skinny. It overlooked a landscape of untouched bush to the east. With the exception of a few taller, older trees, most of what one could see were low-lying bush and shorter African flat crowns, stretching horizontally across the sky. Early in the summer season, the colors of green and blond amalgamated and painted a panorama of bushveld.

As people moved their way into the cemetery, Regina stopped further back with a group of women, many Women of Saint Anne, but others just friends. They formed a cluster, and Regina stood at the top, facing the northeasterly direction of the open grave. She crossed her arms and rested them across the shelf of her chest, and stood like a pillar of strength, with her legs firmly planted and her head lifted high.

She couldn't see much. In fact, she couldn't see anything, really, but the backs of men and the two tall human-high piles of soil lying directly south of Maduzu's grave. What she could see was Winfred's grave. It was never marked by a tombstone or brick decoration, but Regina knew where it was amongst the growing number of plots added each week.

Like that summer day she buried Winfred, Regina couldn't help but feel sorrow that this man about to be buried would no longer have the chance to try to be a good man, sorry that he would never have the chance to change. It was up to God now, to judge if he would go to heaven, go to hell, or wait. Only he knew the truth.

It had been a Thursday when she was told about Winfred. Nearly one year after their conversation under the giant fig tree, her ex-husband's sister returned to announce, "Your husband has passed." And so Regina, both traditional and Christian, adhered to her customs and closed her bedroom door. She remained inside that single room of no more than four square meters until the following Saturday.

As tradition dictates, a group of widows close to Regina gathered together and chose one person to watch over her. Ten Catholic parishioners, mostly Women of Saint Anne, decided that Anna Mdluli was the best person to care for Regina and keep a watchful eye. Anna had lost her polygamous husband a few years earlier, and she was very close to Regina. As soon as she found out, she joined her friend in the closed bedroom.

Anna was in charge of cooking food and making sure that Regina had what she needed. When Regina had to use the toilet outside, Anna would cover her head with a cloth, so that people could not see her, and guide her outside to the tin-walled toilet and back again. During the day, other widows visited Regina, but she was never allowed outside of her room—they were confined to visiting her inside. Traditionally, though, Anna's most important responsibility was to make sure that Regina was not poisoned. It is very common for widows to be blamed for the deaths of their husbands. Some are accused of adultery, others accused of poisoning, and some of witchcraft. Traditionally, there is no such thing as a death by natural causes; there is always a reason behind someone's passing.

On the ninth day, her bedroom door opened once again, and her youngest son Koosh, Winfred's sister who cared for him in his final days, and a relative who planned to drive the vehicle joined her. The four of them drove out of

Acornhoek and north to Klaserie, an old post office and train depot just past the former homelands' border. A Martin's Funeral Parlor hearse waited for them there and followed them back to Regina's home, where Winfred would spend his final night.

Regina's room had been prepared, and it stood empty awaiting their arrival. The coffin was carried through the yard that was never his and into Regina's bedroom. Winfred's coffin was placed on the floor and opened for family members to see his face, once again.

Despite the heat of the summer sun, Regina was covered with a wool blanket by those preparing her husband's burial and supported on each side by strong arms. It was assumed she had little strength to support herself, but Regina was not weak. As custom calls, she looked not to the left, nor to the right, nor toward where she walked. Regina's head tilted toward the ground below. Like blinders, the blanket that curtained her body forced her vision in one direction.

He was buried in the community cemetery near the mission. There was a traditional function, religious program, holy mass, and then the burial. Like Regina, her late husband also walked this journey in the arms of others. The coffin traveled from place to place until he was finally laid to rest.

That evening, ten women remained in her home. Each of them was a widow. Regina stayed with all ten women in the room where she'd been confined for the previous ten days. She couldn't sleep. She knew that they were there to take her, but she knew no more than that. Restlessly, Regina lay in her bed waiting—anxious of what might be to come and unsure of whether to be filled with fear or, since the women around her were all Christian in heart, to be filled with calm. She simply waited. And waited. And waited until the hour was three and the moon was high in the night sky. She waited until the women told her, "It is time."

There was a full moon that night. The women walked in silence by the light of the moon and the Southern Cross above, walking down the dirt roads and passing houses of friends and neighbors. They walked and walked, and, finally, several kilometers away, they arrived at the Nwandlamare River: a place where women fetch water, where their mothers were traditionally courted, vital to the livelihood of each and every villager.

It is at this place that traditions begin and the story often ends.

"They took me to the river, and in the river they gave me laws and some other things. I am not allowed to tell you more than the laws they have given me," explained Regina. It is a mystery to every woman, one solved only at the death of her husband. "I was not afraid," she continued, "because I was surrounded by Christian women."

Although Regina showed no fear, Emerencia was terrified. Every young woman hears rumors about what is happening to the widows down by the river. She had heard that the women are put into the cold water and struck repeatedly. She was afraid that the other widows would beat her mother. She had also heard whispers about the women being cut with scissors on their bodies. But nothing she had ever heard could be confirmed. The widows return home, every time, with a new set of black clothing and a haircut cropped close to the scalp. Regina wouldn't share beyond what she'd been permitted.

The laws presented to her governed her actions for the following six months—simple laws, but crucial for the widowed Shangaan. Regina was not allowed to look in any other direction than forward. There was no looking to her right, no looking to her left, and no looking back. She was not allowed to raise her voice above a soft and respectful tone. Nor was she allowed to walk without her hands behind her back or crossed over her chest. Regina, for the next six months, would honor her husband with these rules of obedience.

She returned home, nearly seven hours later, dressed in black, in which she stayed until her period of honor, obedience, and respect was concluded. Regina arrived where Emerencia waited with tearful eyes. "I was wearing a black dress, black shoes, black jersey, and a black fabric to cover my shoulders," she recalled, "and a rosary."

THOKO

The mountains that would normally grace the skyline to the west had disappeared. From east to west and north to south, the skies were clouded over with bustles of grey and silver clouds. Summers in the lowveld were a constant of highs and lows. For days, the skies would be crystal clear, and the heat would gradually grow hotter and hotter, as if someone was moving the stovetop burner up one notch each day, and when the heat reached the boiling point, when the strength of the sun was too much to bear, the skies would fill with clouds. Much like the day of Maduzu's burial, the skies would billow over in collections of clouds gathering tiny raindrops inside, near bursting point, and eventually letting loose and relieving the dry grasses, the thirsty wildlife, the steamy tar roads, and the lethargic humans below.

Another cluster of women formed to the right, slightly closer to the open grave, beneath a tall tree. In front, just below a low arching branch, Thoko towered above those around her. Although she too could see little beyond the backs of men encircling the open grave, she could see more than those beside her. She could see the small purple tent where Joyce, Maduzu's mother, and Maduzu's three children sat with a clear southeasterly view of the open grave. She could see the green hearse parked between her and the tall piles of red earth, and she could spot the long white trailer to the right where lowering equipment was stored.

Further to the right and closer to the men, almost exactly east of Maduzu's open grave, was the third and final cluster of women. They stood between the white trailer and the purple tent. At the front of this cluster stood six Muchongolo women draped in traditional cloth and wearing necklaces with varying beadwork. They stood two-by-two-by-two, almost alongside the men encircling the grave.

The men created an inner circle, within which the women were not allowed. And the women, because of the awkward position of the grave in the cemetery, formed a half moon on the exterior to the south and west of their male counterparts.

The two men who had led the night vigil and morning prayer stood, slightly elevated, on the western side of the grave, focusing their attention on the clusters of people where Thoko and Dankie were located, occasionally directing their words toward Regina and the women furthest from the grave. JJ, wearing a long blue plastic rosary around his neck, took a step back and allowed George to lead.

"Now that this body is dead," he explained, "the body is no longer in use. God says, when you die, don't worry, because one day you will wake up. One day, you will come alive. All of the graves, one day, will hear one single voice. And after that voice has spoken, all the dead people will wake up and rise."

Suddenly, as if in response to George's words, the six women of Muchongolo burst forth in song. The lead singer, several octaves higher than the others, moved her hands in a one-two beat and began to sing the chorus, "Women *are killers,"* after which the remaining five repeated her words, joined her in clapping the one-two beat, and added two lines periodically.

The men are killed. The women are no good.

The rhythm of the clap shifted the motion of their hips; the women were dancing. In the motion of their chorus, they shifted their bodies from right to left, forward and back. Thoko knew that this was a new song made up just that day for the occasion. She knew most of their songs, and this was not one of them. The melody of the music and the beat of their hands could be plucked from the cemetery, pumped through shebeen speakers, and young people would hum along and dance to the music. But sung with mournful lyrics, with recognizable lyrics and the circumstance under which those surrounding stood, the beat ran only through the bodies of the Muchongolo people. Even Regina, who sings her way through the day, whether out loud or under her breath, stood still.

Women are killers. The men are killed. The women are no good.

As the voices of the Muchongolo women slowed and the beat faded, George broke in with prayer, *"Oh, please God, we have built your child's home. So please, help us to bury him. Now that we are burying him, please, just be with us until we have left here to go home, Lord Jesus Christ."*

To the right of Thoko, a short, round woman raised her head and began the first song of many that would pervade the cemetery as the coffin was lowered and the grave was filled. Unlike the rhythmic dance songs sung by the men and women of Muchongolo, the crowds released a series of softer church-choir melodies, each with the image of heaven or a message to God. The songs sung through the week of preparation, the parlor viewing on Friday afternoon, the vigil Friday night, and the funeral Saturday morning were all chosen spontaneously. There were no plans, no organized series to sing, just a collection of people who could, at any time, lead a song of their choice.

"*Someone is calling my name,*" the first woman led. "*There is no one who is like you, you are our God,*" led the second. And the third, "*Names will be called and I am on the list,*" was initiated and led by Thoko.

As the coffin reached the base of the grave, the two men unlatched the belts from above, let them drop below, slid them underneath the coffin, and pulled them back up the other side. Before the final belt was pulled from the grave, one of the two men had already started to disassemble the equipment and pack up the lever system. As soon as the belts were rolled up tightly, the man with free hands walked over to the tent under which the family was still sitting and began to break down the tent's four poles and pull down the purple roof used as protection from the direct heat of the sun.

With the lever system out of the way, JJ lifted two corrugated metal sheets leaning against the tallest pile of soil and handed them to a local boy who had climbed into the grave with a hammer and nails. A wooden frame had been built at the base of the grave within which the coffin sat and now needed to be closed. The young man slipped the corrugated metal beneath him and began to hammer away, securing the first panel and then the second. After lifting his hands into the air, two men above pulled him up and out. He joined the assembly line of boys between the open grave and the piles of soil.

The boys had formed two lines several meters in length, bridging the gap between the soil removed from the site on Wednesday and the grave that now needed to be closed. The two lines of boys, parallel to one another and facing one another, worked as a team to carry the dirt from point A to point B as quickly as possible. One spade was handed to the boy in each line who stood closest to the pile of soil. He pulled a spade of soil from the pile and handed it to the next boy in line, who handed it to the next and so on and so on, until the spade reached the grave and the soil was dropped inside. The boy who dropped the soil then ran to the pile and dug a new spadeful, handing it down the line once again.

Thoko, standing beneath the only tree inside the cemetery, lifted her left hand above her head and pulled a leaf off the branch sitting just above her black pillbox hat—the one she wears to every burial. As she lowered the leaf to her chest and began to flip and fold its edges, the second song of the burial came to a close, and a moment of silence occurred.

"Naaaaames," she sang. "Names will be called."

She sang with a voice unlike any of the other women. It was soft and delicate but full of force and strength. Her head tipped back, as if she were singing to the skies, pushing her words through the leaves and branches of the tree umbrellaed above her for everyone inside the cemetery and out to hear.

"*Naaaaames,*" she sang with several dozen others in unison. "*Names will be called. I am on the list.*"

Thoko loves to sing. Everyone knows you won't see her in church—she hasn't attended since she became a sangoma—but when it comes to funerals, she is in full attendance. And it's a rare burial day when she doesn't lead her friends and neighbors through several songs.

As if unwilling to give up her role as lead singer to another in the crowd, she didn't allow a second of silence to occur before a new chorus was introduced. If you didn't know better, it would sound as if she led only one song, but in fact she blended one into another, into another.

"*When you were born,*" she started while the final syllable of "list" still hung in the air. "*When you were born, everything is known by God. When you die, everything is known by God.*"

A sangoma and traditionalist, Thoko knew the lyrics and had mastered the vocals of some strong churchgoing melodies.

"*Heaven,*" she began in Zulu, adding just one last song before opening the position as leader to others. "*Heaven is very beautiful. It is home for those people who are good. They will rest there, in heaven. I love my Jesus, because he was crucified for me.*"

Just as Thoko freed the reins, the boys were packing the final spades of soil onto Maduzu's grave. They were fast. They dug quickly, passed quicker, and moved from one position to the next with little fumble. The piles of soil slowly descended, and, in the span of half a dozen songs, the grave was full, and Maduzu was officially laid to rest.

DANKIE

From behind the women of Muchongolo, Dankie could see when the men from Elite began turning the large metal crank attached to two long belts strapped beneath Maduzu's coffin. With each turn, his body had lowered a few additional centimeters closer to the bottom, further and further out of sight.

I will never see him again, thought Dankie, holding back his tears. Lowering his head, as if wishing not to see, not to remember things this way, he spotted Mabel, the daughter of a cousin on his mother's side. Mabel was only three or four, and he hadn't seen her much, but her mother had brought her and her baby sister—who was tightly strapped to her mother's back—for Maduzu's funeral and the lobola function for Dankie's sister Sizele, later that afternoon. Dankie reached down and took Mabel's long skinny fingers into the palm of his hand, holding tightly. She stood leaning her string bean body against his right leg, tapping her white Mary Janes heel to toe, heel to toe.

Joyce's daughter stepped forward with a neatly tied blue-and-white plastic grocery bag. She walked inside the circle of men and beside the grave to hand it to JJ and George. They untied the handles and removed two clear plastic envelopes, each with a sheet of paper and bouquet of fabric flowers inside. The first was from Maduzu's three children. Beneath the bouquet of flowers was a letter written to their father, expressing their love, but also questioning his death and their fate. The second was from the whole Mathebula family. Beneath the bouquet of flowers was a page on which "Rest in Peace" had been written in bold letters. Each plastic envelope and its sealed contents were situated near the top of Maduzu's grave, held in place with several fists of soil. At the foot of the grave, the plastic bag was shoved beneath the soil, half-covered.

Before a new song could be started, JJ spoke quickly, announcing that Teni—a tall and thin elderly man, a representative of the chief—had asked to speak.

"Firstly," he said, "I would like to say hello to everyone. For all that have come here, I thank you very much. On behalf of Chiefs Dwandwe and Xingwane, they say they are crying, like you are crying, the Mathebula family, for this death. We feel sorry for this death. We have lost someone who was working very hard, because Maduzu was always helping the chief, collecting rent and levies when needed.

"There is one thing that I would like to discuss that is important," he explained, lowering the tone of his voice and directing his words toward the group of boys shaking their shoes free from soil after having filled Maduzu's grave. "To you all, the new generation, I did hear about your crying. There are people who think, when you work very hard, that you are very stupid. So to all the people, please remember that this new generation—this young generation, all the young men who dug this grave—they have not been paid. All they were given were cigarettes and some traditional beer. So, I am cross with you, Mathebula family, because you said to the boys that they should just work without any food. Only cigarettes and traditional beer!

"You didn't treat them very well," he continued, facing Joyce and her mother directly, "and I don't like that. That is why I am speaking in front of everyone, so that everyone can hear. These children are not yours, and they are not mine. They are ours.

So you should treat them very well. You don't have a group of children with which you have contracted work to be done. If you did, you should have told us. You should have hired a group of children to dig the grave.

"I should not have sent my lovely boys to come and dig your grave. You said to the boys, 'Did you come here to eat, or to dig a grave?' You should have given them food. I don't like this.

"You, the mother, you don't stay here, but you come here and make your own rules. And you, the sister, you don't stay here, and you come with your own rules. I don't like this. So now, my people," he said, speaking to the community as a whole, "we are going home. So don't go to their home and eat. Just go there and wash your hands and go home. Don't eat, because they said you can't just come to eat. And all I am going to tell you is, we didn't come here to eat. We came here to bury this man.

"I will not go to their home to eat, and you should not go to their home and eat. If I made someone cross, please forgive me, but I had to talk."

The crowd stood silent.

In an attempt to cut through the tense cloud that suddenly fell upon the cemetery and the Mathebula family, JJ stepped forward and suggested that a song be sung, a chorus, before the next announcement, and before the Mathebula family was given the chance to respond.

"Pleeeeeeassssse," belted one of the Muchongolo women stepping forward and toward the soft soil of Maduzu's grave, "*pleeeeeeassssse, ask the preacher to ask God.*"

Following her lead, the five others unleashed in high-pitched vocals, "*Pleeeeeeassssse . . . pleeeeeeassssse, ask the preacher to ask God, Why are people dying? People are dying.*"

The short chorus concluded as JJ cut through the end of a lyric to announce that the brother of Maduzu, dressed in a brown tweed jacket and dark pants, had stepped forward and wished to speak. It was his money and his funeral plan, to which he paid each month and on which his brother Maduzu was listed, that was paying for the majority of the funeral costs. Silent for a brief moment, he pled to the community for understanding and forgiveness, "*To all the women, men, and boys: please, I am telling you that I am good person. It is my sister and my mother that have caused the problems here. They always do things their own way. I don't like this, because people will blame me for their actions. I am now living in Acornhoek, but I will be buried in Rooibok; I won't be buried in Acornhoek. I ask for forgiveness for what has happened. There are a few boys who did hear me telling my mother and my sister not to do what they were doing to the boys, but they just didn't listen to me.*

"Please forgive my family for what has happened. After the funeral, please go and eat. Don't listen to Teni. I understand that he is angry, but please forgive them and eat something. . . ."

JJ, stepping forward to direct the announcements once again, responded, *"Please forgive the Mathebula family, because we always ask God to forgive us as we forgive others. We also have a second and final announcement from Teni."*

"All those people who qualify for food parcels from the government should gather in the soccer field at half past two," Teni said, pointing to the field located just southwest of the cemetery. *"There will be a social worker that will help you learn how to get food parcels if you do qualify. This is a meeting for people who do not receive parcels already, but wish to."*

People turned to chat with one another, mostly regarding the situation Teni brought forth, when the voices of the ten Muchongolo people—four men and six women—began to sing and compete for airspace. But before you could hear the words of their chorus, one of the men began to beat the drum, which drowned out not only those departing and chatting with one another but each of the Muchongolo dancers who were now singing and dancing counterclockwise around the newly filled grave of their friend.

From a distance, Dankie stood watching the men and women of Muchongolo move their bodies, lift their legs, arch their backs, and throw their arms, moving around the grave singing and shouting. "This," he said, "is what killed my cousin." Turning around, he walked through the cemetery still holding Mabel's hand.

Relatives, friends, and neighbors began to disperse out the cemetery gates into cars and on foot. Regina, alongside her best friend, Gertrude, left the cemetery; walked through the schoolyard, across the sandy road, down the narrow footpath passing rows of houses; and arrived at the Mathebula homestead.

Inside, women who had volunteered to cook were preparing to serve those returning from Maduzu's burial. A few had already arrived, but more had come and gone, stopping only to wash their hands in the tin washbasin situated to the right of the homestead's entrance.

Washing one's hands at the end of a funeral is an element of tradition that continues to carry on whether the deceased, or the family of the deceased, believes in Christ or the traditional spirits of *amandlozi* and the ancestors. It's a tradition that, for many, has become superstition.

At the end of every funeral, Regina and other Christians think of the biblical story of King David and the death of his son. King David chose not to bathe while his son was dying and through the preparations of his burial. But when it was all over, once his son was buried and he had said goodbye, he requested a basin so that he might bathe himself.

Traditionally, it is believed that during funeral days a person's blood is dirty, particularly from the time of the funeral parlor viewing through to the cemetery burial, between which the body of the deceased is driven or walked home in a slow procession and laid upon his or her bed for one last night, and during which family, friends, neighbors, and community members sit, in the homestead of the deceased, singing and praying through the night by the flicker of candlelight. At the conclusion of a cemetery service and burial, everyone must walk back to the homestead of the deceased and wash themselves, wash their bodies clean of the dirt, the stain, and the evil spirits. At the entry of the homestead gate, a tin washing basin is placed with a concoction of water, snake poison, and paraffin, where people come to wash their hands and, sometimes, their feet.

Historically, though, this routine came about out of necessity. Before 1960, the ritual washing was to clean themselves after having slaughtered and skinned a cow, dug the grave, wrapped and fastened a body inside the fresh skin of the cow, and then filled the grave. Today, in a nation of Friday assembly-line viewings and Saturday burials where the funeral attendants leave mid-service to pick up the next body, this utilitarian act becomes a cultural custom with greater symbolism and ancestral meanings.

THOKO

Inside the kitchen, Thoko prepared pap on her electric stove. She had already gone to fetch water, prepared the children for school, cleaned the shebeen, and made morning tea for the builders. Pap with marojo would be lunch for the two men. Since the day the tavern started construction, Thoko's list of what to care for had increased, but her excitement—as the foundation was initially poured, and then each brick was placed, eventually resembling walls—supplied the energy she'd depleted with little sleep, a lot of counting, and a degree of worry about which she did not speak.

In July, earlier that year and just before Patrick returned to Rooibok, the police visited Thoko's house, put her in handcuffs, and booked her in the Thulamahashe jail. She had been accused of registering Patrick's daughter Evidence—the mother was an ex-girlfriend—and Shelly's child as her own children and collecting monthly child grants on their behalf. The charges: two counts of fraud.

Thoko was spending money or taking the steps to spend money long before she had it—indebted to many, soon to be indebted to more. Numbers filled her head far beyond banking bricks in the yard. She'd recently paid one lawyer for processing her liquor license, but she'd eventually have to pay for the other lawyer defending her in court. They'd already appeared before a judge three times, each postponed for another month. She owed her close friend Elizabeth money for bail, and she had to pay multiple micro-credit loans each month. Patrick had to save enough for lobola, the bride price for Lizzy, partially Thoko's responsibility after calling her son back from the city. His first installment was scheduled for December. And although she'd made one payment to start construction, additional installments were due.

Leaving the pap on the stove and covering its top, Thoko left the kitchen, located her broomstick, and walked out to sweep up around the site.

The foundation of the six-room building was complete, and two of the exterior walls were progressing at a pensioner's pace. The older of the two men stood on top of a corrugated metal sheet propped between two rusting barrels—an inexpensive scaffolding—adding a new line of bricks along the northern wall. Caking a layer of cement, making a bed for each cement brick, the two men placed the new row, one by one, at a protracted pace.

Thoko walked from the house toward the goat pen with walls made of sheet metal, thick branches, and a rusty spring frame with no evidence of the mattress that once covered its coils. Its roof was made of twigs, thick cement sacks, and ten-cent grocery bags. She walked past and through the chickens and goats that came and went freely, wandering in and out of their pen, in and out of the gate, sleeping where they found shade, and pecking around where they found food.

Thoko stood and examined the walls. None of the window frames being handmade according to her drawing's specifications were complete, but the space for each window was becoming quite clear. As Thoko watched, she could see a long metal wire coil, resembling railroad tracks, being stretched along the top of the brick wall. Wet cement would then cover the tracks, followed by another layer of bricks. Watching the men work, Thoko couldn't help but think that the wall seemed a little crooked. She couldn't help but think—as she had already on a number of occasions—that the northern corners of the building weren't as perfect as a book's edge.

She started to sweep along the fence line beside the road and worked her way closer and closer to the building. The first rains of the season had only teased the dry soil, so her broom slipped along the ground easily, collecting bits of construction debris and trash that had been dropped by the men, shebeen customers, or people passing by. With each sweep, a small plume of dust would rise and fall again.

Lost in the motion of sweeping, she heard something she did not recognize. She looked up to see the two men in the same place, doing the same thing as minutes before, but Thoko could see that her contorted wall was sliding. Her skew wall was coming down.

"Run!" Thoko shouted.

The younger man looked up and ran toward Thoko, away from the building, and away from the old man high on the scaffolding.

"Jump!" Thoko screamed.

The old man, who was standing in the direction that the wall was shifting, jumped from his spot on top of the corrugated sheet onto the ground below and was knocked off his feet by the cement brick he had just laid. Flat on the ground, he had been able to evade all but a few bricks. At first, no one spoke a word. But as he pushed the bricks off and stood again with obvious pain, he looked at Thoko and angrily said, "These windows are too large!"

Seemingly upset and confused as to what had happened, he looked at her again and said, "I've never had a house fall down before. This tavern has been witched. And if it has not been witched, this is because you are building on graves!"

Thoko ruminated for a moment, confused about why he was talking about graves, trying to think if she had ever heard of anything about building on top of graves. No one is buried under here, she thought to herself.

She looked at the man, about to respond, when he said, "This place has been witched, and I will not build in a place that has been witched." Supposedly fearful that he would be witched himself, he started to collect his things to leave.

One of the two men suggested that they visit a sangoma to biamuthi (de-witch) the place, but Thoko was certainly not giving them money to go visit a sangoma when this was not a case of witching; rather, it was an obvious case, to her, of bad building. The suggestion was not recognized, and Thoko agreed that they should leave. The old man, who was clearly injured, gathered his cement mixing tools and the two long metal corner frames that had been on the wall and came down with everything else. He left immediately and started to walk home.

Thoko had hardly moved from where she stood watching the walls of her tavern; watching the bricks she had paid for and her sons had made; watching those blocks of money fall to the ground and crumble, shatter into a myriad of pieces. With a broom already in her hand, Thoko began to sweep. She swept the pieces together into large piles, as she would have done had someone turned her month-end earnings into five-cent coins and thrown them into the sky to land wherever they rolled.

By nightfall, Thoko had swept each piece of cement brick together and had started to smash every bit as hard as she could with the backside of a spade. She smashed for hours. She pulverized each broken segment into the smallest pieces she could manage and often into fine dust. With these, and a new builder, she would start again.

REGINA

Five nights a week, Regina and Emerencia ate dinner in bed. Sometimes Simphiwe joined them. Sometimes she'd be outside playing, already full from the food she had eaten after school, food her grandmother made her each morning before leaving to work. Most nights, it was just mother and daughter perched with plates on top of a maroon-and-pink duvet, talking about their worries, their concerns, their days.

That morning, the Catholic mission had celebrated World AIDS Day with a series of workshops, one for the youth and a second for adults. Regina sat in the front row of the long hall beside a few Women of Saint Anne, listening to Sister Moya, an occasional visitor from Jo'burg, discuss HIV and AIDS in the village of Acornhoek.

When the women left, Gertrude said that she learned two important things: one, you must trust your partner no matter what, and two, condoms are bad. Regina went home and visited Anna to tell her of what she had learned. But there was one thing she couldn't remember—the three Cs. According to Sister Moya, there are three things that entice young women to give up their bodies at an early age.

"The triple C—what does it stand for?" Regina asked.

Emerencia looked at her mother and started to giggle. "Cash, car, and cell phone," she said.

The two women laughed together. During the previous year's World AIDS Day workshop, Sister Moya had gathered unmarried mothers and young women outside of the long hall and in the mission courtyard. Emerencia joined a circle with others and watched Sister Moya pull a beautiful dish from her bag. It looked fragile and expensive.

"Do you see how beautiful this plate is?" she asked the women. "Is there anyone here that wants it?"

Many of the women laughed and replied, "Yebo," or nodded their heads.

Sister Moya started to pass the plate around for everyone to see. But she didn't pass it carefully from person to person. She tossed the plate in the air to one woman. And once she had a close look, it was her turn to pass it along to another in the same way. The women watched nervously, just hoping they didn't drop the plate when it was passed to them. It was tossed and tossed and tossed until eventually it fell to the ground. And shattered into pieces.

"This is your life, girls," Sister Moya said. "Men are playing with your lives just like this."

"If the plate is broken," she explained, "no one will repair it. If you let someone play with your life, they will not stay by to fix it."

Sister Moya told the young mothers, "Tell your daughters that they are beautiful, or they will be taken advantage of by men who do. Take your daughters to restaurants, or they will fall for the men who do. They will think that only a man can do that for them."

Since then, Emerencia tells Simphiwe every morning that she is beautiful. And every month, Emerencia uses nearly all of her child grant to take Simphiwe to Kentucky Fried Chicken. They buy enough food for the whole family. Emerencia has even spoken of saving money to buy plane tickets. One day she would like to board a plane in Hoedspruit and fly someplace. They wouldn't spend the night, because that would cost more money, but they could see the airport and fly back again. Emerencia has never flown before, but she wants Simphiwe to know that they can do these things without a man.

Emerencia had never heard of the three Cs before Sister Moya referred to them that morning, but she knew that there was some truth behind her words. She and her mother laughed and laughed at the alliteration, partly because they knew it didn't apply to them, and partly because it was easier to laugh than to cry.

On Friday and Saturday nights, Emerencia and her girlfriends hang out at Mbebe, a tavern in Acornhoek with a patch of green grass and tall trees. The women sit and talk with friends while drinking ciders. The men gather in circles, not far from them, drinking beer. The DJ plays the sounds of Sophiatown from the 1950s, African jazz, township-inspired music of the Drum era. They listen to Mandoza, Brenda Fassie, and Arthur Mafokate.

Emerencia's friends sit back and watch the men pass, looking for key chains and fancy cell phones. Most of her friends won't date anyone who doesn't have a job. Many of the men drink beer, leaning against their cars, moving to the beat of "the Kwaito King" pumping from the speakers. Emerencia is shy compared to her friends. She's never looked for men with money, although she's been with the same man, her child's father, for eight years. They aren't married, but she'd stayed with him in and out of employment. Her friends, though, say that men must provide them with cash, but the men also must have accounts—Truworths, Jet, Exact. They must have a store card to give their girls to go shopping, but the girls also need cash to buy themselves expensive cosmetics, like L'Oréal and Avon, and good food, like Chicken Licken and Kentucky.

The girls lie in the grass and laugh under the stars. They dress in tight jeans with hair that took hours, if not days, to relax, popcorn, s-curl, braid. They look for men wearing expensive clothing. And the men must be able to buy them drinks. If the men have a car, they will always hold their keys in a prominent place or sit leaning against the front fender. And if the girls are interested, they will rarely wait for the men. They'll walk right up and tell them they would like something to drink—as honestly as they will later ask for money and for department store account cards.

Girls go to town and are attracted to the men with things they don't have at home. In the rural areas, there aren't too many men who are based locally, full-time, making money. The men with good money are either teachers or politicians. Most of them are married with many girlfriends.

The girls want something from them. Most of the girls are poor and have little money at home to buy new clothing or cosmetics from the pharmacy. Emerencia's friend, a daughter of another Mapusha weaver, dated a married schoolteacher while she was still in high school. He taught at another school, but they met at a municipality-wide athletics competition. He approached her and they started to talk. Soon after, he started to visit. He would give her cash to buy clothing and would bring her nice things. Eventually, those visits turned to trysts, and, soon after, she was pregnant. Once she was pregnant, he was no longer interested. She threatened to file for maintenance (child support), but he convinced her that it would be too expensive for him, and his wife would find out. So they agreed he would help when he could. Though, he rarely did.

"Is it true?" Regina asked, referring to the three Cs.

"Yebo," Emerencia said to her mother in reply. "But it's mostly happening in Jo'burg. Girls here don't really look for triple C. Look at all the girls that get pregnant. If they were looking for triple C, they wouldn't get pregnant."

THOKO

Lindiwe, who had been called by the ancestors to train as a sangoma, didn't arrive as planned.

The third of the month came and went. Thoko had been preparing for her arrival for several weeks, although the death of her sister's nephew by marriage certainly distracted her for a short period, but, just a few days past month-end, one of Lindiwe's family members came to visit. Thoko had been airing out her dozen or so goat- and cattle-skin drums—usually stored inside the ndumba of her mother's ancestors—leaving them outside to tighten in the heat of the sun.

The family member explained to Thoko that their elders had not been able to return and prepare a celebration for the ancestors, announcing that Lindiwe would be entering sangoma training. As Christmas was approaching and most people were returning home from work just past mid-month, they would have the chance to prepare for the celebration in a few weeks' time, after which Lindiwe would be able to start with Thoko immediately.

Lindiwe, like most people, needed the three months not only to take the muthi prescribed by Thoko for her illness but also to collect the money with which to pay Thoko for training. She needed three thousand rand in order to start training, and that is often the entirety of one person's salary for three months. Lindiwe needed the help of her family members, including the elders, returning in a few weeks for the holidays and summer break, in order to pay. She was not doing well. Although her family didn't share specific details with Thoko, the muthi wasn't strengthening her. It wasn't taking away the pain and uselessness of her legs. Her weakness was actually increasing, and the training was a last hope for a turnaround.

As much as Lindiwe needed to collect the sum of money for training, Thoko needed to collect an exorbitant sum of money for the construction of her tavern. The tumble, several weeks earlier, caused her purse strings to tighten and her plan to shift askew. The cogs inside Thoko's head needed to churn overtime to push money here, pull money there, and fill the holes that needed filling.

When Thoko is short on cash, she heads into town to Get Ahead or an equivalent alternative. Get Ahead is a microfinance company that works with men and women locally to gain credit and keep cash in their back pockets. Thoko has an ongoing loan with Get Ahead in order to keep both the tuck shop and the shebeen stocked. The loans last only four payment periods, and since they are given out in groups, rather than to individuals, she really needs to visit the offices only when the loan needs renewal and upgrading. Each payment period, one of the group members collects everyone's payment and goes to the office in time for their due date. If loans are paid for on time, the renewal allows for a credit increase. Starting with a loan for five hundred rand, Thoko, after cycles and cycles of proper repayment, will eventually qualify for four thousand rand each period.

Thoko's money troubles weren't limited to the tavern construction. Actually, the legalization process of registration and liquor license acquisition was probably the most significant cost in one lump sum that Thoko had ever paid. Before the first summer rains, Thoko's payment to the white lawyer down in Hazyview, who was handling the process and paperwork on her behalf, required an up-front payment of six thousand rand for both government fees and legal services. On top of that, the cost of transportation to file paperwork, appear in court, and visit the tavern site required an additional two thousand rand.

The tavern walls were growing slowly, and the tavern's opening date kept getting pushed. The original builder required an up-front payment of fifteen hundred rand to dig the foundation, pour the concrete, and begin constructing the walls. When the walls were finished, a second and equal payment was due. With the collapse and crumble of the northern wall, and his premature departure, Thoko didn't pay him any more, but she did lose her initial payment. The second builder required three thousand rand to start off where the other finished, although the roofing, plaster, and interior tile work would be extra.

Thoko didn't believe in banks, so—by default—her bedroom became her vault, and the key hanging around her neck or on a spiral bracelet around her wrist opened the safe. Thoko's room is dark, shaded by thick white lacy curtains. Behind her door, a dozen bras hang from a hook shoved into a wall crack. Above her bed, her two hats and several scarves decorate the wall. And her wardrobe is closed and locked, clearly stuffed to the brim with items sticking out the edges of its double doors. In the center of her room, the queen-sized bed is propped up by two stacked cement bricks at each corner—she is afraid of the Tokoloshe, a small hairy creature (often compared to a baboon) that pulls people from their beds at night to kill them.

She never used to lock her room, but after her children started pinching bills or coins here and there, she started to close and lock her room every day, while she was home and while she was away.

REGINA

The mountains were missing again. Heavy rains through the night pulled a curtain of fog and cloud over the impala flats and brought an abundance of bird life. A flock of chittering red-billed quelea flew through the mission like acrobatic pilots, looping in and out, over and under, every move tight and precise. Hundreds skimmed the mission's green grass—around the keyhole tree, past the pink flowering bush near Mapusha's entrance—and dared to slide past the circles of barbed wire that kept the barking dogs in and the community out. They flew in three packs, each in complete unison with their team, crisscrossing one another, singing a jumble of harsh and melodious notes, like prattling children running through the eagerly anticipated puddles and raindrops.

Each rainy season since the flood of 2000 had been weak, with little rain and poor crops. A good rainy season can mean the difference between full bellies and hungry ones, between an abundant stock of mealies, peanuts, groundnuts, and pumpkin to last the year and a bag of mealies barely making it through a month.

The sound of rain—*tho, tho, tho*—promises good crops. In Shangaan tradition, a sighting of the bateleur eagle's zigzag flight signals water for drinking and growing, as well as deathly strikes. Black millipedes are a sign of forthcoming rain. And the sacrifice of a black sheep is made to please the ancestors, releasing black smoke in the air, in hopes that it will form into clouds and burst with precipitation.

Lightning had dominated the previous two evenings, filling the sky, striking like spears into the lowveld villages below, dancing in circles, assaulting the innocent, striking homes, crops, and the shadiest of trees. Lightning means both goodness and anxiety for the Shangaan and Sotho people. Witches work to reel in the power of the white light in the sky, in hopes to harm individuals and families through *vuloyi*. When someone's home is struck by lightning, witchcraft is blamed and sangomas are consulted. Lightning brings misfortune as well as much needed water for crops, livestock, and people residing below.

Rain from above means hours of relief from fetching water. When rain falls on Regina's roof, the slight incline slides the water down a curved track made of corrugated sheet metal that turns two times before releasing the stream into a tall blue barrel sitting behind her house. Heavy rains fill the barrel up quickly and offer Regina and Emerencia water with which to cook, clean, and wash.

Without rainwater, they rely on fresh water from the borehole (which had been broken for nearly a year), or they must fetch water from the dam or natural spring. Regina, who admits more and more that she has grown tired with age, often uses a portion of her salary to pay someone to fetch water for her, filling her largest containers.

Even when the borehole worked, their connection to the water pipes in Rooibok was weak. When the borehole motor was powered by electricity, the push was strong enough to bring water to the single tap in their yard. When the motor was changed to diesel, the strength decreased, and their tap became useless. This meant fetching water from the house of another Mapusha woman, down the road, during the limited hours the motor was running.

The rain let up, maintaining a slow and steady rhythm amplified by the tin roof of the leaking studio. As Gertrude swept water out the studio's open double doors, visiting youth from outstation parishes were just starting their final day of weeklong discussions on AIDS and HIV. They were sleeping, eating, and conducting workshops in the two old classrooms across from the long hall.

Squish-Squash, Squish-Squash, Squish-Squash, announced Regina's shoes. The soggy soles of her feet were heard coming before she was spotted walking through the mission's back entrance. The sky was still dark since the sun was trapped behind the mist, and cloud coverage blanketed the landscape. As if it were closer to nightfall than just after sunrise, the lights inside the mission compound and on the classroom buildings were still on.

The two women were dressed for a banking trip. Gertrude wore a long green jacket with a red plaid skirt, and she'd pulled her hair back with a neatly tied black and white scarf. Regina wore a khaki-colored suit and a fuzzy red beret, and she'd made sure not to forget her umbrella, assuring that she would look her best.

Gertrude and Regina travel to the bank once a month to collect salaries for each weaver and spinner at Mapusha. Although their bank has a branch in Acornhoek Plaza, they insist upon traveling the extra forty kilometers to withdraw from the Hoedspruit branch. *The lines are shorter, and the tellers are more helpful,* the two explained. Usually this means three taxi rides there, and three taxi rides back: Rooiboklaagte to Acornhoek's main street; Acornhoek to Plaza; Plaza to Hoedspruit . . . and back again. Often, they try to coordinate with anyone they know who may be driving back and forth—sometimes it's Judy, sometimes it's a local car owner, but, more often than not, the taxi is their only option.

Although it wasn't month-end—when lines stand stagnant for hours, snaking out doors, around corners, and full of all walks of life—the women were still emphatic about going to Hoedspruit.

Regina and Gertrude climbed inside a vehicle waiting outside the studio and started the first half of their travels. Knowing that their return trip would be by taxi and take much longer, they sat back and enjoyed the ride through town, peering out the vehicle, watching people on the roadside and taxis crammed with travelers.

The amount of litter on the side of the road is a fairly good determiner as to how close you are from Acornhoek's town center. The more litter you see, the closer you are. And when you see a "No Littering" sign beside goats chewing a banana peel, chickens pecking through a makeshift dumping ground, or plastic bags caught in the wind like tumbleweed, you'll know you've arrived. When people say they are going to "town," they are referring to the space between the first and second turnoff to Tintswalo Hospital—past Mapulaneng Technikon College, Martin's *funerals you can afford*, and Tswelopele Funeral Parlor—and before Plaza, the police station, and the newly installed, and only, traffic light.

They were anxious. They weren't sure if the money they were traveling to collect was actually in their bank account. At the end of November, they were short. They normally need 8,850 rand each month to pay all twelve members, but when they arrived to collect, the account balance was only 8,747 rand. Nervous that they would need some money left in the account, they choose to pull 8,200 rand, shaving a few salaries below expectations.

Judy, who was in the United States visiting her sick parents, had told them that money would be deposited soon from a UK woman who had made orders that were already delivered, and a few donations were expected to come through via the South African Development Fund. But neither deposit appeared on their bank statement at the end of November, which meant that only one week later, there was a chance it was still outstanding. And if they couldn't pull the money by December 9, they wouldn't take their usual month off for Christmas holiday.

Each woman was a nervous wreck that she wouldn't be able to make the purchases she'd been planning. Regina intended to save as much as she could afford for a new house. Anna needed the money to buy her son something nice and to offset her medical bills and food costs. Gertrude was hoping to spend her salary on bags of cement and building supplies to continue her half-constructed house. The other women had similar needs and wants, but their greatest fear was any sign of trouble, any sign that Mapusha was slipping back to where they'd been when mission priests left the project and the women behind.

Gertrude had already started building her new home. When it is completed, her nearly blind husband joked, they will open a hotel for people to stay, but not South Africans; he wants to host Americans and Europeans. Realistically, the new house will finally allow them to pull down a row of tin shacks, where many of Gertrude's children and grandchildren lived. Everyone would finally sleep surrounded by cement walls and, if Gertrude had her way, under a roof of clay tiles.

Regina was following in Gertrude's footsteps and had started saving for a new house, one that wouldn't leak in her bedroom, one that was made of cement rather than mud-brick, one that she didn't have to worry would eventually crumble at the pounding hand of summer rains.

Anna was receiving financial help from Mapusha for medical bills and food, but she wanted to take care of herself, and she wanted to show everyone that she could get healthy. Anna was eager to find a way to return to her spinning wheel, more than anything, but, since she wasn't strong enough to plant as much as she usually would, the December salary would help balance out her crop losses.

The women passed through the doors with built-in metal detectors and into the lobby of Hoedspruit's Standard Bank. The lines were short, and the people were quiet. Gertrude pulled an empty fabric bag from her purse and unzipped it. Regina held a sheet of paper listing denominations, quantities, and account details. The two anxiously stood in line and watched the other customers closely.

A barefoot Afrikaans boy in a local school uniform was walking from man to woman in line. "Oom," he would say, requesting that they purchase raffle tickets to benefit his school. "Tannie," he greeted, with very little luck in sales. He passed by Regina and Gertrude as they looked at one another trying to figure out what he was selling.

The line moved fairly fast, sifting a business owner with a bag of deposits to one window, a mother with trailing children to another, and a safari guide with knee-high socks, short shorts, and epilates to another. Gertrude and Regina waited their turn and were eventually directed to a pleasant Afrikaans woman in the farthest window. Regina apprehensively approached. She handed the teller the slip of paper and her ID book. "We would also like a bank statement," she said. Gertrude waited with her open bag on the counter. The woman greeted them formally and started typing into her computer. She smiled and walked away to collect a printed statement and a handful of plastic ziplock bags to separate each denomination. As the teller pulled a stack of fifty-rand bills to count, Regina's tense shoulders relaxed.

DANKIE

Vultures can spot a meal several dozen kilometers away. As they circle in the open skies above, competition joins the orbital flight, and, together, they all drop down into the bush, perching on dead trees, where they can watch their prey closer.

The lappet-faced vultures, the first to dive in, have a hook on their bills, equipping them to break tough skin. The survival of other vulture species is dependent upon this trailblazer's work. Once they have started the job, others are able to join.

* * *

Once a month, a government grant truck arrives in each community. They resemble small bread delivery trucks, and there is a driver, a grant agent, a government computer, and a finger scanner inside. Lines form and last for hours. Each person has his or her fingers scanned under a bright green light and grant-card details cross-checked with the computer. Everyone over sixty or on medical disability collects a monthly grant of 840 rand. Mothers earning less than 800 rand qualify for monthly child grants of 180 rand per child, to help pay for school fees and uniforms, food and tuck shop sweeties. The small armored truck distributes on the spot.

The best customers are those with cash in hand, and the only people being handed cash outside of month-end are grant recipients. Vendors situate themselves so that the recipient lines have to pass through them. Blankets are set up to their right and their left selling kitchenware, clothing, fruits and vegetables, freshly cooked meals, baked goods, and anything you might find in a corner tuck shop or the Indian store in town. Each blanket is its own store, and each owner is out to sell.

Expensive items like secondhand clothing or seamstress-made pinafores and dresses can be purchased on lay-buy. Lay-buy allows customers to purchase on credit . . . a little now, a little later, and another payment to finish off the sale. Purchases on credit are a risky affair for small-business owners who pack up at the end of each night and mark their storefront with a neatly laid blanket. But, if you're a grant-line storefront, you know that you're likely to see your customers again. They won't avoid you because of late payments when they know it would mean not collecting their monthly grant. They cannot spin lies about having no money when they are standing in line to pick up their grants and walk away from the collection counter with crisp cash in hand.

One brown elephant could purchase two bags of homemade *magwunya* buns. Dankie had baked them over the fire at home after watching his cousin Patrick run an assembly-line operation using a small toaster oven. Half of them were burnt, but he threw them in as a bonus to customers who purchased a nice batch.

Dankie sat alongside several other men selling the same product to mothers and pensioners. The recipes were nearly identical. The only differences that set them apart from one another were their sales tactics and the names they gave to their home-baked goods. Some called them biscuits, others sweet bread, some even called them cookies, but Dankie called them scones.

He wasn't aggressive like the men equipped with years of audacious sales tactics. He sat leaning against walls, behind lines of blankets, or beside bakkies filled with goods for sale. He didn't set up along the line where people walked and window-shopped with empty pockets, waiting to fill them, only to walk home with half of what they came for. Dankie made a poor salesman, but he wasn't willing to jump in the front lines and learn how to circle above his prey and dive in for dinner.

His cousin Patrick was the first man out there pecking and pecking until he broke the skin and got what he wanted or made it easier for others. He had much more of an enterprise compared to Dankie's casual sales, and he was quite successful with child-grant recipients. Patrick looked as if he was from the city, and when women passed him, his height, masculine features, clean appearance, and fashionable attire caught their eyes. Patrick's expensive jeans caught a second glance from many young mothers.

Dankie's shorter frame, tired wardrobe, and youthful baby fat drew in more pension than child-grant collectors. He was quiet and would very often rely on someone coming up to him, rather than approaching those passing by. His stock was small, since he had to travel by minibus taxi to and from each line. And some of his best sales were made sitting quietly with his oversized bread crate in the back of a taxi.

Becoming a better salesman would be admitting that his test scores might not be good enough to attend university. For now, he was trying to earn a little extra cash—something to get him through Christmas, to buy a new cell phone, and maybe to visit his sister down near Nelspruit in the village where they live amongst the boulders. Selling scones was to pass the time until his matriculation scores came through and real decisions had to be made.

As the lines moved forward toward the truck, recipients were checked and double-checked. One year earlier, the government initiated a crackdown on grant fraud. They were out to catch grandmothers who registered their grandchildren as their own, for mothers who were earning more than eight hundred rand but still collecting, for illegals registered for grants under fake IDs, and for guardians collecting pension for recipients who were no longer living. Amnesty was offered to those who were willing to come forward and cancel their illegal registrations, but very few people took the opportunity, causing the government, with the help of social workers, to file formal charges against each fraudulent collector.

Dankie's mother was in the midst of filing for her pensioner's grant, having recently turned sixty. His sisters collected child grants for each of their children. His cousins were collecting child grants for their children. And his aunt, Patrick's mother, had been charged with child-grant fraud five months earlier.

REGINA

Every morning, Regina made food for Simphiwe and hid it inside the house. If she was the last person to leave for the day, she would lock up and stash the keys to each bedroom and to the fridge padlock in a secret place.

Mapusha had closed for the month, and the women had exchanged long days of spinning, weaving, and dying for even longer days of loosening soil, planting crops, and weeding fields. Emerencia was still working at Buzi Cash and Carry. And summer holiday had started for Simphiwe.

Regina joined Gertrude and two other women from Mapusha in the gated land across the dirt road from the community crèche, just south of the mission grounds. The property was divided into four almost equal squares, and each woman took a portion. Inside the gates stood a small whitewashed building with butler doors. Regina and another woman from Mapusha used to rent the space and run a tuck shop, so long ago that neither can remember when. Today, the women use the land to plant maize and peanuts, adding to the fields they have at home.

Only the older generation work in the fields. The women of Mapusha say that the young women complain too much and aren't strong enough to do the hard work. Passing through Rooibok, MaRoman, and other communities throughout the village, you'll rarely see women in their twenties and thirties in the fields; rather, women like the original members of Mapusha, in their fifties and sixties, are the ones tilling, planting, and weeding. Women like Regina supported their families with maize for maize meal, peanuts and pumpkin leaves for marojo, and groundnuts for more protein.

Emerencia left early each morning by taxi. She worked Monday through Saturday as a temporary holiday worker, earning fifteen hundred rand—more than double what she could at Mapusha and almost as much as her mother earned after adding her salary and her pensioner's grant together. Emerencia couldn't pass up the opportunity to better her life, and money meant easier months and easier days. It meant buying new clothes and making sure that Simphiwe was taken care of. More money meant saving faster, which, in turn, meant that they could build a new house sooner.

While Regina was in the field and Emerencia checked customers' till slips against their bags, Simphiwe stayed near home. She would spend her days playing among the mango, guava, and granadilla trees or in the homesteads of neighbor children. She would play with her two chickens or chase away the neighbor's black hairy piglet that liked to come mingle near their pigpen.

When she was hungry, she would run home, find the hidden keys, and dash inside for a snack. But she always needed to keep a watchful eye, just in case her uncle Aubrey—her mother's older brother—could see her. She was terrified of him. She would look around the house, behind the kitchen, and near the pigpen. As soon as she knew he wasn't around, she could take and return the keys as freely as she wished. If she knew he was around, she kept a watchful eye.

Aubrey wasn't like everyone else. He didn't live in the house with three generations of women. He lived in his own single room on Regina's property, behind the main house, separated by a link fence, and alongside one of Regina's fields.

Aubrey didn't eat dinner with the women, either. He would collect his food at dinnertime and return to his house to eat. They lock the fridge to keep their food for the month safe. "He will eat everything. He will eat the whole chicken if we don't hide it," explained Emerencia. "We hide everything."

He didn't work. He spent most of his days hanging out in his room with closed doors, sometimes on his own, sometimes with schoolboys from the community. Mostly, he smoked *boxers* (tobacco rolled in newspaper) or *dagga*.

And he smelled. Aubrey didn't like to take baths. He would pour water into the plastic washbasin and go inside of his room, but when he came out again, the water was still clean. He would, however, make sure to bathe at least twice a month—for grant pickup day and to visit the hospital.

Once a month, Aubrey would travel into Acornhoek to Tintswalo Hospital for his shot. If Emerencia or Regina didn't go along with him, he would most likely never go. And even if they got him there, it didn't guarantee that he'd get his shot. In the past, he's tricked Emerencia into letting him go to the bathroom, while she maintained his place in line. He would stay in there so long that she would reach the nurse without him, losing their place and needing to come back another day. He infuriated both his sister and his mother.

If he didn't get his shot, he would scream and yell. He would go crazy. He would lose his mind as he did after his father left them. Everything was fine before then. He was a normal boy going to school. But when Winfred kicked Regina and her children out of their home, and he said he was planning to marry another woman, Aubrey had a nervous breakdown. He was hospitalized. Ever since, he has relied on medication to get him through the day, to allow him to function at the most basic level.

Aubrey receives a medical disability grant of 840 rand each month. He collects the money with his mother and immediately hands it over, keeping 200 rand for spending money. If he doesn't, he will use it all on tobacco for boxers, on dagga, and on beer in just a day or two, leaving nothing for food or electricity. Every day, Aubrey goes to his mother and collects 6.50 rand for a large packet of tobacco. He finishes one packet a day. Sometimes, though, he buys a matchbox of dagga for 3.80 rand, half the price of tobacco to roll, but only quarter the amount. The rest of the money stays with Regina, who makes sure he has food to eat, toiletries to care for himself, and new clothing to wear.

Simphiwe looked to her right and looked to her left. She pulled the key from its hiding place, went inside, and unlocked the room she and her mother share. Inside, she found the food her grandmother had made for her that morning. She nibbled on the hard maize meal porridge for a short while and returned as quietly and cautiously as she had entered. She put the food back in its hiding place. She relocked her bedroom door. And, looking around to see if Aubrey was near, she replaced the key in its secret hiding place.

As soon as Simphiwe was out of sight, her short and stocky uncle Aubrey emerged. He'd been hiding in the distance, watching her the whole time. As fast as he could, he grabbed the keys, went inside, and foraged through the room, looking for food. Aubrey had a habit of breaking into the house to eat whatever food he could get his hands on. He also steals Simphiwe's things, just to make her angry. He will take her toothbrush and her Colgate bubblegum-flavored toothpaste, her toy cars, and the books she has been given as a gift. He brings them into his house, where she is surely not to go looking. Emerencia, who hides her cell phone for fear he will take it, has compared living with Aubrey to jail: "He listens to his mind only."

But Simphiwe knew she wouldn't have to worry about him much longer. Her mother had decided to send Simphiwe away for the coming school year. Emerencia was working at Buzi Cash and Carry to save money for a new house and for driver's school. She wanted a driver's license, and she knew that all the hours required for lessons and driving time would prevent her from being home with her daughter. Theresa, Emerencia's oldest sister, had agreed to take Simphiwe in January, the start of the school year. Theresa was a community crèche teacher and could be home with Simphiwe before and after school. Emerencia would take her on the weekends, when she could.

Regina had no say in the decision.

THOKO

The heavy rains had prepared the fields. Thoko's hands and knees were stuck in the moist, sandy soil planting rows of maize. She had tilled, loosening the hard and stiff bed of the previous year's small crop, and prepared to place each seedling neatly in a row, coddling it to grow into tall and fruitful maize stalks. Summer had arrived and was now in full force. The rains had started to show up on a consistent basis, always arriving just in time to cool off the bodies below in desperate need of a temperature drop. Like a pot of water boiling over an open fire, the temperature slowly grows higher and higher. And just when it is ready to boil over, just when everyone is ready to call it quits, the rains cool off the land, halt the rapid boiling, and bring the people down to a livable level of heat. With torrid temperatures and steady rains comes a season full of life and birth—the first days of watching the maize begin to grow, pushing its way through the earth and into the air, where it scrambles to soak up the soil's limited nutrients and the moisture of much-needed rains.

Thoko was in her field behind the three mud-packed, single-room buildings in the southeast corner of her homestead when the news of Lindiwe arrived. Thoko had been expecting her for weeks, just waiting to hear when her family planned to bring her through for the start of her training. Two of her relatives arrived to inform Thoko of her student's death, to tell Thoko that Lindiwe had died of AIDS.

Sangomas generally learn how to mix muthi and how to use new ingredients through the advice of their ancestors given to them within dreams or while connecting on a spiritual level during ceremonies. Thoko's father, who was also a sangoma before passing away nearly twenty years ago, tells her when to go out into the bush and what to gather. If she has a client that she's been unable to cure, he will often come to her as a voice after dreams (in which she sees snakes) to teach her about a new muthi mixture to use. This, Thoko explains, is how sangomas learn to cure new diseases, more recently HIV/AIDS, and solve new problems that were not around during their training or the lives of their ancestors.

But in this young woman was something more. What Thoko will never know is if she missed something, or misread something, or both. What Thoko will never know is whether the opening of the small, white whelk's shell with orange and gold leafing was facing the thatch of her ndumba that day—whether the encasing of a snail that stuns its prey, rendering it helpless, and the "bone" that symbolizes the HIV virus eating away at someone's insides lay open on her sangu waiting to be read. Was the sign there but missed, or did the ancestors never give her the opportunity to discover that the frail daughter, who had become a child once again, debilitated by pain and a deteriorating illness, was actually positive? Was actually, at that point, dying of AIDS? And had she known, what would have happened differently?

Or, was this the case of something else altogether?

Thoko has seen the prevalence of HIV/AIDS pass through her gates and into her ndumba more and more during the near decade she has practiced. She agrees with scientific evidence that the virus is located within the blood and passed along sexually, but it is the root cause and the method with which to treat and cure the virus that she sees differently. Thoko purports to have cured seven people of HIV/AIDS.

Like a majority of elders within her community, she believes that breaking traditional rules, rules mandated by the ancestors, causes HIV/AIDS. "*You get this disease when you have sex during funeral days,*" Thoko explained.

The information highway in Thoko's community and similar rural communities—ever more true with its increased remoteness—travels mouth to mouth more effectively than through the text of a newspaper, the pictures of health care pamphlets, and the words of an educator or health representative. *Maveriveri* (rumor) and *ku hleva* (gossip) spread faster and are taken more seriously than the words of any expert or source originating outside the community. In Shangaan culture, rumor and gossip have distinct differences, the first being merely a telling of tales without proof. The latter, translated directly as "telling secrets," tells tales of proven fact. Maveriveri and ku hleva are both significant factors in people's understanding of HIV/AIDS.

Rumors from the mouths of the elderly in Thoko's community generally equate the AIDS pandemic with the rise in young people breaking the rules of sexual behavior. With an estimated one thousand South Africans dying daily as a result of HIV/AIDS, the "dirt" that causes the virus that some people call HIV and that others call the destruction of milawu (the rules of sexual behavior) has greater prevalence than ever before. Inside communities like Thoko's, where six of every ten girls are pregnant before the age of twenty-five, milawu seems a logical cause of the virus that is killing at a rapid pace.

Young people, particularly men, have ignited rumors about a white doctor who invented condoms and gave them away for free. Word spread that he put the virus inside of those condoms and was trying to prevent the black South African population from increasing, thereby decreasing their power. The coincidence of timing, between the change of government from apartheid to a democratic republic and the campaigns to promote safe sex, indirectly supported such maveriveri and continue to do so.

Some believe that AIDS is passed through flu shots offered each year. Others explain they would never buy the eighty-kilogram bags of mealie meal because the virus is put in there since white people don't buy the large bags. And the fear of being included in rumors and gossip is one of the many reasons only 3 percent of young people who are HIV positive actually know their status.

HIV/AIDS discussions are still relegated to quiet ku hleva (murmurs outside of funerals and inside homesteads), and moments where a family admits that someone has died of AIDS are still scarce. The blame is attributed to breaking traditional rules, to witchcraft, or to illness that struck the weak, immune-deficient body. And death certificates distort the truth when the cause of death is documented as the most recent illness of those struck by the pandemic, most often to prevent losing insurance payout if the truth were revealed.

The young girl diagnosed by the ancestors, via Thoko, as having been born to become a sangoma could have been one of many girls who travel from the rural communities where jobs are scarce in hopes of finding employment in the city, falling into the trap of selling themselves within the townships for shelter, food, and money. She could have been one of the nine women raped every twenty-six seconds within South Africa's borders. She could have erroneously trusted that her partner was monogamous, or her partner could have falsely trusted her. She could have made mistakes on her own, carelessly choosing to ignore the reality of what sex could bring amongst a triangle or pentagon of partners. Or she could have fallen prey to one of many cultural and social conditions that affect her chances of contracting HIV, and, untested, she could quickly slide below the two hundred T-cell count.

"She didn't tell me she had AIDS," said Thoko, fictitiously curt. Her eyes stared into the green grass growing like an island between her ndumba and Western-style house, staring into nothingness, staring to stare, staring to avoid eye contact. Her long gangly arms and legs sat fidgeting as she continued, "Had I known, I could have helped her."

Thoko sat there surrounded by over one dozen goat- and cattle-skin drums of various sizes and a newly collected bag of bones with which to train the young girl who had now passed and been buried. She explained again that she didn't know. She wasn't told. The bones did not reveal the girl's status. All of this is Thoko's truth, a truth that will morph itself over the coming months from having never been told; to having known her status, providing muthi; and back again to having never known.

DANKIE

Dankie was afraid to open his eyes. This was the day matric results would be announced—and announced not just to him privately, but in the newspaper for everyone to see his success or his failure. Lying across his bed, Dankie could feel the morning heat fill his room. He could hear his mother, the children, and the chickens outside.

Thousands of kilometers away, the minister of education spoke in front of Parliament. Her voice reached living rooms and bedrooms, mothers and fathers, students and dropouts, from the Atlantic to the Indian, through the radio waves of SAFM.

In this year's comments I intend to limit reference to the past and to attempt instead to provide signals for the future. This is because the matric class of 2005 is the class with which our new system began. We have now come of age and are at a point at which we should indicate to South Africa what kind of "adult" we intend to be.

We can say to South Africa today that the effect of the 2005 results will be to make the education sector strive hard to be a confident, competent, achieving sector, one that provides young people with the tools to take full advantage of the opportunities presented by a growing and progressively transforming democratic South Africa.

Our education system has come of age, our matriculants have come of age by reaching this point in their education, and our schools, parents, teachers, and communities have come of age by supporting us and steering us to this point of achievement.

Today we will give some sense of how education must perform in the future and some insight into indicators that suggest that we can and must perform better.

Throughout the month of December, Dankie had seen ads in the newspaper and heard public service announcements on the radio explaining how students could register to have their results sent to their cell phone the night before they were printed in the newspaper. But Dankie decided that he couldn't handle the sight of a text message. At least a newspaper can be left behind, handed to a neighbor to be taken away, used to start a fire or prepare meals over. A text message in his cell phone could haunt him. He would forever see his results etched in his head, a vision of the small screen announcing his failure or success. "If they were bad results, I would read them over and over and over again. I would not erase them. It would not be for me." If it were failure, he knew it would never leave his mind.

The *Star* and the *Beeld*, both national newspapers, always print a matric results supplement for each province. Had Dankie stayed with his sister and brother-in-law in the boulders, he wouldn't have been in their paper. Although they reside in Mpumalanga and Rooibok is part of the province's northernmost village, Acornhoek schools are actually part of Limpopo Province's Department of Education (one example of the long and strange historical division of government services in the area).

The only place to purchase a newspaper would be in town, and Dankie had spent most of his scone profits on taxi fare to and from his sister's home, on Christmas presents, and on drinks with his brother-in-law, so he decided he'd wait for newspapers to filter into Rooibok as people came and went throughout the day. The lines that had been forming for hours outside shops filtered in as doors opened at eight in the morning and cleaned off the shelves by ten. The bundles delivered to newsboys selling on the street vanished equally as fast.

Dankie stayed inside the house for most of the morning. He was afraid to walk outside and come across a newspaper or someone who had already caught glimpse of the names. Eventually Dankie wandered out of the house to see what people were saying. Since his home was farther west, down the slope of Rooiboklaagte, heading toward the river, he knew he wouldn't see too many people gathered together, but word would spread quickly in his direction as mothers and sisters came to collect water at the spring and men grazing cattle brought the herd to drink fresh water.

Dankie slid through the sheet of link metal serving as a door to his mother's homestead and walked northeast along a pathway to his neighbor's homestead. As he walked, he could see young people and old people talking. Some were crying. Some were smiling.

"*Congratulations*," came jumping toward him by a neighbor and classmate. "*Congratulations! We saw you in the newspaper!*" Dankie's insides skipped, but his heart froze. He didn't know whether to believe him or nor. And if, in fact, his name was printed in those pages, was there an E next to his name? Was there an E symbolizing "Exemption"? Had he really passed and passed with Exemption?

The news came from the mouth of a classmate with empty hands, so Dankie began to walk faster until his walking was really running. He passed around and through homesteads dotting his community, heading uphill. From neighbor to neighbor and their neighbors. The first had nothing. The second was empty handed as well. But the third had people piled inside a dark living room peering over an open newspaper.

The dark room was filled with sadness and tears. The mother living there had collected a newspaper in Acornhoek that morning in hopes to spread joy through her family, but instead only sadness came. The student in that house had not found his name in the paper, despite peering over and over again, despite having read through the short list of Moholoholo High School students.

Dankie called, "Tama," as he entered and stood there with very little to say. A family member kindly handed him the paper to sift through. He held it, staring at the front page. He opened to the center, where the results were lined up like daily stock numbers. He scanned page one, past the As and Bs, looking further for the schools that started with M: Mohlodi, Mohlopheng, Mohlotlwane, Mohola Hlogo, Moholoholo.

On the list of surnames under Moholoholo High School, there were only twenty-three of the fifty-eight students who tested. Dankie moved his finger down the names, looking for M. Down, down, down, and there it was—Mathebula. Dankie Mathebula.

But that was it. There was nothing after his name. There was no E.

Only 40 percent of Moholoholo students passed compared to 70 percent of students who passed the previous year. Across the country, 68 percent of twelfth grade students passed their matriculation exams and only 17 percent earned University Endorsements. On the radio, the minister of education was talking about Dankie's class—the first class to begin schooling outside of the apartheid government:

Today we acknowledge and celebrate the achievements of the class of 2005—a special cohort of children, graduating in a special year, the year of celebrating the Freedom Charter. The class of 2005 started school in 1994. They are the first cohort to learn from start to finish under a democratic dispensation. They are the first cohort to learn the values of equality, non-racialism, and non-sexism at school. They are our measure of how our system is growing and maturing.

The family offered him the newspaper to take home and share with his mother, since there was no need for them to keep staring at its pages. With a smile across his face, so large his scarred lip began to crinkle, he walked through the footpaths back to his home and called for his mother. When she surfaced from inside, he announced his results.

She looked at him, not seeing that he had a paper in his hand, with a face of hesitation. Her eyes told Dankie that she wasn't sure whether she could believe him; she wasn't sure if he was lying or covering up for his failure.

"Read this," he said, handing his mother the open paper. "Read this."

She pulled the crinkled pages from his hands and looked for his name. As Dankie pointed to his Afrikaans name printed beside a select few of his classmates, Maggie looked up with near tears in her eyes.

"Crazy boy!" she screamed with elation. "If I had money, I would buy something for you to show you I am happy." Maggie had worried for weeks that Maduzu's death had destroyed her son's chances of passing this year. She'd seen her son study for months and worried that the same noose that stole the breath of Maduzu had stolen all of his hard work. With her arms wrapped him, she confirmed, "You've done well."

That weekend, as the sun set over the escarpment for the final time that year, Dankie's family gathered inside the fence of his homestead to celebrate his accomplishments. With a golden glow in the background, the sound of voices—dozens of voices, of uncles and cousins, friends and family, and several classmates who had not seen their names in the paper—filled the yard. In harmony, they sang to Dankie with thanks and celebration: "People mustn't be afraid to have a baby, because one day something like this will happen."

REGINA

Three nights a week, Regina sits glued to the television watching *Smackdown*. Her favorite wrestler is Rey Mysterio. He is five feet six and wears a red-and-white pleather headmask with a gothic cross on his forehead. Almost always without a shirt, he battles his rivals with signature moves like the 619, West Coast Pop, Frog Splash, Sunset Flip Powerbomb, Droppin' the Dime, Sitout Facebuster, and the Tilt-a-Whirl Headscissors Takedown. Branded across his glistening, rock-hard chest in convex Blackmoor lettering is the name of his home country—Mexico.

Regina watches Mysterio and other WWE wrestlers spin in the air, body slam one another, balance on the ropes, leap into the ring, and get taken out by folding chairs, almost as religiously as she attends Sunday mass and Thursday Saint Anne meetings. She leans in front of the television in the small sitting room of her two-bedroom house every Saturday, Sunday, and Wednesday night, rooting for the underdog.

"I don't want anyone to touch him," said Regina, describing the flying wrestler with eagle wings running across the cheeks of his mask.

There is only one thing that prevents Regina from watching Smackdown, and since Simphiwe moved out, it's more frequently an issue. Regina is afraid to turn on the television. If it's time for Smackdown and there is no one around, she moves her chair to the front doorway and keeps an eye on passersby. If schoolchildren pass or a neighbor is on the road, she will call them into her homestead and ask them to flip the switch and turn the dial to Channel E. When Simphiwe was around, she would turn on the television and move the chairs front and center, preparing for the two of them to cheer, yell, and jump around as they watched the wrestlers slam into one another. But Simphiwe was no longer there.

It's not just the television Regina is afraid of; it's actually anything electric. Regina is fearful of being shocked. Although Emerencia generally wouldn't go along with her mother's idiosyncrasy, Simphiwe has always been good about turning things off and on: the iron, stove, television, light switch. The stove shocked Regina one day, and she's been terrified of it ever since. She refuses to touch the iron because it is old and the plastic wire cover is starting to wear away. And she doesn't listen to the radio, because she'd have to plug it in and turn the dial. Emerencia was in town late working at Buzi, which meant that she was rarely home in time to turn on the television for Regina, but that would change soon, since Emerencia had decided to quit and return to Mapusha.

When Judy visited Emerencia at Buzi with a tourist from America, she asked why Emerencia didn't want to work at Mapusha. Emerencia explained that there was more to it than wanting to work one place over another. She and her mother wanted to build a new house, and working at Buzi would help them save enough money to do so.

When Judy and the tourist left, they talked about ways to get Emerencia back to Mapusha. And their push came in the form of a gift, or news of a gift, to her mother. The tourist had committed to raising eight thousand rand to help Regina build her house, and they promised to send her the money in one year, enough time for Regina to save the rest of the money on her own.

Regina had built her home with her own two hands. When Winfred told her that she was no longer welcome in their home, she gathered what materials she could, collected secondhand window and door frames from a priest in the mission, and started on her own. She had help in building a wooden frame for each wall, and she began packing homestead soil inside, only releasing it from its mold once it hardened. Regina did this all the way around and coated the building with a layer of cement, like icing on a cake. She also poured a rounded cement stoop around all four sides, making sure it had one last chance to gain strength.

Regina and her five children—Walter, Aubrey, Theresa, Emerencia, and Koosh— moved into the two-room house on their new plot, half the distance to the Catholic mission and Mapusha's studio than their previous. Once she was settled and had enough money to build herself more rooms, she built a second house as well as Aubrey's single room away from the main house. Using mud bricks and cement coating, Regina later built a two-bedroom house, only a meter or two away from the original, with a small joining sitting room and an outdoor kitchen.

When Regina heard of the foreigner's gift, her emotions were of immediate excitement followed by sudden anxiety. Gertrude had been building her house for over a year. And it still stood incomplete. A few of the younger women were saving for their first homes, trying to make a life for themselves out of their mother's residences. And pretty much everyone was ready for a housing upgrade.

Regina knew that she couldn't tell anyone. She was afraid they would be angry with her. She was no more deserving of a new home than any of the twelve women at Mapusha. With the realization that this was actually going to happen, Regina started thinking of her new house in real terms. She visited the man who sells housing sketches and examined all of the plans he had for three-bedroom homes. She wanted one room for herself, one room for Emerencia, and one room for Simphiwe. She wanted a bathroom inside and a small kitchen to prepare her food before cooking outside. She wanted a big living room like Anna Mdluli's so that she didn't have to lean against the fridge as she watched *Smackdown* or hear others watching television while she was in her bedroom. She wanted a place where she could invite her friends to talk and drink tea. She wanted everyone to have privacy and wanted a bedroom for Simphiwe so that she didn't have to sleep with her mother or grandmother every night—so that Simphiwe had space for her own things and no excuse to rummage through Regina's things.

Regina found a perfect match. The man who sold her the plans said that she would need 3,000 cement bricks to build the house. Regina started to calculate everything she would need before she could hire a builder to put it all together. And she would have to reclaim the bricks she had given to others in the past. There was a neighbor, not too far away, who owed her 150 bricks. He would have to make her 150 new bricks to use. And Gertrude had borrowed 200. She would have to pay her back in time to start building in one year. And there was a man who borrowed 100 bricks from her almost twenty years ago. She would be sure to reclaim those, as well.

When the others found out, they were upset. They wanted help too. They were scared to talk to Judy about it, though, because they thought she would tell Regina. Over the years, people always said, "Don't tell secrets to whites. They don't know what a secret is. They will tell everyone. They don't believe in secrets." The women were afraid that Judy wouldn't keep their private feelings to herself. They were afraid that, if she were told of their jealousy, she would tell the next one and the next one, like gossip. They were afraid that she would go tell Regina. But eventually, because the women talked amongst themselves, someone told Regina that bad things were being said about her.

She nodded her head and said, "*Yes. I know.*"

THOKO

A miniature bug of a car crawled its way up the road bordered by grasses taller than some men and by maize that grew from inside each homestead. Detouring around each ditch caused by the consistent summer rains, the driver eventually parked outside of Thoko's gate. Patrick climbed out of the passenger door, and a middle-aged stocky white man of nearly the same height in a button-down shirt and dress pants climbed out of the driver's side, looking around, taking in a 360-degree panorama.

Thoko came running from inside the house, where she had pap on the stove, to greet the man, her lawyer, Louis Hugo. Louis wasn't really a lawyer—he was still taking his exams—but he was taking care of Thoko's liquor license application for a law firm in a village a few hours south.

Thoko had first been introduced to Louis nine months earlier. A local man advising her on the liquor license had accompanied Thoko and Patrick to his office. Thoko trusted him immediately because they were inside an official office. In a village where architectural plans are purchased on the side of the road or from inside someone's house, and roadside vendors offer credit, office space symbolizes success and wealth, as well as a sense of authority and validity.

Louis Hugo had first visited Thoko, not long after their initial meeting, to photograph the empty tavern site so as to complete the initial application. Those photographs and the paperwork were filed with the liquor board, and then the waiting game began. Patrick called Louis frequently, checking on the status of their application, but each call was received with about as much information as Louis had—nothing. Nothing had come back. Louis called Patrick on his cell phone a few days earlier to share the bad news. The Liquor Board had lost the paperwork, and everything needed to be refiled.

Louis emerged from his car and passed through the gate with a small one-touch digital camera in his hand. "Hello—how are you?" he said, looking at Thoko.

"Inkomu" replied Thoko.

Looking around, Louis examined the full picture. The second builder, Tlanga Sithola, was inside the roofless walls with his wife and a local woman wearing a yellow hat. Outside and to the left of the tavern was a newly dug ditch from which sand was being pulled. Inside, Tlanga was mixing cement, sand from the ditch, and water on a corrugated tin sheet with a boxer hanging from his mouth like a hinge. The cheap tobacco encased by newspaper had fallen limp after hours of his moist lips gripping it as he worked.

Thoko and Patrick, who were standing beneath a trio of mango trees where the only breeze could be caught, watched Louis as he walked around the tavern, covering all four sides and taking photographs of every angle, every direction. With each step counterclockwise around the building, he would look down to carefully avoid any debris on the ground or standing water from the previous night's rains.

Outside the homestead gate, the sound of a man screaming caused Patrick and Thoko to turn and face the gate. A medium-height, thin man who Thoko described as "mad" entered through the gate and approached Thoko. The two tried to quiet the man as Louis rounded the tavern wall, heading in their direction. The man stood in between but slightly behind them, and Thoko slid closer to Patrick to eliminate him from Louis's view.

"Eh, *madam, I am hungry. I need a cool drink and bread,*" said the man. Thoko didn't turn and face him, nor did she respond to his request and jabbing gibberish. She continued to watch Louis, and Patrick pointed the man toward the homestead gate.

"I am not a very good photographer," said Louis, approaching the mango trees with a low giggle in his voice. Patrick laughed in response, and Thoko—without knowing what Louis said—lifted her head in the air and joined in with a belt of laughter.

When Thoko found out that Louis had called and told Patrick that the paperwork was lost, had gone missing in the system, her immediate reaction was to consider him a crook. "*I'll come after that white man,*" she had said. "*He must make it right.*"

Just as Louis was leaving, a bakkie of supplies for Patrick's new house arrived. He was building a single cement room for Lizzy and himself. He planned to seek freedom with his fiancée in a house two blocks away with no electricity, across the street from a water pump, and only a short walk to his church—living alone, away from Thoko's shebeen and customers.

DANKIE

Dankie had a plan. Although he couldn't go to university, he wasn't willing to give up his dreams of becoming a police officer. His adamance that school was the only way to become a detective was starting to soften; he found solace in the idea of climbing the ladder through the system, from the bottom rung to the top. Dankie never wanted to be like the police officers he grew up around. He didn't want to be one of the men he sees in the police station who seem bothered by people seeking their help, often dismissive. He didn't want to be like the officers who stand on the side of the road, parked beside other police cars, talking to young girls, eating nice food. He never wanted to become a traffic cop who sits on the roadside with a radar, stepping in front of speeding vehicles, seeking bribes. He never wanted to be someone his community didn't trust. Dankie wanted to help solve crimes. He wanted to help his neighbors feel safer, and be the one to put criminals in jail. He wanted to stand up for women like his mother.

But to climb up the ladder, Dankie would have to earn a position within the police academy, and classes were accepted only twice a year. Before he could even apply, though, he needed a driver's license (compulsory for all police officers), which requires driving school, hours of clocked driving time, a written test, and a driving test—all of which requires money. In total, from start to finish, getting a driver's license takes two to three months and costs approximately three to four thousand rand, the price of one semester at the University of South Africa. Selling scones was not going to be enough. Over Christmas, when Dankie was visiting his sister a few hours to the south, where people have built their homes amongst the mountain's boulders, he met a few men who work in forestry with her husband. They live most of the month in a small mountaintop staff village called Elandshoogte, and they spend their days working in rows and rows of pine trees. News reached his brother-in-law, who later called Dankie to offer him a job in the trees. It was only temporary, but they were hoping he could earn enough money to go to driving school.

*   *   *

Elandshoogte sits where the mountains touch the clouds. Perched on the edge of the Drakensberg escarpment, the small village of forestry workers has a view rivaled only by aircraft. Surrounding the clusters of square cement staff housing lined in rows and laid out in blocks, a mosaic of indigenous and commercial forests paints the valleys, darker where the land creases and hills roll into one another, lighter in areas of grassland and open space. Wrinkles in the earth, where water can gather and rivers meander, are darkened by indigenous growth, filling the space with the pointillism of lush green figs, jackalberries, fever trees.

The village itself is nowhere as striking. Part of Sappi forestry land, the village is rented by a subcontractor for staff housing. It hasn't expanded far beyond its basic needs, consisting of a long hall where the village's sole teacher runs a one-room schoolhouse, of ablution blocks and washing stations for cleaning up, of a small tuck shop where things can be purchased on account, of offices for both the subcontractor and Sappi, and of open space for children to run, men to gather, and laundry to be hung.

Dankie had never lived outside of Rooibok, nor had he ever lived with men. Other than growing up beside Jack and having his neighbor stay over the year he lived alone, he was most comfortable surrounded by women. Although living next door to Maduzu opened windows into the lives of older men, he certainly had little reference to prepare him for the days and nights of the village in the clouds.

Someone is always awake and someone is always sleeping in Elandshoogte. During the day, lorries travel with mostly men and a few women into the trees. The commute varies, depending on which section of the plantation is being worked on, and it can often last an hour. While the day shift are spread throughout the plantation, the night shift are at home, either closing their curtains and spreading the sheets they've nailed to the walls or sitting in friends' rooms, playing cards, drinking beer, watching TV, or smoking boxers, dagga, and cigarettes.

At night, the men returning from the day shift continue games, keep the television going, or sneak off to sleep. But in a world where women are scarce, and wives are even more absent, so much more goes on behind closed doors.

South African men are historically absent members of the household. It's more common than not for a husband to spend all but the final weekend of each month living in a staff village like Elandshoogte, surrounded by other fathers and husbands. The women who do live there are generally single or employed alongside their husbands. More commonly, girls passing through the village are selling themselves to both day and night workers, and single women become the work "wife" for an already married man.

Young sex workers catch lifts on trucks on the highway and hang on until they have wound their way up the cliff-side road and into the residential clusters.

Out of management's sight, what happens on the mountain stays on the mountain.

REGINA

Regina boarded a taxi with Gertrude and headed down the eroding dirt road toward Chochocho. In Regina's hands was a neatly wrapped package. She'd known the day was coming for six months, and she had saved close to one-quarter of her month's salary in order to purchase a new skirt to celebrate the end of mourning and the removal of Gertrude's cousin's black clothing.

Regina spent the entire taxi ride holding on to the neatly folded and carefully wrapped skirt in her lap. She knew how special it was, as she remembers every gift given to her on that day, from a duvet and dresses to blankets and a washbasin. Regina and Gertrude—who were dressed in their best skirts and blouses—eventually arrived, after a bumpy, crowded, and sticky ride, to a celebration several dozen times larger than Regina's with loud music and dancing everywhere. Almost everyone wore their church uniforms: Catholic, Nazareth Baptist, Zionists, and a few of which Regina was unsure.

When a woman is widowed in Shangaan and Sotho culture, she is required to mourn by following a strict set of rules and wearing black for a period of six or twelve months. Shedding these clothes was like breaking free from shackles and finding oneself again. The celebration associated with removing one's mourning clothes is a day every widow understands. Regina remembers the day she was permitted to end her mourning with great clarity.

Regina followed the rules she had been given, but the day eventually arrived that she could shed the black clothing that bound her to the husband who had left her behind long before he was buried. It was a day with no tears and only celebration.

It was a Friday. She didn't plan for anything special to wear. It was more about not having to wear black, rather than about wearing something new. So, when she slipped out of her black clothes and placed them in the pile with the rest, she slipped on an old dress and the new pinafore that her sisters and aunties had made to cover the clothing she would wear after she removed the black.

That night, Regina gathered in the yard with the women of her family. She had pulled together every piece of black clothing she'd worn over and over again: three skirts, two blouses, two dresses, one shawl, three *doeks* (scarves to cover her hair), and one pair of *takkies* (sneakers). Together they followed Regina as she walked away from the house, through the trees, and behind the tin-walled toilet, where she dropped everything on the ground. She was tired. It was as if wearing black clothing had drained the energy and life from her and releasing them would allow her the chance to rejuvenate. Someone came past her and poured paraffin over everything. Then, Regina watched someone light a match and toss it in the middle. The flame flew up quickly and then sunk back down, burning the clothes slowly until they were nothing, as if they had never existed.

The next day, everyone gathered in Regina's homestead to celebrate. She dressed in her church uniform, the bright purple dress special to the Women of Saint Anne. Tea was steeped first thing in the morning and served with cookies. Father Miguel had come to say early prayers and then returned to the mission.

The Hlabane family and the Mohlolo family each brought a goat for the celebration. The Hlabanes gave their goat to Winfred's family, and the Mohlolos gave their goat to Regina's family. Each slaughtered and cooked the other's goat, symbolizing that they trusted Regina again, that they continued to get along and loved one another.

A cow and chicken were also slaughtered to feed everyone. Regina and her family had prepared beetroot, rice, and biscuits and offered juice, canned beer, and traditional brew. Regina doesn't normally drink, but she had Redd's from the can that day. It was a day to remember, a day to pull away the darkness and become happy once again.

Regina had pulled the hi-fi from her bedroom, and the dial was turned to church music for everyone to listen to, passing the "happy-clappy" music Regina doesn't like and eventually stopping on her favorite church gospel station, but nothing worth dancing to, since Regina doesn't consider herself much of a dancer.

DANKIE

Dankie and his niece Busisiwe went to town on Saturday morning to shop. Busisiwe, only a year younger than he and the daughter of his eldest sister, was starting tenth grade at Moholoholo High School. Busisiwe had a little girl whom Maggie cared for while Busisiwe was at school. The only money she had came from the 180-rand child grant collected each month and what little her grandmother or mother were able to offer her.

They had traveled by taxi to Acornhoek Plaza, where the shops were bustling and the serpentine lines for the ATM could have prevented anyone from reaching a retail counter before noon when the shops close. Dankie had withdrawn cash the previous day in Nelspruit as he boarded the first of five taxis home, knowing, for the first time, after just a few weeks of temporary work in the trees, that he could provide for someone.

The two stood outside of Jet and Dankie pulled two crisp blue buffalo—200 rand—from the 1,019 he had earned for the two and a half weeks of temp work in the trees. Busisiwe needed a new school uniform.

She walked inside toward the school uniforms with an excitement, a confidence, and stared at the wall of uniforms of blue, green, maroon, black, and brown. Moholoholo High School students wear blue uniforms. She sifted through each item slowly, as if to make the moment last longer. She pulled a crisp, white collared shirt that had never been worn before—or at least out of the store—and held it out to examine. It was perfectly white and thicker than the thin white shirts that you can see through. Then she pulled a blue skirt from the rack, short enough to look good with her new black knee-high socks, but not short enough to attract attention.

She carried all three items to the counter as Dankie watched from afar like a father providing for his daughter. Each item was carefully folded and placed inside the plastic Jet bag for everyone to see that she had just been shopping.

REGINA

It was the end of the day, and the sound of belly laughter traveled through Mapusha's open door, wide-open windows, and gaps in the roof, out into the empty mission grounds.

Inside, Anna Mbetse leaned with her back against the counter, laughing with Gertrude. Regina tidied the space around her loom. Lindy and Anna Ndzukula swept their work area, and Lizbeth, Wonder, and Emma chattered with speed and giggled over one another's words. The laughter was contagious as it pinged in the air and echoed off the tin roof above.

Every day, it's the same routine. Just a few minutes before 4:30, the ladies walk around, clean up where they can, and close every door and window, laughing or skinnering like school children on afternoon tea break. And suddenly, the vibrations that fill the room are quelled as if a curtain has been drawn over each mouth.

Since the first days of Mapusha—when the mission's brothers, priests, and nuns were actively woven into the lives of each mother and daughter, sister and cousin—the women have closed their days exactly the same: in prayer.

"*Close the door,*" Anna Mbetse said.

Everyone formed a circle in the center of the studio. Other than the sound of the mission dogs barking, there was total silence, not even a breath could be heard. Regina, who was standing beside the door, moved across the circle to stand opposite her loom.

"In the name of the father," they said in unison, tracing the sign of the cross from forehead, to breast bone, shoulder to shoulder. "We pray with you day and night. You are the creator of the Earth, our house, our child. . . ." But then the voices of Tsonga and Sotho began to beat at a different pace and a different rhythm. The women unraveled the single thread of their prayer and allowed their own words and their own concerns to come untangled and be revealed. Some of the women pray the same prayer every day with the exception of the occasional need or request. But others talk from the heart with new requests, new thanks, and new worries to report.

Anna Mdluli, the object of Regina's prayers for months, stood close to the door between Regina's bench and the old vertical loom. Her string-bean frame stood tall, and her head was held high as she recited her prayers with strength and volume. She spoke above the rest as if to make sure God could hear her over all the others, that God would listen to her despite the others. And when Regina's soft voice, almost a breathy undertone, had trickled off, when Lindy's nearly silent prayer was done, when the two other Annas and Gertrude and Wonder and Emma and Lizbeth finished with their report of thanks and requests, she still prayed on.

When Anna's voice halted, a second of silence remained, assuring everyone was done, and then the curtain lifted. The room began to rock again with voices and laughter and chatter.

The women began to disperse this way and that, toward the tuck shop across the road, out both front and back entrances of the mission, and around the back of the studio through the soccer field and toward the homes in MaRoman. Regina stepped onto the sandy patch in front with a sturdy hoe swung over her right shoulder. She began to walk down the driveway. Anna and Anna followed under the great fig tree, over the cattle grids at the mission's entrance, and around the corner onto the dirt road leading to Rooiboklaagte A.

As the three turned right and walked south down the road, Anna Ndzukula began to sing, softly at first, growing louder with each step and each line of the song. Her little body balanced on the edge of the road where grass met a drop down toward the sandy road. She walked teetering on the edge, singing the words of her mother and aunties.

Regina walked ahead of the two Annas (the third, Anna Mdluli, had gone home) down the dusty road parallel to the mission fence. The two dogs that live inside the mission's barbed-wire compound were barking louder and louder, but they couldn't seem to maneuver themselves close to the fence line, since the interior fence separating the buildings from a large garden had barricaded their path. They stood barking as close as they possibly could.

"Ma chan chu lani mali ya malungu," sang Anna in a high-pitched voice.

As the women sang, the sound of the rickety hoes clinked against their wooden sticks (to which they were loosely fastened with bent nails), and the shuffle of the sand and gravel crunched below their feet, augmenting the rhythm of the music.

When Regina was young and her family worked on the farms of white men, they would hoe and weed, and sing the whole time. They would sing songs that told stories or explained how they felt at that time. Singing, according to Regina, offered them strength and speed. Their hoes would match the rhythm of their words and the pace of their song, working faster. Before they knew it, they were done.

"Wah, Wah," she said, swinging her free hand into the air and slamming it down toward the earth like a hoe. "Wah, Wah," she said again, motioning. "While they are weeding, they are singing."

"Ma chan chu lani mali ya malungu," they sang in unison, "ah haaaaaa!"

"Wah, Wah," she continued, pretending to swing a gardening hoe (while keeping the hoe in her other hand still). The women sang a song about working in the fields for a white man. They sang of needing to work very hard in order to earn their money. Over and over again, the words would repeat: *you must work, work, and work to get your money.*

"Ahhhhhh, eiiieeeeee," she bellowed, leaning forward and popping back with laughter.

Balancing her body on the edge of the road, Anna Ndzukula placed one foot in front of the other, swinging her white plastic bag and resting her hoe over her right shoulder. As they rounded the corner along the southern fence line of the mission grounds, past the community crèche with broken windows and stained walls, a small three-room building with clean, whitewashed cement walls came into sight. Around it was a chain-link fence forming a perfect square.

The white building with butler doors was Anna Mbetse and Regina's old tuck shop. Too many years ago for either woman to count, they sold sweeties, maize meal, cool drinks, candles, and many other conveniences at the shop. It is closed up today. "No money to stock things," Anna explained. Regina pushed the gate door open and entered. Anna Mbetse followed, moving immediately to the left, and Anna Ndzukula followed, walking toward the center of the land, to put her things down beneath a tall shady tree. Since the tuck shop was no longer in use, Anna and Regina drew imaginary lines down the middle from north to south and east to west, dividing the plot into four equal squares to farm on. Anna Ndzukula was designated the southwest; Gertrude was in the northwest; Anna Mbetse was assigned the southeast; and Regina took the northeastern corner, sharing her field with the old building.

Anna stood beneath the tree and pulled two clear plastic sheets from her white bag. She leaned forward and wrapped each plastic bag around her ankles and over her shoes to protect herself from scratches and her shoes from dirt. Regina, who was now standing along the southern wall of the building, surrounded by waist-high mealies, did the same.

Regina's plot was the same size as the other three, but the tuck shop consumed at least one-third of the farming soil. She had carefully planted maize along the southern side of the tuck shop wall in clear, neat rows that eventually traced around the backside of the building. She split her land in two halves: mealie to the south, peanuts to the north.

Gertrude eventually arrived, joining Regina, who was standing beneath the shadowy tree and examining Gertrude's crops. Her short and skew maize stalks filled one-third of the block, and the remainder had been filled with newly planted peanuts. Crowded by weeds equal in size and height, the peanuts looked as if they were drowning in overgrowth. As Gertrude walked into her rows of mealie, their lean toward the east became more prominent and more concerning. She had planted later than the others, but she was confident it would be fine. While the two Annas and Regina were starting their third day of weeding, Gertrude was just beginning.

The women picked up their hoes and bent forward, forming a perfect L without the slightest arch in their backs. And they began: *Wah, Wah.* Unlike their mothers and grandmothers, they don't sing in unison or think of the money they are going to earn—possibly because there is no money to earn. While their families used to hoe in the fields of white farmers, they now farm for their own subsistence.

On the southern side of Rooiboklaagte A, just on the edge of Rooiboklaagte B, was Farm Champagne, a 257-hectare citrus farm, and Letsitele Valley, a 15,000-hectare commercial farming cooperative. In those fields and the fields throughout the province, the voices of many men and many women still fill the rows of mangoes, paw paws, oranges, lemons, maize, potatoes, sugar cane, bananas, tobacco, and coffee, each day.

Regina bent forward in the first row of her tall, blond stalks and began to swing. The golden blanket of maize seemed to swallow her from sight, but if you got close enough, you could find Regina by the sound of her soft hum.

As the sun set behind the escarpment in the skyline, the rays of the summer sun came closer and stronger. With each strike into the earth, a new bead of sweat began to form, and new pools gathered along each brow and the edge of each hairline. As they straightened their backs at the end of each row, the pools of salty perspiration came sliding down foreheads and into eyes like an abrupt landslide into the valleys below.

Like clockwork, though, the ladies pulled small cloths from their skirt pockets and dabbed the pools before they straightened their backs and started a new row.

The day was coming to a close. The sound of cattle walking past, the sound of children returning home, and the sound of metal hoes slicing into the rocky soil composed the late summer soundtrack. In the distance, as the slope of Rooibok leaned toward the valley and into the escarpment's base, small plots of farming dotted the landscape between homestead clusters with silhouettes of mothers and grandmothers striking away.

THOKO

Thoko sat silently on a rectangular cement bench with her arms crossed, holding her black Christian Dior knockoff tightly against her chest. She wore her best red dress with a lace neckline, a thin jacket covering her shoulders and arms, a pair of recently cleaned one-inch heels with large gold buckles, and a stiff brown fabric wrapped around her head hiding her short unkempt hair. Thoko dressed this morning with the intention of looking her best, to present herself as a law-abiding citizen. She crossed her right leg over her left and began to bounce her foot impatiently.

To her left, Lizzy sat casually with her feet dangling, not quite long enough to reach the floor. Her curly hair looked like twisted twine kept in place by a black crochet band. Her earlobes held two large gold-plated hoops, and her closely fit pair of jeans and simple V-neck T-shirt emphasized a list of assets that don't run in the Makwakwa family.

Juxtaposed against her future mother-in-law, her curves seemed curvier, her lips seemed fuller, and her clothing was in a different league. Where Lizzy had two front teeth lined in gold casing, Thoko had one wide gap. Where Lizzy's hips and backside added shape to skirts and pants, Thoko's slim sides caused fabric to hang just as it did in the shop she bought it from. While Lizzy's feet dangled and her height was average, Thoko towered above other women and was taller than or equal to most men. Lizzy's breasts were full and robust, perky and young; Thoko's bra served more to carry her canister of snuff than to provide support.

Next to Lizzy sat Thoko's oldest daughter, Shelly, and across from her sat Elizabeth, Thoko's best friend, whose eyes seem glued to the doorway over which a grey sign read: Criminal Court B. Several cement benches and blocks surround the building, where defendants sit and wait to be called and family wait in support. Thoko had been told to arrive by 9:00 that morning, but her watch read 9:15, and she was still waiting.

Deedlee dee dee dee . . . Deedle dee dee daaa . . ., rang Thoko's cell phone.

"Kunjani," Thoko said as she lifted the large stiff knot of fabric on the right side of her head and slid her cell phone over her ear. Almost immediately, the doors opened, and a court clerk walked out holding a stack of brown government folders. Thoko didn't finish the conversation or even say goodbye. She turned her cell phone off, slipped it back into the mesh case hanging around her neck, and tucked it beneath her neckline. She sat up straight and listened.

"Robert Mathebula."

"E. Mnisi."

"Lloyd Mathebula."

Pause.

"Lloyd Mathebula."

He stopped for a moment, peering into the brown paper file when a short-haired woman, a prosecutor, wearing thick gold hoops and tall wedge heels, carefully walked down the steps, pulled the next file, and called "Thokozile Makwakwa." Thoko stood up, said, "That is us," and began walking around those still seated, up three steps, and through the doors. This was the seventh time Thoko had been there for the same case. She knew exactly where she needed to go and wanted to make sure she got a good seat.

The room was small and cramped. There were six or seven old wooden benches to the left and fewer to the right, while the front half of the room squeezed two witness boxes with red carpeting and a crooked microphone; a table for the defense and prosecution to share; several chairs and stools, each of which revealed more cushion stuffing than cover; and a tall and long judge bench with enough room to fit three or four seated judges. The judges' bench had sections of rotting wood, the wall behind it had water damage, and the majority of the ceiling panels were missing or water wrinkled.

Although the building and its contents looked as if they should have been condemned, this room reflected the state of most functioning government buildings in the rural areas—the municipality buildings, police stations, courthouses, and jails were all in disrepair. None was soon scheduled for reconstruction.

Thoko walked down the short aisle and sat in the second row. Her daughter took a seat in the first row, directly in front of her mother, while Lizzy and Elizabeth sat behind her. *Clog, clog, clog.* The sound of the prosecutor's heavy shoes announced her entrance and pulled everyone's heads from conversations or quiet thoughts.

Thoko sat with perfect posture. Her purse was on her lap, and her hands slid along her dress and down her legs, straightening the material and wiping away any dust from sitting outside. She followed by reaching beneath the lace neckline of her dress to pull out a canister of snuff, hidden away in her bra. With her right pointer finger, she scooped out and balanced a small hill of ground tobacco. Bending her shoulder downward, she lifted the snuff to her left nostril and *Kudzaha.* She breathed in deep. One more time, *Kudzaha.* This time in the right nostril. As quickly as she pulled the canister out, she snapped it shut and shoved her left arm back under the neckline of her dress.

A white man in a grey pinstripe suit, the only white person before the bench or preparing to witness, walked down the aisle and placed a stack of files on the center table. He hung his black robe over the back of a blue ragged chair and started to flip through a pile of files. He pulled a green folder with "Thokozile Makwakwa" written across the top and placed it on the table's podium.

The man turned around and looked into the crowd of people filing in, to call out, "Thokozile Makwakwa," in a blank questioning tone. He called out as if he had never met her and didn't know what she looked like, despite having seen her monthly since the previous August. Almost immediately, Thoko—still holding her purse tightly—stood up halfway, signaling her presence. He nodded and turned around to open the folder.

Suddenly, Thoko heard people talking of an immediate courtroom change. Her lean body maneuvered out of the row, through the aisle, and out of the door, all the while signaling the others to follow. Lizzy, Elizabeth, and Shelly shuffled along with the crowds and caught up with Thoko.

Together, they walked past Criminal Court A, through dozens of people waiting their turn to contest fines in Traffic Court, past a cluster of shady trees under which women had laid their grass mats and unpacked their plastic bags of snacks and lunch, past the metal detector and turnstile entrance, and around to the north side of the building to the final door on the right labeled "Criminal Court C."

Thoko walked through the doors and found a clear bench to sit. Shelly took a seat two rows in front, beside the man with crutches, and Lizzy and Elizabeth took up seats in the row to her right. Although similar to the previous room in layout, this was certainly an upgrade, clear of water damage and rotting wood, not to mention the addition of several air conditioners turned on high.

People filed in and sat where they could. The bench went from two to three to four and five until one man even tried to slip a quarter of his rear on the sliver of bench remaining. Thoko leaned her head back to give him a look, and he took the hint, finding space elsewhere. In front of her, she watched a man examine the room with a careful eye until he decided to skip the edge-balancing act and plop himself between two people, forcing the body of an elderly woman at the end to fall off.

Just as the movement began to settle, a man wearing green pants and a colored dress shirt walked in, crossed the front of the room, and took a seat next to Shelly.

"He's the social worker," Lizzy whispered, leaning toward Elizabeth's ear.

In his left hand were several manila envelopes, one of which had three names written in large block lettering across the front, filling space from left to right, top to bottom: T. Makwakwa on top; S. Makhuvele in the middle; and S. Mondlovu on the bottom.

He called the name "Susan Makhuvele" into the air, not looking back, not looking forward, not looking at anyone in particular. The name hung in the air, causing heads to perk and scan the bodies packed shoulder to shoulder.

The problem is that Susan Makhuvele didn't exist. Susan Makhuvele was the name on a fake ID book that Patrick's ex-girlfriend was using. She was an illegal Mozambican immigrant, which meant that she did not qualify for South African benefits like child grants. This is why Thoko had registered for Evidence, her granddaughter, in the first place. Susan Makhuvele was the name Suzette used to file for a child grant, after Thoko had already registered, collecting each month and handing the money over for Evidence.

Susan Mukhuvele's real name was Suzette. Suzette and family crossed the border into South Africa through Kruger National Park during the Mozambican civil war. Her father was Portuguese and her mother was Mozambican Tsonga. She had lived with her mother in South Africa since they crossed on their own through the bushveld filled with lions, elephant, hippo, crocodile, and more. Her mother settled the family in the apartheid-era homelands and has lived there ever sense.

Suzette, Patrick's ex-girlfriend, walked down the aisle and toward the social worker. She was dressed in a flared, dark denim skirt and matching jacket, with a pair of floppy sandals that showed off her recently painted toenails. Suzette was half the height of Thoko but more than double the width and blessed with a curvy African mother's body.

The door in the rear opened slightly, and the sound of a cell phone sang loudly, filling the room of no more than seven-by-four paces. Thoko giggled when she peeked around heads to see that the ring belonged to her white lawyer. She saw everyone reaching in pockets and digging in handbags, looking for cell phones to turn off. She cocked a tiny smile, knowing that she had already turned hers off and tucked it away for later. Eventually her lawyer took his seat at the center table.

And once again, the green folder bearing Thoko's first and last name was pulled from his briefcase and propped on the center table's podium.

The room was quiet, but still full of chatter, until the door in the far corner of the room opened, and the judge walked through, causing everyone—policeman and defendant alike—to jump upward in the air sending chairs and benches squealing across the dirty floor. Everyone's eyes followed the round judge as he closed the creaky courtroom door, stepped up to the bench, and took a seat. He towered above the courtroom.

The prosecutor—now in her long legal robes—announced each case title, and the defendant stepped into the witness box to the left with any witnesses on his or her behalf, and the witnesses on behalf of the state filled the box to the right.

The near-bald judge in robes and with a red sash over his right shoulder spread his papers across the bench. He pulled a pen from the side to begin writing. His eyes were on his papers while each case was called. His pen moved around the documents sometimes with diligent speed; other times his movements could have been construed as tangents of doodling. Once each defendant stepped onto the stand, the prosecutor, the government-appointed lawyer, and the many witnesses stood erect waiting for him to look up, to speak.

His silence was deafening, and he seemed gangrenous on the bench. He would repeatedly lift his head in the air and stare at the ceiling as if there were directions written on its panels. The process was painful and drawn out, but expected. After pulling his head from the air, he would begin with his chorus for the day, "Remand," meaning that the case had been postponed. "You'll come again to the court on the . . ."—filling in the blank with 14, 17, 20, or 22, each followed by the month of March.

Remand. Remand. Remand. Remand. Remand. Remand. Remand.

Each was followed by the restatement of his statement by the prosecutor and then a translation of the statement to the defendant in his or her preferred national language (of which there are eleven) by the court's official translator, who sat beside the defendant's stand.

"July 2005. The state versus Thokozile Makwakwa," announced the prosecutor.

Thoko slid past the legs beside her and down the aisle, taking the stand to the left. Her daughter crossed her path, moving to take position in the witness box to the right. Suzette joined her. Squeezing in behind them, making sure to find footing on the box's red carpet, was the social worker.

"I call Susan Makhuvele and Shelly Mondlovu."

Silence.

Eyes in the air.

Elbows on the bench.

"Remand. You'll come again to the court on 20 March." Thoko looked down at the translator beside the box to make sure she understood exactly what had happened, to have it repeated to her in Tsonga. *Remand. 20 March.* It didn't change in translation. It was the seventh "remand" since her first court date in August of 2005, one month after her arrest.

The next morning, Thoko brought Evidence into her ndumba, and they sat together. With her legs sprawled across the floor, she pulled her bag of bones from behind the curtain. She reached next to several food-coloring bottles filled with powder of deep brown, milk brown, and mustard yellow, picking up her beaded sangoma necklace, leaving the two bracelets behind.

Wearing a blue cotton dress, with Ric Rac ribbon of yellow and red lining the cuffs of her short sleeves and outlining the V neckline of her dress, Thoko looked far more domestic than usual. Over the skirt of her dress was a plaid traditional cloth, and covering her hair was a culturally patterned cloth, haphazardly wrapped.

"*20 March*," said Thoko. "*We go to court again. What will happen on 20 March?*"

She flipped the bag upside down and gathered the bones from every direction, placing the cowrie shell on top of the pile held in her two slender hands. She bounced her cupped hands against the sangu several times, filling the room with the sound of shaking bones, but, unlike usual, the raspy voice trapped inside of her—only to be released behind the closed doors of her ndumba or outside when she's tapping into the ancestors of her mother and father, the voice that signified the intensity of concentration and the seriousness of consulting the wisdom of those who have passed from this mortal world, the second in the two-part harmony of *throwing the bones*—wasn't anywhere to be found.

Bouncing three times, she released the bones across the mat to read the ruling for 20 March. Scattered in every direction, the bones tumbled and halted, positioning themselves like a constellation of stars, like a game of connect the dots.

Examining closely, but quickly, Thoko announced, "*They say free!*"

"*Free, free, free,*" she shouted. With each word *free,* she pointed to different bones.

"*The other lady—Suzette—will be guilty.*"

"*Shelly and Patrick's ex-girlfriend will cry, because I am free.*"

As if the force of freedom shot her head back and tipped her mouth open, Thoko released a laughter laced with revenge, cackling like a mischievous hyena.

She swept the spread bones once again, cupped them into her hands, bounced several times, released again.

"*The grant will cancel,*" she proclaimed. "*Shelly and Suzette's grants will be cancelled,*" she said, pointing toward each bone.

"*These two girls will lose their concentration, because the grant will cancel. The grant will cancel,*" she explained just as the rooster released a *cock a doodle doooooo* from just outside the ndumba door and someone slipped a single-rand coin into the jukebox, releasing the sounds of reggae into the morning air.

"*I will be free,*" she said again.

Repeating the sweep, bounce, and release process, Thoko tossed the bones out to be read once again, asking for further information on the day.

"*They will arrest them. The two of them,*" she said, pointing next to the two coins beside one another and two small animal bones beside them resting on one another. Looking at the two bones leaning against and crossing one another and symbolizing the police, Thoko said, "*They will cancel the grant.*"

Shaking and releasing once more, Thoko interpreted, "*They will want bail. They will want money.*"

And again, "*They will arrest them. They are guilty.*"

DANKIE

It was month-end, and Dankie was returning to Rooiboklaagte like most of the men and brothers and cousins he knew. He was far more confident, after a few visits home, in his journey between the village in the clouds and his mother's home on the impala flats of Acornhoek.

In Dankie's absence, his mother, Maggie, had started to build a new home in the yard of her existing two-bedroom house. She'd received a surprise deposit in her bank account one afternoon totaling 2,800 rand and quickly withdrew the amount in case someone noticed the mistake. It turned out, however, that the money was actually hers. It was back pay for her pension. She should have been receiving monthly pension for more than a year, since she turned sixty-one.

Dankie was earning 1,500 rand for his month of work in the trees. And one of the reasons for his trip home, like others, was to distribute his paycheck where it was needed: 250 rand for food and taxi would be set aside for himself, 70 rand went to cool drinks for his mother (20 rand of which came from his brother-in-law), 500 rand went into savings for a better life, and 700 rand went to his mother for their home. She needed more bricks and supplies than her pension check could afford.

After many sleepless nights, he was ready to leave the mountain and head home to his mother and his community for a few days. He was eager to see the start of their new home, to play snooker in the shebeen, and to see a few friends. More importantly, he'd hoped to escape his cousin. For more than a month now, Dankie had seen or heard his cousin Maduzu at least once a day. His voice would find him in his sleep. His face would look at him in the trees. And the memory of him and the rope and the knife would fill the room when he sat alone. Dankie was afraid to tell anyone what he was seeing. But he wanted so badly for someone, anyone, to make Maduzu go away.

Most of Dankie's visits were spent with his mother and at funerals. The days would fly away quicker than the Tokoloshe could run, and Dankie was always sad to leave again on Sunday morning. But that weekend, as he was packing his bags to return south, he heard Maduzu in the distance. The songs of Muchongolo. He ventured outside and across the empty plots to ask his neighbors, the weaver and the retired sugar mill man, about the music.

"There's Muchongolo across the way today," said the retiree on his way to church.

Dankie didn't go back to the house. Nor did he rush to catch his taxi. Instead, he walked the windy paths of Rooibok until he reached the source of the music. Muchongolo dancers and spectators were crowded around—in a circle where the past is surrounded by the present, where xintu and xilungu battle.

In the 1930s, Muchongolo was a wedding dance, and was danced only when a man and woman were marrying. Muchongolo teams from the bride's community and from the groom's community were invited by the bride's parents, and beer was brewed. The bride's Muchongolo teams would express mock anger and fight the groom's team for taking the bride away from their community. What started as custom and play eventually got out of hand—politics and civil strife invaded tradition—and injury or death was often a result.

After the initial native policies of 1948, legislation that is considered the start of apartheid, lobola became a burden. Stock limitations reduced cattle herds, which reduced each family's ability to pay lobola in cattle. Many parents stopped helping boys pay for their brides, and the boys started to pay in cash with installments as one would do to pay off store credit. This meant that there became less and less Muchongolo traditions before and after weddings.

A decline in elaborate weddings caused wealthy businessmen and shop owners to invite and sponsor Muchongolo dance teams from the surrounding villages to dance on Sundays, at their homes or stores. They would sell sorghum beer for profit and awarded prize money to the best team. This caused even greater issues than the violence that took place at weddings. This began to pit villages against one another, creating fights and feuds.

In 1961, there was a Muchongolo dancer from a nearby community killed during a competition. Dancers were also going to sangomas for muthi to strengthen them during competition and for muthi that would help them defeat particular teams. There were even rumors that certain teams would put human skulls inside their drums for strength.

Muchongolo eventually evolved from wedding dances, to business-based competitions, into formal stadium competitions (tamed by the local Christian elite), and eventually back to a more traditional, less formal competition across the villages. In 1994, the Ngungunyane Traditional Dance Association was formed, and teams blended based on tradition more than ethnicity.

Shangaan Muchongolo is the most traditional. Men dress like Ngungunyane's warriors. They carry knobkerries or sticks in their right hands and cowhide shields in the left. Knobkerries represent a willingness to defend their village against foes. The shield represents man as the village's protector. Many men wear goatskins around their shins, hang wildebeest hair from their waists, and wrap red and green beads around their necks. White represents ancestors and wildebeest power. The women of Muchongolo, wearing bright blue and yellow, represent the virgins from the original bride party of marriage rituals where dancers first began.

Today, there seems to be a class system within the spectators. The dancers are in the middle; there are rows of chairs around the dancers where men in suits, local dignitaries, sit; and behind them the regular spectators sit.

As Dankie approached, he walked through an informal lot of parked cars. He knew exactly what was happening inside many of the cars, and, for that reason, he kept his head down and his eyes on his feet. From visits with his cousin over the years, Dankie knew that the aggressive sexual dances inside the circle leaked outward.

Muchongolo dances and music are like stories. It is a war of words and songs and images in which teams hash out contemporary hardships like wife problems, cheating, poverty, HIV/AIDS, and witchcraft. In many cases, they're quite improvisational. And throughout most competitions, sex is the most frequent topic. Rapid and aggressive dances represent nights with prostitutes and girlfriends. Less about love, more about power. The slower, more concerted dances with rhythmic pelvic movements represent procreation with your wife. And while Muchongolo has evolved to represent a battle between the past (xintu) and the present (xilungu), some say that while older men act out the past in the center, younger men reflect the present on the periphery.

Inside many of the cars, rapid and aggressive dances are easy to find.

Once inside the circle, Dankie could see his cousin's Muchongolo team preparing to battle. He stayed behind other spectators to make sure he wasn't seen. He didn't want to answer questions or see his cousin in their eyes. He didn't really know why he was even there. Maybe it was to bring Maduzu back to his people, or maybe it was to push him away from Dankie's memories and visions. Was he trying to tell Maduzu to go away? Or was he trying to reconnect with the man who'd been haunting him, truthfully, since he cut him down from the rafters with a bread knife? Or was it that Dankie was afraid to admit he was becoming a man like Maduzu?

Maduzu's team began to dance, and the sound of the drum pounded Dankie like a semiautomatic. Like the guns he sees the security guards carry in the city and larger villages. Each pound brought him back to the day Maduzu was carried home from Elite. Each pound escalated his anxiety and insecurities. Even with his eyes wide open, he could see Maduzu. He was everywhere.

THOKO

The rain continued to turn off and on, keeping the ground soft and the maize green. The chickens in Thoko's yard kept cover inside their pen to the right of the gate's entrance, and the goats that hadn't crammed themselves inside with the chickens were curled up on the ledge of Thoko's ndumba, hiding under the lip of the roof and avoiding the wet wind hitting the building's opposite side.

Patrick was inside the house with six other men talking business, and Lizzy was in back checking on the buckets and washbasins that lined the rear of the house and collected water as it fell from the skies. The men inside were talking about banding together as a single business rather than individual producers and sellers. Each of them sold magwunya to pensioners and wanted to find ways to save money and make money. The common consensus was that they needed a loan, but they knew that loans were given only to companies and that they weren't large enough to register themselves as a company, nor would they qualify for any Black Economic Empowerment grants if they applied as individuals.

Their ideas seemed to fly around the room, but none were really caught. Each wanted to work together, but no one wanted to work together. They wanted to call themselves a single business, but most insisted that each have his own equipment and that each were responsible for his own stock and his own sales. What some were willing to share was transportation. Taking taxis back and forth with crates of scones was too expensive as individuals, and they wanted to purchase cars, but no one had a driver's license. And even if they had the money, the used car dealer said he would not release a car unless someone with a driver's license picked it up.

While the men talked in circles, Thoko started on her way home from town. She had left early that morning during a downpour with Elizabeth for court. This time, Thoko was there to support Elizabeth in a case against her and her sons who beat up a pair of drunken robbers breaking into their house. After the monthly visits to court since the day Elizabeth bailed Thoko out of jail, Thoko knew Elizabeth deserved the companionship and moral support.

As the rain increased its volume and pressure, as if someone was controlling a faucet up above, shouts and screams from the back of the house could be heard. Through the shebeen and the kitchen's back door, Lizzy ran for help, still screaming, but Patrick knew what was happening only when she entered the living room and said, "Water. There is water coming from the ground! Quick, we need buckets!"

Patrick ran out the front door and to the right, around the house, to where he could see the black hose that led to one of the community boreholes pouring with water, jumping up and down as the pressure fluctuated, streaming like a small water fountain. As Patrick stood and looked at the hose and the puddle forming around it on the ground, Lizzy was dragging buckets from inside the house. Anything she could find—cooking pots, washing tins, and twenty-liter containers—was attached to her arms or fingers. She dropped everything, grabbed the hose, and directed the stream into a twenty-liter canister.

"*It's time to celebrate!*" said Patrick. The hose that looked like a straw stuck in the ground had been dry for months, just over a year.

In 1994, when the municipality paid to install water pipes throughout the community, Thoko was one of the many locals hired to dig trenches and install pipes up and down the grid of homesteads in Rooibok A. She helped lay the thick black piping nearly two meters below the surface from the main road leading toward Dingleydale down to the river's edge, snaking pipes up and down, up and down, until every available plot in her community could access water. Once the pipe system was in place, people who could afford to dig and connect their own pipes to the main line could have access to water from inside their homesteads. How far those pipes went depended upon the money people were willing to, and had to, sink into water infrastructure, but most people were happy enough to connect to the main line with a single pipe that stopped just above the surface with a tap to turn off and on.

Thoko, though, understood the challenges of water pressure and strategically installed her water pipe. When the pressure is down, the water sits like a light stream at the base of the pipe. A trickle. The majority of people installed their pipes at the top of the main line, which means they can access water only when the pressure is high, but Thoko and a few others connected with the main line at its base, which means that even during low pressure, water will find its way through an open tap.

When the pressure dropped, caused by the switch from the borehole's diesel-run motor to an electrical motor, Thoko's homestead had a line of people sitting on buckets and in wheelbarrows, waiting for their turn to fill up. The queue was good for business, as people waiting for several hours would get hungry and purchase Cheese Nips for fifty cents or bread for two rand fifty or cool drink for seven rand fifty. Eventually, though, the tap broke, and there was only the hose left, turned off and on with a kink in the line.

As the rain fell from above and the water continued to stream from below, Lizzy sat on the edge of the house and monitored.

REGINA

It had rained for three days. The main road through MaRoman into Rooibok had become two slowly meandering rivers bordering an island of water-filled potholes. Cars, with their fog lights switched on, cautiously crawled along the edge of the road with one wheel vibrating over potholes and the other rolling through flooded green grasses, as tall as those who *famba* with their open umbrellas. In the distance, trees and homesteads painted misty silhouettes of purple across the veldt. A curtain of fog and cirrus clouds resembling pulled cotton just before it hits the spinning wheel had fallen over the lowveld and stolen the mountains from the skyline.

Children were on their way to school, walking along the snaking paths within the tall grasses that swallowed them whole. Only their umbrellas bobbing up and down above the grass line—painting the dreary morning with red, yellow, white, green, blue, purple, and flower-patterned canopies of plastic—could be seen. As the little ones came into sight crossing the trimmed grass of the soccer field, they crossed through several dozen cows and oxen grazing both east and west. A tall man followed the cattle headed west, down the slope in the direction of where the mountains usually stood. Dressed in a blue jumpsuit, he swung a long stick in his left hand, up and down, up and down.

Heading in the opposite direction, a man of equal stature, dressed in a long yellow rain coat with calf-high black rubber boots, seemed to move at a pace equal to, or slower than, the grazing herd he followed. He zigzagged his way through the soccer field, along the road's edge, over the flooded and ineffective cattle grid, and into the mission grounds bringing up the rear of his desultory cattle.

A collective of birds seeking refuge inside the tall mission trees sang like the church choirs Regina loved to listen to on her hi-fi, blending into one strong voice. In the distance, the sound of the morning train passing through Acornhoek toward Thulamahashe could be heard.

After years of drought, the grass in the mission reflected the days and weeks of heavy, steady rains, kept near ankle height by the teeth of local livestock ambling in and out each day. Between Mapusha's studio and the main entrance to the mission, the cracking foundation and remnants of old walls from the mission's first construction in 1954 had disappeared under the lush green blades inching toward the sky.

The clank of the cowbell tied around the neck of the wide ox with black patches and long crooked horns beat at a consistent rhythm. Tails swung left to right and right to left. Young cows moved like unattended children around trees, behind buildings, and in the opposite direction inside the mission grounds. As the man began to direct the herd back toward the skinny gateway in the back of the mission, Emma and Lizbeth ducked inside the covered church stoop and shook themselves and their umbrellas dry.

It was past nine when Lizbeth looked to Emma and said, "Regina is late . . ."

Over the fresh cattle tracks in the mission's sandy soil, Regina and Anna Mdluli walked through the mission's back gate. The man in a yellow raincoat followed his herd down a dirt path leading away from Rooibok. Balanced on top of Anna's head sat a white plastic bag filled with Tupperware and jars of food. Anna had tied a blue-and-purple plaid cloth around her body like a cape on top of which she'd wrapped a clear plastic sheet of equal size. Regina was wearing an orange plaid blouse, a flowered skirt, and a doek around her head and carried a black plastic bag. Her black shoes crunched against the soggy soil, gaining amplitude and speed as soon as she spotted the girls waiting.

As Regina pulled out a ring of keys and reached toward Mapusha's front door, the girls began to shuffle toward the studio. Immediately, inside, Anna Mdluli filled the teapot with water and plugged it in, and the others checked for any leaks in the roof.

Anna pulled a wide smile and clapped her hands together when she spotted the white plastic bag left at the studio for her by a friend. She knew exactly what was inside. Regina walked toward her to see what the commotion was about, and then Gertrude and Anna Mbetse, just entering the studio, quickly joined. From inside the bag, Anna pulled a square plastic container of minced garlic and a squeeze bottle of honey. The women immediately picked up each, examining the contents and labels. They immediately followed with curious chatter.

The garlic inside was to help clean her stomach and heal any infections or ulcerations. Two spoons of garlic a day in her marojo, and Anna won't even notice the bitter taste of the full cloves she dislikes so much.

Anna peeled the corner of the green top to the minced garlic and peered in like a child examining the glass jars of sweeties that line the counter at a tuck shop. Gertrude handed her a spoon, and Anna immediately pulled a heaping spoonful out and shoved it into her mouth.

"The honey is for my tea," said Anna to the women, with remnants of garlic still in her mouth. She picked up a ceramic mug and said, "This is for Anna. Two cups a day for Anna. No sugar. Tea with honey. It is better."

Knowing that she was supposed to have only one spoonful, a sneaky grin began to crawl across her face. The women howled with laughter as Anna held her ceramic mug against her chest like a treasure she had finally found.

Anna loved her sugar. She would boil a cup of tea on mornings like this one and heap four or five tall teaspoons of sugar into her small ceramic mug, plop a bag of Five Roses inside, and pour the recently fetched and boiled water.

"Ey! We have had a lot of rain," Regina said, shaking her head.

"Is the maize going to survive?" Anna Mbetse asked.

"Yes," insisted Gertrude.

"They will survive the rainfall. But if the rain is too hard, the maize will die," Anna Mbetse surmised.

"Yes," Gertrude agreed, "you are right. If we have more heavy rainfall, then the maize won't survive."

Regina explained, "The maize that we planted during the first good rains— the second planting—ey, there is nothing! It was too hot two weeks ago. The third planting—they are very good."

With the taste of the garlic lingering on Anna's palette, her thoughts immediately turned to food. "Yesterday," she interrupted, "I left Mapusha and decided not to cook at home. But this morning, I am really hungry. I did eat today with my medicine, but I am hungry again."

"You must eat lots of food because of this medicine," stressed Regina.

"It is because of the treatment," Anna said to Gertrude. "If I could give you one tablet, Gertrude, you would understand."

"No," said Anna Mbetse, cutting Anna's words in half. "You are not allowed to share your treatment."

Anna Mdluli replied, shaking her head, "Yes. I know. That is why I said, if I were to give you the medicine. It is better now, because I don't have to visit the hospital very often. I go once a month. My soldiers are now ninety-eight. At first, I was fifty-three. So now I am ninety-eight. That is good."

"And I gained three kgs," Anna said proudly. The ladies all laughed.

"What were you weighing, at first?" asked Regina, looking at Anna's stringy frame.

"Forty-two," she replied.

"You should weigh yourself—we have a scale in the stockroom—to keep track," suggested Anna Mbetse.

"You should weigh yourself after eating food every day," suggested Gertrude.

"No," Anna Mbetse said. "She should weigh herself here at Mapusha before she goes to hospital."

"I have someone I met in hospital," said Anna Mdluli, ignoring the discussion of when and how she should weigh herself. "She said before she got a government grant, her soldiers were thirteen."

"The mother of Tulape," Anna Mbetse interrupted, "her soldiers were seventeen. But, she has now gained weight."

Anna Mdluli continued, "I was so surprised the other day. I took the letter from Nurse Stella to give to Tulape, and she was so surprised."

"I was better, not like Tulape," she said. "I was also better than that woman I told you about earlier. Who I said she is receiving a government grant. This woman says she was working at the farm called Mablanga."

"There is a girl that I know," added Anna Mbetse, "that stays next to my child's home, Dikeledi. She is very sick. And she also can't walk. And this girl is the reason why Gloria divorced her husband. Her husband had an eye for this girl who is sick now."

"This girl," Regina inquired, "did she have a stroke, or does she have other diseases?"

"No," Anna Mbetse explained. "She has this same disease, and some people will get stroke."

"If you have stroke, then it is not easy to recover," Anna Mdluli commented. "After six months you may recover and start getting the treatment. Does she go to Tintswalo?"

"Yes, she does go to Tintswalo," said Anna Mbetse.

"It is hard for those people who cannot walk," said Anna Mdluli, remembering her bad days. "If the transport does not take you into the hospital, then the nurses must come and fetch you at the gate."

The conversation continued like a four-woman ping-pong game, until suddenly Gertrude started to say something and then hesitated. She cut herself off and looked around for permission to continue. She wanted to give words to what everyone was thinking, to talk about the topic that had Rooibok whispering behind closed doors. The women all nodded their heads.

"Father Miguel is no longer here. He went somewhere . . . he went somewhere because he is in love with a young girl, this side," Gertrude said, pointing north toward MaRoman.

"He is no longer going to be a priest," Gertrude added. "The girl—oh—she is very young. Twenty-five years."

"No, she's not twenty-five," Anna Mbetse chirped in, "eighteen or twenty years."

The women bickered amongst themselves until they could agree that the girl was no more than seventeen or eighteen years old.

"He's old," Regina said, stretching the word old. "Father Anton says he's forty." Regina giggled with an out-of-mind, out-of-belief laugh. Anna Mbetse joined.

"He was always going there, bringing groceries. Always bringing her somewhere. Nelspruit. Taking her just to take her," ranted Anna Mbetse.

"He already paid lobola," stressed Regina, thinking about the sacrifices families make each year to gift the fathers both food and finance. "Last Sunday, they were at Thulamahashe holding the parish council. He told the council members, 'I am going before June.' It was Sunday. Monday. Tuesday, he went away."

"They say, he didn't say why," said Regina. Knowing that the priests stay for three or four years and then return home for a few months—Regina explained—everyone expected him to leave soon. "So, many people thought, maybe it is his time to go home?"

"It was not a secret, the way he was. And the little sister, the small one down there," Regina said, pointing toward the girl's home, "was speaking to everybody. Even the boys, his friends, they were speaking, because he was always going there to that family."

"The parents liked this. They did agree with Miguel being with her. If they didn't, they would not allow this. If it were me, I would not allow this," said Anna Mbetse.

"Yes," confirmed Anna Mdluli. "The parents approve of Miguel."

"The parents like this," Anna Mbetse said, "because when Miguel went to their home and took their child out, they said, 'Oh, my child is in love with a father.' They said, 'Father likes my child.'"

"Yes," jumped in Gertrude. "The parents like this. Because if they didn't, they should have stopped father from doing that."

"Miguel had many boys as friends," Anna Mbetse added, referring to the rumors that once flew around Rooibok relating to the group of young boys he kept close. Many people made accusations.

"I don't understand why girls are getting involved with priests," Anna Mbetse said, bringing the conversation back in focus. "Is it because we are poor, and we need them to buy us things? I was told, one day by the husband of a friend, that Father Miguel was going there every day. Like the girl's home was his home, and I heard long before that they were leaving."

"Lindy doesn't believe that the girl is pregnant," said Anna Mdluli.

"I believe the girl is pregnant," Anna Mbetse interrupted, "because now they are running away. If she is pregnant, that would be the reason for them to run away."

"I believe so too," said Gertrude, "because if she wasn't, he would have waited until June. He promised us that he would leave in June. So why did he hurry up? That means the girl is pregnant."

The women all stared at one another.

Breaking the silence, Gertrude said, "The girl's brother mentioned that they are still here in South Africa. They are still preparing to leave South Africa. That means they are still here. They haven't left yet."

"So where is the mission car?" asked Regina. "Father Anton has no idea, because he tried to call Miguel, and his cell phone is off."

"You know," said Gertrude, "the first time I heard about it, I couldn't say anything about this. I just came here and closed my mouth."

Anna Mbetse added, "I was so hurt when I heard from my sister that Father Miguel was in love with this girl. I was so hurt. Even if I could, I wouldn't tell anyone. But, then I heard people talking about it. So there was no use of me keeping quiet."

DANKIE

Bodies were packed like pilchards in the company lorry as it crawled up the mountain. The final leg of five from Rooibok to the staff village of Elandshoogte was slow, hot, and cramped. Dozens of men stood shoulder to shoulder, leaning against one another for relief in the two-hour ride from Nelspruit, over the Fish River, over the Crocodile River, over the Fish River, again, and through the Sappi entrance where the slow climb began. Bags of clothing and newly purchased groceries filled the floor below, piled where space allowed. The seats that bordered the sides of the truck were filled with women who worked in the trees alongside the men, and wives who looked after children and fulfilled more domestic roles within the village. Children sat on laps, at fathers' feet, and lay wrapped on the backs of women and girls.

"They transport us like cattle or timber," Dankie complained. Every time he stepped inside the lorry, to leave or return to the mountain, he worried. About the children struggling to hold on to their mothers. About the little fingers and toes in danger of a heavy foot. About the infants squashed between their mothers and strangers beside her. About the absence of seatbelts for women and children, who shouldn't be traveling like a wholesale delivery. The trapped air grew thinner as each passenger took in oxygen and released carbon dioxide. Steeping like a sangoma's infusion, the air began to taste and smell of sweaty armpits and dirty diapers, trapped.

Stewing inside of Dankie was the decision he needed to make about whether or not to accept a promotion from temporary worker in the trees to assistant supervisor. As he stood inside the lorry with his coworkers, he grew even more anxious. He feared the reaction of those nearly twice his age and half as willing to work through the day. He feared most the men from Mozambique—those who questioned Dankie's ability to be a team player each time he told them that working together would be more productive in less time. He was afraid that everyone would blame his promotion on family ties and favoritism. He was afraid that they would hate him and possibly hurt him. As he rocked back and forth inside the truck, Dankie couldn't help but think just as he did when school frustrated him. "I don't deserve to be here. I deserve to be like someone who wears designer clothes."

The lorry slowed and opened its door, letting in oxygen to breathe and off-loading its passengers. Dankie shuffled out beside the others and headed toward his house, looking for his brother-in-law. He was afraid, but he decided to "accept the challenge" that was staring him in the face. "I know if I do something like this, it will take me somewhere." He could earn more money faster, and he could gain the experience of leading people. He was petrified, in and out of cold sweat, bouncing between a rapidly beating heart and one in near arrest. But if he were going to work side by side with the men whom he already feared, why not stand above them? Why not take a position that could help balance the powerlessness his age created? During his bumpy ride up the mountain, Dankie had decided to accept the promotion. The little village perched on a mountain plateau surrounded by rocky outcrops and forestry rows was going to be home longer than originally expected. Dankie had already started calculating numbers in his head. He knew that the previous assistant earned about three thousand rand each month, which was nearly double what he had been making as a temporary worker and ten times what he and his mother were living off the previous year. He could set aside a certain amount each month to start saving for driving school, keep a little bit in the account for emergencies, give his mother as much as possible each month to complete her new house, and help pay for his niece's expenses. Dankie had every rand of next month's paycheck accounted for in his mind. But as quickly as he counted his earnings, he lost them.

REGINA

Regina and Gertrude leaned against the large unused loom, watching out the window and eating portions of maize grown in Anna Mdluli's yard. They watched through the open pane as Emerencia greeted two American tourists and a young South African couple that brought them from a lodge in a nearby game reserve for a lunchtime excursion to Mapusha's studio.

An hour later than expected and half the number of guests, the women weren't sure if they would arrive at all on account of the rain, but two is better than none.

Across from them and staring into the large wooden beams that made up the long horizontal loom, Anna Mbetse sat on a knee-high wooden stool, eating a portion of maize with her left leg extended. To her right, Anna Mdluli sat on the floor with her legs stretched out across a grass mat, pulling kernels from their core and eating them one by one.

Anna Mdluli had packed the maize in her white plastic bag and carried it to Mapusha on her head along with her lunch and midday snack of marojo and stiff pap. The recently picked maize with juicy white kernels was more than a snack to share with friends. For Anna, the maize was celebration. The maize was victory. The maize was survival. She planted only inside the gates of her homestead this year, but she had planted all the same.

"Anna is planting sweet potatoes," Regina said, breaking off a portion of her maize for another woman to eat.

Anna's little body hardly filled the grass mat, and her bare toes seemed to mirror her excitement, wiggling back and forth. She looked up and moved her arms up and down, motioning like a runner or someone doing bicep curls. In her own way, Anna was proudly telling everyone that she had strengthened her muscles with her pair of sand-filled dish soap bottles.

"Hellooooo!" greeted the South African woman with the tourists as she stepped through the door. "Hello!" replied the women as they turned their heads in her direction and slipped their corn into the palms of their hands as if it weren't there at all. Walking toward her to greet them properly, Gertrude, Regina, and Anna Mbetse slyly slipped their cobs into the pockets of their skirts and dresses.

"How are youuuuu?" she blanketly asked as the young girls sat up from their table in the far corner; Lindy and Anna Ndzukula walked from their spot on the floor opposite the spinning wheels; and the ladies with corn in their pockets circled around for a compulsory greeting.

All the while, Anna Mdluli was still sitting on her grass mat, slowly pulling a yellow tin bowl of water from beside her feet and washing her hands. Before she stood, she stretched her arms out toward her toes and slapped the excess water off her hands and onto the tops of her bare feet. When she found her footing, she joined the others just inside the door, greeted as expected, and returned to her grass mat in front of the spinning wheels to continue pulling raw wool as she and Anna Ndzukula had done all morning.

Anna Mbetse had returned to warping her horizontal loom. Lindy returned to work on her tapestry. Lizbeth continued sewing blue beads onto a cotton bag. Wonder returned to pull threads from a turquoise cotton tablecloth to make fringe. Emma slipped her needle back into the black cloth of embroidery. Gertrude wandered the room as if looking for something, and Regina sat in the center of her bench to pick up where she had left off before lunch.

As the business manager and only girl comfortable enough to speak English to tourists, Emerencia continued her tour inside. She walked the tourists through the process of dying, spinning, and weaving. She'd started outside, circled the exterior of the studio, and walked past the fire pit where wool is dyed and hung to dry. Inside, the women greeted their guests and returned to their work, looking busy.

The sound of the spinning wheel had begun to whirl as Emerencia walked toward Anna Ndzukula and Anna Mdluli. "First, we buy raw wool," explained Emerencia, pointing to Anna Mdluli's pile of pulled wool. "It comes in a big bail and looks like stringy cotton. Then we cut the wool and prepare to spin by making it soft. It is pulled apart to make it soft, and then we spin the wool."

Anna Ndzukula lifted her head and smiled a crooked, toothless smile, as Emerencia began to describe the spinning wheel on which she was working.

She understood very little of the English Emerencia was speaking, but with the two foreign women looking in her direction, it must have been her cue. Anna guided the wool in her hands and let the strands slip into the spinning machine to twist and rotate into rolls.

Regina watched through the warp of her loom. As she shifted her foot back and forth on the loom pedal and slipped each color into its place, she scanned the movement of the two tourists and their camera, which had a very long lens and a very bright flash. She watched through the slivers of space between each line of warp on her loom, watching her youngest daughter guide the visitors through the studio teaching them about every stage of their work: pulling, spinning, dying, warping, weaving, and finishing.

Dangling from her partially completed tapestry were the colors of Rooibok on a summer evening just as the sun slips behind the Drakensberg. Six variations of blues and purples blended like rolling hills across the warp with the occasional thread of khaki shining like the blond grasses of the veldt reflecting off the last light of the day.

When the tour wound down and the tourists were free to walk around and look through the studio's storeroom for rugs, tapestries, bags, painted shirts, table runners, and embroidered cloths, the tourist dressed in khaki pants, a white T-shirt, and a long khaki safari vest found her way back to the studio's entrance and just across from Regina. The tourist stood leaning against the open door, butt up against a trash bin for support, photographing Regina up close.

Regina watched through the warp to see what exactly the woman was up to, only realizing that she was snapping away as fast as Anna's spinning wheel moves in circles. *Snap Snap Snap Snap* went the camera as Regina provided one wide smile and returned her focus on the tapestry in front of her. *Snap Snap Snap Snap* the camera went as its owner stepped closer and closer.

The sound of someone's voice outside carried through the door and, suddenly, Regina looked up and waved her left hand, rapidly moving it to the left of her loom so the tourist woman could see. "Goodbye!" she said. "Goodbye!" She thought it was time for them to leave, completely forgetting the final thank you. As she realized her mistake, she stopped herself from repeating "goodbye" several more times and returned to weaving.

As if deflecting the mistake, Regina stretched her legs, stood up from her bench, and took her place in the center of the studio, to the right of her loom. The younger girls began to move the long wooden benches around, screeching their legs across the cement floor. The rest of the women began to circle around, forming a horseshoe closed in by the line of benches for the two tourists and their two South African drivers.

Anna Mbetse, with a swollen knee about which she could not explain, sat behind Regina and on top of Regina's loom bench. Beside her, she saw Regina's blue pocket-sized prayer book; she picked it up and started flipping through.

The room was suddenly dead quiet. And then Regina's voice reached into the air, "Kuuuuaaaaa Mapusha / Reya lemane / Kuuuuuaaaaa Mapusha . . ."

Suddenly, Emerencia stopped her mother, realizing that she forgot to explain the song to the two tourists sitting on the long wooden benches. "This is the Mapusha song," she said. "We want to thank you for coming." She looked to her mother, who was preparing to begin her lead again. The women end the song on one final stomp, and everyone bursts into laughter. "If you enjoy what you hear," Emerencia said, cutting into their trailing mirth, "we have a CD that you can buy after the show for fifty rand."

Regina stood taking a deep breath, turned to look at Anna Mdluli sitting behind her, and turned back again toward the tourists.

Emerencia explained that the next song was about Elijah from the Bible. "We sing about the Bible story of Elijah, and we are asking Elijah, take us to Heaven with him."

"Our last song is the South African national anthem," announced Emerencia. Originally a Methodist hymn from 1897, absorbed into poetry thirty years later, the Xhosa lyrics of this song became a symbol of the pan-African liberation movement across southern Africa and became, eventually, the unofficial, anti-apartheid, South African anthem. "This is special for us, to our people, because in the apartheid times, we were not allowed to sing this song," she continued. "If the police would find us singing it, we would face some serious charges."

After the first democratic election of 1994, after Regina voted for the first time and walked around with an inked thumb—the mark of a voter—the national anthem came into question. Mandela, the president of new South Africa, chose to excerpt both official and unofficial anthems throughout the country's history—the Afrikaans "Die Stem van Suid-Afrika" and Xhosa "Nkosi sikelel' iAfrika"—and to integrate multiple languages. This composite of the old and the new—with lyrics moving from Xhosa and Zulu to seSotho and Afrikaans, and closing in English—represented the inclusive nation Mandela sought to foster.

"When Mandela became president ten years ago, we were allowed to sing this song. The only time before that time we would sing this song was at a funeral," explained Emerencia. "We would sing verrrry, verrrry low, so that the police could not hear us."

Nkosi sikelel' iAfrika
Maluphakanyisw' uphondo lwayo,
Yizwa imithandazo yethu,
Nkosi sikelela,
thina lusapho lwayo.

Morena boloka setjhaba sa heso,
O fedise dintwa la matshwenyeho,
O se boloke,
O se boloke setjhaba sa heso,
Setjhaba sa South Afrika—South Afrika.

Uit die blou van onse hemel,
Uit die diepte van ons see,
Oor ons ewige gebergtes,
Waar die kranse antwoord gee,

Sounds the call to come together,
And united we shall stand,
Let us live and strive for freedom,
In South Africa our land.

Lord, bless Africa,
May her spirit rise high up.
Hear thou our prayers,
Lord bless us.

Lord, bless Africa,
Banish wars and strife.
Lord, bless our nation,
Of South Africa.

Ringing out from our blue heavens,
From our deep seas breaking round,
Over everlasting mountains,
Where the echoing crags resound . . .

Sounds the call to come together,
And united we shall stand,
Let us live and strive for freedom,
In South Africa our land.

AUTUMN

DANKIE

Dankie walked inside the fire-blackened kitchen of his house in Elandshoogte, looking for his brother-in-law, hoping to share his decision to accept the promotion. But what he found was the voice of someone within the village telling him that someone was looking for a maintenance man who could read and write. Immediately, Dankie's mind twisted back into fear, away from the confidence he had started to nurture. Apparently, while Dankie had been walking the footpaths of Rooibok, a man, whose company is outsourced to care for the pipes and electricity in Elandshoogte, had inquired amongst the staff, looking for a man with literacy skills to hire. No one really knew of Dankie's promotion, so they suggested him as a candidate. The position would keep him on the mountaintop but away from the trees. With little thought, Dankie rang the man and said, "I will do it."

They arranged to meet the following day. Trusting that the job would be good and that the man would arrive, Dankie didn't board the lorry the next morning. While his coworkers headed into the trees for a day's work, Dankie waited in the staff village for his meeting. He didn't tell anyone what he was doing. He waited and waited. No one arrived. He called the man's office and was told that they could meet the following day. Dankie agreed and, once again, watched his coworkers board the lorry without him.

Eventually, an Afrikaans man driving a maintenance bakkie arrived in the village. It was midday, and no one was really around. Dankie walked with the man through the village, into areas he had never entered, discussing the way the electricity and the pipes worked on the mountaintop, from building to reed sewage system to dams. The man, who had a team of plumbers and electricians in Nelspruit, needed a middleman to keep an eye on everything, reporting specific items when they required repair. *Sounds easy*, Dankie thought. *I can do this.* And so, he accepted with little question and little thought.

For months, Dankie would ask himself questions every day, stressed out by his surroundings, his job, and his choices. "I am still young. Why do I do something like this? Maybe the problem is that my father left my mom and is no longer supporting my family. I ask myself a lot of questions that sometimes get me angry." When Dankie feels like he's unable to move forward or is progressing too slowly, the emotion seems to take over his every thought. Even while he was still in school, his worries would sometimes interfere with his work: "I would even get a poor symbol, because I was writing a test, thinking I had nowhere to go."

Dankie's new position wasn't really a full-time job. When everyone left for the day, he would linger in the house a bit to pass the time, eventually leaving for his three-hour inspection. If he dawdled, he could stretch the time, but with his checklist in hand, he would walk through houses and maintenance rooms, water stations and ablution blocks. He would write down any signs of wear and tear, or vandalism. Dankie kept an eye out for units where the residents had taken it on their own to rewire according to their needs, prevalent when stealing electricity from your neighbor. And he would keep an eye out for damage that needed immediate attention. These problems made uncommon appearances, but when repairs were necessary, he would walk up to the main office and hand in a report to be faxed to the Nelspruit office.

Dankie had accepted the new position hoping that it would give him direction, give him some place to go. But he was bored. Although he was no longer in the trees, dealing with men who disliked him, he wasn't happy. He didn't feel fulfilled. Dankie wanted more for himself and for his days. He continued to wake before the sun each morning to cook his brother-in-law breakfast and clean the house. Despite the dilapidated bachelor conditions of the unit, Dankie's cleaning habits—something his mother never understood—continued. When he finished the day, he would sit and play video games with a friend who worked on the night shift, but even that was too little to fill his day.

What he hadn't questioned was the pay. Dankie had assumed that he would at least earn the same pay as he did temporarily working in the trees. As things worked out, that was partially true. The daily pay equaled his temp rate, but what he hadn't realized was that his workweek shrunk by one day, losing Saturdays, and more deductions were made from his salary. Since Dankie was no longer working for the company who rented the village, his new boss had to pay rent to his old boss for his shared housing. Additionally, deductions for things with acronyms that Dankie didn't understand had been pulled out. But, what was most aggravating was that Dankie was left in the dark regarding the various deductions. Unlike his previous employers, the man from Nelspruit didn't give him a pay slip.

THOKO

Thoko and Shelly sat inside Criminal Court C, once again. Because this was Thoko's eighth court date since being arrested nine months earlier, she knew that the state was required to either act on her case or drop it. Remand was not an option this month.

Grant-fraud cases were being conducted across the country, and newspaper articles were documenting win after win on behalf of the government. Some of the cases were focused on recipients who were double registered, were deceased, or never existed. Others looked to catch people who were informally earning more than the permissible maximum salary, something that could evolve into both fraud and tax cases. And many were against illegal residents, using fake ID documents to register for grants.

As Thoko sat beside defendants and witnesses dressed in their best and crammed shoulder to shoulder, she knew the one thing that could cause the case to crumble—and it was all about Evidence. Or, really, the mother of Evidence, Patrick's ex-girlfriend, Suzette. She was nowhere to be seen.

Thoko watched as people filed in, lawyers took their places, and the judge took his seat, closer to the ceiling than the floor. She heard people talking, but, with her limited English, all she heard was jabber. What she could identify, though, was her name. The prosecutor said her name, but what she'd said before or after was a mystery. Thoko stretched her body taller, pulling herself from her seat without actually standing, as if getting closer would turn their words from English to Tsonga. Her lawyer, in the same grey suit as the April court date, spoke briefly, gathered his things, picked up the green folder with Thoko's name on it, and walked out the door, giving Thoko the signal to follow. She practically leapt from her seat, stepping over people, telling Shelly, Lizzy, and Elizabeth to follow. Outside, the lawyer started talking, and Lizzy translated for the others. He explained that the case had been dropped. It all boiled down to evidence. There wasn't enough, and the state was dropping the case. Thoko was free to go, and she shouldn't worry, he explained. They can't reinstate the case in the future, so she shouldn't have any further troubles.

The women, standing just outside the courtroom's open door, subtly shouted for joy. Elizabeth snuck away to collect the bail she had placed for Thoko nine months earlier. She pulled out her wallet in which the receipt sat—still as crisp as the day she slipped it beside ragged bills. Thoko then asked the man, via Lizzy, how much she owed him. Before he could answer, she started explaining that he should give Lizzy his bank details, so that she could make sure he was taken care of. He only laughed, explaining to Thoko, who towered above him, that he was appointed to her by Legal Aid, and his services were free of charge. Thoko was further overjoyed, and then muted by an angry police officer closing the courtroom door.

Shelly and her mother, who just took a seat outside the courtroom door, looked at their watches and realized it was only 9:40 A.M. Each month for the past eight, Shelly had to miss school to attend court. Whether their case was "remanded" by nine or past two, she never made it back to school for the day. Since her principal required a note from the courts verifying her absence, and the judges wouldn't write something up until their dockets were complete, she sat outside the entire day waiting.

Shelly was repeating grade twelve. She didn't pass the previous year's matric exams, so she returned to school, but not Moholoholo High School. Since she was repeating, and students can repeat their matric exams only twice, Thoko agreed to pay the higher school fees required to send Shelly to Acornhoek Academy, across the street from Elite Funeral and the Tintswalo turnoff. Shelly walked there every day.

Thoko anxiously awaited their return home; she had many things to do. That morning, she had removed thirteen handmade goatskin drums from storage and lined them up against the front of her house to dry. When people pass by and see this, they know that Thoko is preparing to train a new sangoma. The drums are normally stored inside the ndumba of her mother's ancestors, alongside crates of empty bottles, bags of cement, buckets, window frames, and anything else that needs a temporary home. Thoko was preparing for the arrival of two girls, one in her early teens and the other in her twenties—sisters, both called by the ancestors.

REGINA

Regina looked at Father Anton, unsure as to what she should say, as the words came out of his mouth and slapped her in the face. *The bishop has said that Mapusha must pay rent.*

All Regina and Gertrude knew was that they were being told to pay rent for the studio. After more than thirty years, they must pay for their presence in a building they built with their own sweat, a building they gave life to each day and repaired when its roof leaked, its door was kicked in, its windows broke.

Father Anton was the only one left at the mission. It was him and the two dogs that barked at the women each morning. Except for Grace, who came in and out each day to clean, and David, the night security guard, the mission was empty. In just a few months, two priests had come, and three had gone away, leaving only the oldest. Father Anton had been at the mission for several years.

"The bishop asked me what financial contributions Mapusha was making to the church in exchange for water, electricity, and the studio," he elaborated. "We will let the parish council decide on the rent at their next meeting."

Regina diplomatically nodded her head and said that they would need to speak with Judy. The two women returned to the studio and explained to the others what was happening.

THOKO

"Where does MaSociatie stay?" asked a police officer leaning from the window of the lead vehicle. Behind him, five additional blue and whites caravanned through the streets of Rooibok in search of MaSociatie, in search of Thokozile Makwakwa.

Sitting on the stoop of her home with her long angular legs jutting to the left and right, Thoko watched six police vehicles—one from each surrounding village and two from her own—approach and park in front of her homestead. Although she'd been told by Louis Hugo via Patrick that the police would be completing a final inspection of the tavern site within a few days, Thoko was surprised to see the train of police from Acornhoek, Bushbuckridge, Hazyview, Hoedspruit, and Thulamahashe. The last time the police had arrived at her door, she was arrested and taken to Thulamahashe jail.

She stood to greet the eighteen men piling out of their vehicles, two of whom entered her home with a notebook and camera. Looking in every room, they snapped digitals of each (excluding bedrooms) and documented the shebeen separated from the rest of the house by only a deteriorating wooden door with orange paint. One of the two was scribbling in his notebook, looking up and down between his notations and what was in front of him. The other snapped the small silver one-touch in each room. Thoko watched—as they investigated the interior of her home—with no real knowledge as to what was actually being written or why her house had anything to do with the adequacy of her new venture.

The two men walked outside, and Thoko followed. *"What is that?"* asked one of the men, pointing to the partially complete building, the reason for their inspection.

"The tavern," she responded.

The fourteen others were walking in and out of the windows and doors; into the room where Thoko envisioned cases and cases of cool drink, bottled beer, and mixed spirit drinks packed side by side, from floor to ceiling; into the room where Thoko planned to place a desk, chair, and brand new computer for the stock-take, accounting, and sales software she was shown during a week-long tavern management course in the capital; into the large entertainment room where Thoko planned to have an upgraded snooker table and jukebox building upon her already existing business partnerships; and into the back room where pap, chicken feet, fried mopani worms, and snacks would be prepared for sale. Before the two men joined the others, one turned to Thoko and asked, *"Are you married?"*

Technically, Thoko was married, or at least had been. She wasn't any longer, but she had given birth to four children with the same man. Despite this, she still carried the surname of Patrick's father, her first and only husband.

"Yes," Thoko replied to the policeman, cocking her head upward with legitimacy. Walking counterclockwise around the tavern—which stood with four exterior walls waiting for plaster, a dirt floor within which a field of weeds were growing, and an absent roof—the two police officers wrote and snapped stills of the progress, capturing the builder smoking a boxer and his wife sitting in the front left windowsill missing its frame.

The more than dozen men eventually transitioned from close inspection to hang around and dawdle. Other than checking the distance between the tavern and the closest school or church, Thoko wasn't sure what they were looking for, but she surely wasn't asking. She stood tall beside the three mango trees in the center of her homestead, not far from where her maize was nearly ready to harvest, and watched the uniformed men chat until, eventually, they piled back into the half-dozen vehicles. As quickly as the caravan arrived, it left, with scribbles in a notebook, pictures in a memory card, and a tick off the list of Thoko Makwakwa.

REGINA

Every Tuesday of Lent, the Women of Saint Anne gathered at one of their homes for the stations of the cross. Every woman had the chance to host, and a few had the opportunity to host twice, but Anna Mdluli was simply happy to be strong enough to gather women together in her home. And, of all days, it just so happened to fall on Human Rights Day.

Thirty-six years earlier, before any of the second-generation weavers had been born and early in the elder weavers' marriages, long before any of them joined together in the studio at looms and behind spinning wheels, a peaceful protest of apartheid pass books and laws turned violent. Three hundred police officers in Sharpeville, one site of many protests around the country on that day, opened fire into a crowd of thousands. Igniting several days of township rioting and marking the start of the armed resistance in South Africa, the Sharpeville Massacre illustrated a brutality via which more unarmed protestors were shot in the back than not, brought international attention to South Africa's apartheid laws, and would, two years later, lead to Nelson Mandela's twenty-seven-year imprisonment.

Now, decades later, gathered in the outdoor room at the end of Anna Mdluli's porch, the Women of Saint Anne were circled around, legs in the center and backs against the walls, verbally walking the stations of the cross. Jesus is condemned to death, carries the cross, and falls the first time. He meets his mother, is helped by Simon of Cyrene, and has his face wiped by Veronica. And, yet, he falls again. He meets the women of Jerusalem, only to fall a third time, soon after. His clothing is taken away. He is nailed to the cross. And dies. Removed from the cross, he is laid in the tomb. And then, stopping there, the women are in waiting for him to rise again and ascend into heaven. As they closed their recitation of the stations, they paused for a moment—waiting for Regina to tell them about her meeting earlier that morning.

Regina had gone to the mission first thing to discuss security with several church leaders and Father Anton. The mission had been broken into the previous night, and Father Anton called a neighbor's cell phone to plead for help. The security guard was nowhere to be found, and the usually barking dogs weren't enough of a deterrent.

"We decided to fire him," explained Regina, referring to the absent security guard. "We said, if he can't look after Father Anton, if he decides to sometimes sleep in the mission, he is not doing his work."

What they didn't know was that Father Miguel had made a deal with David, the security guard. Father Miguel would give David the night off if the father had a girl with him. Regina and Father Anton may not have known, but the young people in Rooibok did. It wasn't clear whether or not there were set evenings that David could take off, or even if he understood why he was getting the nights off, but what David did know was that he could go home and sleep on those nights, and he was happy to do so. It was a Sunday night, and things were quiet.

Unfortunately, Father Miguel was gone, permanently. David took the night off, returning on Monday morning to an upset priest and a group of even more disturbed parishioners. "It was my day off," David said in his defense. Shifting the conversation abruptly, one of the women started to tell the story of her son in the hospital with TB, and then another shifted even faster to the subject of church lessons.

"There is this man who came to me," said one of the Women of Saint Anne, "and he is asking for a church lesson, because he wants to get baptized. I am so hurt, because I really don't have an idea who is going to help him. I think we need to get someone to help."

She continued with great concern, "I also heard about another man who said he went from church to church all over the country, and he decided to become Catholic. I think he would also like some church lessons."

Regina took a deep breath to gather her words and replied, "I don't know what will happen, because Satan has done his work. We don't have anyone who teaches church lessons. Gertrude's daughter, Susan, is the only one who teaches the children, and the adults, they don't have anyone. I heard that the one who was teaching the adults wrote a letter to church saying she is no longer interested."

Regina's words were stuck in the thick air that filled the day. The women waited a bit before chatting amongst themselves, until Regina continued,

"I should make this announcement in church that there are three people needed to help because Jesus said there is too big of a job here, but I really don't have people to help me."

THOKO

Thoko ran, barefoot in a dirty blue dress, from the house and into her ndumba with a plaid suitcase in her left hand. Inside the door, she dropped the suitcase and slid the white curtain hiding her muthi bottles. Thoko bent down on both knees and started sifting through the dusty bottles, carefully scanning and pulling each item on the checklist inside her head. With four bottles pulled, she turned around and placed them beside the suitcase. She straightened it with both hands, slowly unzipped the top, and flipped it over, revealing an empty interior.

Very carefully, Thoko packed three brown opaque plastic bottles that clinked and rolled around; a tall skinny bottle with dark yellow liquid (shaken slightly, examined for any signs of leakage); six iron hooks; a razor wrapped in newspaper; a small packet of sewing needles; an envelope of premixed dry muthi; and a small sheet of newspaper crinkled around a muthi ball, glued together with animal fat. Lastly, she placed a wooden spear—just short enough to fit diagonally—and a wildebeest tail inside and zipped the suitcase closed.

She ran out the door and back inside the house, returning in a black pleated skirt and sandals. Before picking up her suitcase and closing the creaky door of her ndumba, she wrapped a traditional cloth around her waist with snake emblems throughout—signifying the snake bites her father used to cure— and put on her beaded necklace and bracelets. With her suitcase and purse in hand, she passed through the front gates and into the passenger seat of the vehicle waiting to take her to Green Valley.

Three days earlier, a woman in her twenties with dainty features had come to visit Thoko in her ndumba. Xisiwana had arrived by taxi with her fourteen-year-old brother and thirteen-year-old sister. She had cared for her siblings since the death of her mother ten years earlier and had come to Thoko on her neighbor's recommendation.

The three worried siblings sat across from Thoko inside the darkness of the round, closed-in room and watched her throw the bones. They listened to Thoko's diagnosis, the words of their ancestors, possibly the warnings of their mother. Someone was trying to witch them. Xisiwana had watched her siblings through several weeks of restless nights, tossing, and cold sweats. The two would wake while the moon was still high and tell their sister that their father and his new wife were chasing them with knives, trying to kill them. The visions grew stronger with each night, and eventually the children's nightmares seeped into daylight with similar visions while they sat in school or walked down the road.

Thoko mixed two packets of muthi for the children and instructed Xisiwana. The first muthi was soft and to be used only once. Thoko explained to the older sister that she needed to take a razor and place small cuts on the children's bodies along their hairlines and near each major gland, into which she would have to rub a bit of wet muthi. The second muthi was an infusion. It should be boiled on the fire outside, and the children needed to hang it with a cloth over their heads, inhaling as much of the steam as possible.

Together these would help rid the children of the witches' hold. The muthi was not enough to stop the witches from trying to kill the children, explained Thoko. She would need to biamuthi the house, strengthening and protecting it from any witch's bad muthi, sometimes called black muthi. Xisiwana gathered the newspaper packets and left with the children, having agreed to biamuthi the house as soon as Thoko could travel to where they lived in Green Valley.

Green Valley is a small community that sits on the western edge of the village of Acornhoek, tucked against the lowveld's domineering rocky escarpment. Thoko traveled along Acornhoek's tar road through town, past the Women's Development Bank, past the hospital, past Plaza, and to the only robot in town, where the distance taxi rank sits below the tall and wide flat-crowned acacia. Thoko sat with her suitcase on her lap, keeping an eye out for the right-hand turn where Green Valley Wholesalers, a petrol station, and street vendors sit and a dirt road heads toward the mountains.

As the car pulled into a petrol station full of taxis and children buying sweeties on this Sunday afternoon, Thoko jumped from inside, dusted herself off, and started walking down the center of the road toward the mountains with her purse in her left hand and her suitcase in the right.

She met Xisiwana along the way, and the two ambled along the grid of roads until they reached the homestead gate. Immediately, Thoko asked Xisiwana for ten liters of water in a large bucket. She walked into the yard, closing the gate behind her, and approached the house, where she opened her suitcase. Around her, Xisiwana and the children watched with curiosity and awaited instruction. Thoko removed the yellow liquid muthi from her suitcase and poured it into the bucket, mixing it with her wooden spear. Returning the wet spear to the suitcase and picking up her wildebeest tail, Thoko stood up and carried the bucket to the gate entrance.

Thoko dipped the thick tail into the water and began to mumble to herself. Like a cardinal walking down the aisle, blessing parishioners with holy water, she pulled the tail up toward her shoulder, snapping it back down and sprinkling the gate's entrance. Thoko walked through the homestead's entirety, showering the sandy soil with her muthi mixture. As she looped toward the mountain side of the yard, around the house, and around the storage rooms to the front left of the house, she returned to where her suitcase sat, and walked through the front door. The muthi-soaked tail rained inside each room, until every part of the homestead had been purified and strengthened.

Returning to her suitcase, Thoko removed the six metal hooks, packet of sewing needles, and dry muthi wrapped in newspaper. She met Xisiwana beside the gate, where she waited with a spade. Thoko dug holes approximately twelve inches deep in six places throughout the homestead—at each of the four corners, in the gate's entrance, and in the center of the yard. Inside each, she placed one metal hook, a sewing needle, and a mixture of dry muthi before covering them with dirt. She explained to Xisiwana and the children that these hooks would trap any witch coming into their home with intent to harm. If witches entered, they would not be able to leave until they were spotted. They would be trapped until Xisiwana or her siblings released them.

Finally, Xisiwana collected hot coals, upon Thoko's request, in a metal spade, which she placed in the center of the homestead. Pulling the crinkled newspaper from her suitcase, Thoko unwrapped a small ball the size of a marula and placed it on the hot coals. The ball that Thoko had prepared at home was made from the fat of elephant, lion, cow, hyena, and wildebeest, in addition to a small mixture of dry muthi. A repugnant smell immediately hit the air and shifted around the homestead, inside and out, for the next three hours, preventing the possibility of a witch casting any animal into the homestead.

Leaving the smoking ball behind, Thoko asked Xisiwana to call her if anything happened. She packed her suitcase and headed back up the Green Valley road as the sun started to slide behind the mountains.

Historically, witchcraft was taken care of from inside the community rather than bureaucratically or democratically. If a family's house were struck by lightning, the family would seek out the witch responsible by having a sangoma set a trap for the person "witching." And the sangoma would assist in protecting the family from further witchcraft, further attempts on their lives. Some people took the situations into their own hands, lynching and burning those suspected of witchcraft. But in the previous decades, witch hunts became illegal, and the government, both apartheid and tribal, deemed witchcraft a nonissue. Now, anyone involved in witch hunts could be tried and sentenced.

In 1990, six years before Xisiwana's mother passed and four years before the first democratic elections, there was a series of unexplained deaths, deaths too close together and too unexpected for people to consider natural. During a period of twelve days, six young men were killed in a car accident, an elderly man committed suicide, and a woman was found dead outside of her home with multiple stab wounds. On a day when five of the nine funerals took place in the same cemetery, a member of the community spoke out to the mourners.

Recollections of the day are varied, but what is agreed upon was the man's call for action: *If five people die every week, more than twenty will die in a month. If things go on like this, we'll all die. You yourself may be next. The priests should pray to God to stop these deaths. If these deaths are man-made, the ministers should pray that the witches must stop. The witches think they are safe because I told [the chief] to stop burning them.*

Several elderly mourners in the crowd responded in shouts: "Tsamayang baloi!" *Away with the witches!*

Over the Christmas holidays of that same year, Green Valley residents commenced a witch hunt. A group collected two rand from everyone present to pay for a sangoma to assist them, but the sangoma was reluctant to help, and the meeting was unsuccessful. Some say the meeting place had been witched. After a few simultaneous incidents, delegates from the community were sent to consult a powerful sangoma near the border of Swaziland: a young boy had been found hanging from a tree, noosed by the sleeves of his own shirt; another young boy died after complaining of a headache and vomited blood; and a migrant worker home for month-end had been found naked and confused in a fruit store after a night in the shebeen, unsure as to where his clothing, his ID book, his salary, or his bank books had gone.

A message was sent back to the community via a traffic policeman, naming thirty suspects with a request of seventeen hundred rand for the sangoma to sniff out the witch. A group of men forcibly collected the suspects, put them on a bus, and sent them with the money to the sangoma several hours south.

Once identified, several men and women were told to climb on the roof of the bus and confess, to declare that they were witches. Some swore at the crowd, while others confessed and named names of others inside the community practicing witchcraft. Some were accused of laying *xifolane* on the road at the site of the car crash, while others were accused of keeping zombies in their homes. The same group of men responded by searching the homes of each accused. Inside the home of a man who supposedly was keeping a zombie in his coal-burning stove, a decaying piece of meat was found buried in the dirt floor beneath the stove. When the owner refused to eat the meat, it was determined that his refusal signified that the flesh was not that of a cow or goat; rather, it was the flesh of a man.

Along with this man, who had no chance once he refused to eat the buried meat, several people were hung that year in Green Valley. Witches, or those accused of witchcraft, were punished by the community who acted in ways that they believed protected their people. Xisiwana, and the entire adult community in Green Valley, remembers the hangings well.

Several days after Thoko performed the biamuthi on Xisiwana's homestead, the children's nightmares had waned to near extinction. They were sleeping through the night and no longer complaining of seeing their father and his new wife running after them with knives. There was nothing unusual to report to Thoko until, one afternoon, low-mumbling screams were heard coming from the yard.

Xisiwana was inside the house with the children when the sounds reached her ears.

She stood up from the worn green couch and peered out the window with enough distance to prevent whoever was outside from seeing her. In the center of the yard stood her father, who was mumbling and emitting a muted, underbreath scream. *He's gone mad*, thought Xisiwana as she watched him—a man she was very afraid of—standing as if frozen in place.

Since he had moved from the house with his new wife and child into a new homestead in Green Valley, he frequently arrived with an ugly demeanor, always accusing Xisiwana, his second-eldest daughter and third child, of being a witch, playing with snakes, placing black muthi for him in the doorway. She would just look at him when he ranted, keeping quiet.

This time, he walked through the door and to the left inside the living room toward his old bedroom. Since he moved from the house, his room remained empty but locked. He pulled the only key from his pocket and unlocked the door, stepped inside, and locked the door behind him. He was inside for several quiet minutes. Eventually, he came back out again, locked the door, and sat in the wooden framed chair just below the window and beside the front door. Xisiwana sat still and quiet on the green couch, pretending to watch television. Her father, who still had not said a word, closed his eyes and fell asleep.

Thirty minutes later, he jolted up and stared at his daughter sitting on the couch.

She turned to look at him and was confronted by angry eyes that felt like daggers flying toward her. He said nothing. He made no noise. He simply stared and stared. After minutes passed, he stood up and walked out of the homestead yard. He never again returned.

DANKIE

Dankie placed a two-rand coin on the snooker table to save his place in line and handed money to a small child for a bucket of traditional beer. It was ten in the morning. He knew he was related to the little one somehow—either the child of his mother's sister from another father, or maybe her daughter's child? But Dankie wasn't interested in figuring it out or being polite today. He wasn't interested in much more than drinking beer and ignoring the fact that he had twenty rand in his pocket when most men were buying food and drinks and clothing for their families and girlfriends.

Dankie spun around with the Crack! of a snooker break. Its force boomeranged off the tin roof and back down to many of the already woozy men below. Many flinched. A few faces winced. The newcomers simply watched attentively. Fifteen red balls and singles of yellow, green, brown, blue, pink, and black shot in every direction. Two friends from high school had started. Dankie was up next. He'd play the winner of this frame.

A different little one came back in the room through the kitchen of the house and handed Dankie a yellow bucket of beer. The cup didn't look very clean, but it was better than what he'd get in the clouds, so he just drank. As the door swung shut behind the girl again, Dankie caught a glimpse of his cousin Patrick and a young man from church baking biscuits.

Three men who'd been inside through the night leaned in the darkest corner of the room and bantered about the blue, pink, and black balls—the big hitters—five, six, and seven points. The odds of getting them in one of the four pockets were smaller, but their values were exponentially higher than the one-point reds. Dankie always played it safe. He shot for reds, and, if one of the single colored balls happened to cross his pathway, he would take his chance, but he wasn't one to chase a lottery ticket.

His cousin, though—he would always go for the big win. "*Less in quantity, higher in quality,*" he'd say every time he beat Dankie. But it didn't make sense to him. It felt like hunting for a leopard in the bush when there was a herd of impala grazing on the lawn.

His cousin seemed to walk around with a sense of ownership or dominance wherever they went, whether he was in his mother's shebeen or selling biscuits and sweeties to people in grant lines. Dankie didn't have the sense of ownership over much more than his Bible and the few trinkets Jack had given him over the years. And the teacher on the mountain was right—he didn't hold his head very high. He didn't show any signs of winning. What Dankie knew he needed, more than he needed money at this very moment, more than he needed a better job, was the confidence in himself to do those things. To do anything.

Without Maduzu, he seemed to have lost his way.

It'd taken Dankie hours to get home the previous night. The rains were terrible, and the roads were eroded and undrivable. A small canyon had developed in the road leading down to the river and past his house, so large it seemed to have eaten a few cars and had the potential of swallowing small children. Tributaries were flooding, and memories of the rushing water from 2000 were on everyone's minds.

When he walked inside his mother's house, she wasn't there. He knew he couldn't go to the town or play snooker at the shebeen or he'd spend money intended for his mother, so he decided to go for a walk. He didn't know where he was going, but walking was better than wallowing. And lately, nighttime was better than day.

The next morning, Dankie was inside his bedroom, where he used to listen to church broadcasts. The radio was on, but it was screaming music louder than the shebeen. He emerged with a sweat too late in the season to disguise as the summer heat. He'd closed his bedroom door and made sure to keep his eyes down, unwilling even to look at the chicken that had made its way into the house. He had a girl under his peach blanket, and she'd been there all night.

Dankie pulled a bucket from the back of the house, filled it with water, and walked to the back of the plot, behind a tall tree, facing Maduzu's home.

THOKO

Thoko and Patrick sat in the living room waiting for his cell phone to ring.

Thoko, with her arms stretched out across the back of the couch's wooden frame, faced Patrick, who leaned with his legs up against the couch and stared at the closed curtains behind his mother. Neither were really talking, but behind the wall against which Patrick was leaning and on which a black-and-white portrait of himself hung, a young boy from church was inside the kitchen baking biscuits.

The boy shifted between the twenty-liter bucket filled with dough and the flour-coated kitchen table where he rolled it into small balls, placing each on a thin cookie sheet. When a sheet was filled, it was pushed to the side, and another was started. When a sheet's batch had cooked, expanding into one another, creating a single biscuit with twenty bumps, it was pulled from the grease-coated convection oven. They were then cut and left to cool on the linoleum table and replaced with a new sheet in line.

The boy was helping Patrick, his religious teacher, since Lizzy was visiting her family just outside Pretoria, and Patrick's weekend was filled emceeing the ninety-ninth birthday celebrations for the grandmother of his pastor's wife in Mobogwane, fifteen kilometers away. Earlier that morning, Patrick and Thoko had sent two relatives, Thoko's eldest sister (Patrick's elder mom) and a cousin (Patrick's uncle), to visit the Sithole family—Lizzy's mom and dad—in the village of Ramogodi in the province of Gauteng. The two boarded a long-distance taxi just on the edge of Acornhoek, beneath the giant acacia tree, with a neatly folded and stacked collection of gifts that Thoko had handed them earlier that day. They carried one blue-and-yellow duvet, one blue apron with yellow flowers, a dark blue traditional cloth, a bottle of XXX Brandy with ten rand taped to the outside, and two canisters of snuff with ten rand folded inside. The two traveled more than five hours over the mountains and through the highveld maize belt before reaching the taxi rank in Pretoria. Lizzy was waiting for them there.

Their visit, dictated by both purpose and protocol, was five months later than originally expected. The date nearing winter had been set not long after Patrick asked to postpone the original date in early summer, and Lizzy was anxious. The two family elders had arrived to pay lobola and propose the marriage of Patrick and Lizzy. Lizzy's older sister Gloria, who had been married and was now separated with two children, lived with her parents Selena and Benet Sithole in a five-room tin house.

Her mother (of the Ndebele tribe) had been a domestic worker for the majority of her life, excluding the short period during which she trained and worked as a sangoma. Her father—a Mozambican Tsonga—had been a plumber for the duration of his life.

Just a few weeks more than one year earlier, Lizzy had met Patrick at the Conquers Through Christ Church in Pretoria. She was visiting a friend at the born-again Christian church where Patrick was teaching. Lizzy grew up going to the Roman Catholic Church with her father, and she had rarely attended a born-again congregation, where voices exalted and arms waved.

Patrick saw Lizzy from afar and came into the room where she was standing to say hello and ask for her cell phone number. When he finished teaching, she was still lingering, so he asked her to join him for a cool drink at the tuck shop. After a short walk and a nearly finished beverage, he gave her five rand to catch a taxi home. Almost immediately, he called her number for permission to visit her home the next day. Lizzy, who was mesmerized by the tall, thin, and handsome churchman, said "yebo."

Now, Patrick's elders were welcomed into the Sithole home and offered a room to sleep for the night. In their hands, they carried the gifts given to them by Thoko, on behalf of Patrick, as a portion of lobola to be paid for Lizzy.

Traditionally, lobola—the payment to the father of the bride-to-be, grant-ing permission to marry and signifying an official engagement—was paid in cows, but had Thoko collected eleven cows for her relatives to travel with in tow, their transportation would have been a great problem, not to men-tion the challenge as to where they would store the cattle upon arrival to the country's third-largest city. Today, lobola is typically paid in cash and goods. The father of the bride-to-be sets the amount. If the father is no longer alive, or if the bride's father is not around, the second in line of male elders stands in. The price, like the traditional payment of cows, is determined upon the promising assets of the woman. If your daughter is exceptionally beautiful, then you would ask for a larger payment. If your daughter has already given birth to children, especially from another man, then you would ask for less, since with her comes an instant family and more mouths to feed (although that doesn't necessarily mean that the children would be permitted to come along with her to her new husband's home).

If David Mondlovu were to marry Thoko, he would have to pay lobola to her elder uncle since her father is no longer living. Taking Thoko's age into consideration and the five children (of which four are David's), her elder uncle has set her lobola price at two thousand rand, considerably less than what she would have been worth as a childless girl. Despite Thoko's reputation as MaSociatie, her lobola price wouldn't be affected by her successful businesses or traditional standing as a sangoma.

Several hours after the arrival of Patrick's elders, Benet Sithole arrived with Mrs. Ratlhogo, a friend of the family. She was asked to join them to speak and negotiate with Patrick's relatives regarding the lobola payment. At first, the collection of gifts was given to Lizzy's parents via Mrs. Ratlhogo. Then the two handed her 900 rand. Mrs. Ratlhogo took this money to Lizzy's father, who turned around and said, "No. It is not enough." Mrs. Ratlhogo bounced back and forth between the two pairs until, eventually, a number was finally agreed upon. They had already decided that Patrick would need to pay 6,000 rand for their youngest daughter, but the decision that needed to be made on that day was how much he must pay up front, like a down payment on a house or a deposit on lay-buy. Eventually, Mrs. Ratlhogo was able to stop the negotiations at 1,480 rand, which included the ten-rand bill taped to the brandy bottle, and the bills folded in each snuff canister. A final 50 rand was fined to Patrick for having postponed the initial date, not to be subtracted from the 6,000-rand total payment.

While the negotiations took place, Lizzy was elsewhere in the house, Patrick was emceeing the birthday party, and Thoko was preparing food for the night vigil of a man in her burial society.

Although the proposal had been accepted, Patrick still needed to pay the balance of 4,520 rand and purchase several additional gifts: a short knife, a suit, shoes, and a cane for Lizzy's father; a dress and shoes for Lizzy's mother; and a traditional cloth for Lizzy with which to cover her skirt while cleaning. But from that moment, despite all that remained to be paid, something changed. Patrick and his family, who had already been referring to Lizzy as his "wife," were now in charge of making decisions for her. And so, when Lizzy told Patrick that she would like to stay with her family for another week before returning to the lowveld, Thoko refused. Although Lizzy and Patrick were only engaged to be married, in Thoko's eyes Lizzy was now her daughter-in-law, and she needed to return, immediately. The next morning, Lizzy returned to the lowveld, where her future mother-in-law was waiting for her.

REGINA

Regina stood over a boiling pot inside the three-walled outdoor kitchen on the mission's grounds, just beside the back entrance. Anna Mbetse and Regina had been preparing food in the mission since early that morning. Teenagers from the outstation had arrived and would be staying on the mission's grounds until Easter Monday, so the women of Saint Anne who could spare the time were in charge of preparing their meals. The old classrooms were filled with laughter and commotion as the boys and girls prepared to reenact the Passion of Christ. Boys were dressed in old choir gowns and priest vestments, while most of the girls wrapped themselves in traditional clothes with a pattern of Daniel Comboni's framed face throughout—similar to cloth worn in support of African political leaders. Daniel Comboni, an Italian Catholic bishop, was the founder of the Comboni Missionaries who settled across the continent in the mid-1880s, building communities under the vocation of "Save Africa through Africa." Acornhoek mission was a product of Daniel Comboni's work, nearly seventy-five years after his death.

Anna Mbetse stood between the old classroom and the long hall, wearing a blue dress covered by a full-length apron with frills along its edges. She was holding a twenty-liter bucket, half-full of beans, beneath a tap for them to soak. Regina stood above the boiling pots with billowing smoke.

Inside, Emerencia, Simphiwe, and Walter's daughter were sitting in the front pew to the left of the altar, waiting for everyone to file in and take their seats for the Passion of Christ, a stations of the cross reenactment. On her lap, Emerencia held the only daughter of her eldest brother, truly representative of the Rainbow Nation with Zulu, Shangaan, and Sotho blood running through her veins. Less than two years old, Walter's daughter sat quietly on her auntie's lap in a blue halter dress and bare feet.

"Momma," said Simphiwe, looking up to her mother with stress-crinkled eyes, "I am worried about Jesus Christ." Rolling her eyes, Emerencia put her arm around her daughter and pulled her in closer.

The front of the church was filled with children from the outstations involved in the reenactment, and the remaining pews had been filled by women and some men who had arrived from the city for Easter weekend. There was very little youth from Rooibok and MaRoman. Emerencia was the only one of the younger women from Mapusha present, and the gap between church members that were Simphiwe's age and members that were Regina's age was significant.

When the bishop, Father Anton, and another priest from the outstation walked down the aisle, everyone sang. When the bishop—wearing a giant gold ring on his right hand and a long, large gold cross that caught the late afternoon sun streaming in—reached the front, he kneeled down on a sangu. He laid his entire body flat against the mat in prayer. Everyone followed by kneeling on the cement floor or the skinny, warped wooden kneelers. The bright sun shining through the window cast an elongated shadow of Simphiwe kneeling in prayer across the front of the church floor, just before the altar, just below the bishop's feet.

The bishop eventually stood, dusted off his long white robe, and straightened his red vestment, which had gold embroidery of a cross. Father Anton—wearing brown pants, his square eyeglasses, and a pair of Birkenstocks with socks—stood to the bishop's side and started to speak to the congregation in Tsonga with only a thread of his Spanish accent sounding through.

It was Good Friday, the anniversary of Christ's crucifixion and the day the Comboni Missionaries describe as "Sorrowful Friday." It has been translated into variations from language to language, but in Regina's eyes, it is the day she realized something was wrong—the day she realized she had reason, other than the history of her faith, to be full of grief.

It was the early 1990s, and Easter was approaching. The long weekend typically signaled the arrival of men from Johannesburg and Pretoria to see their families. Regina waited anxiously for the bus to arrive, and she was not the only wife surrounded by little ones in anticipation. When the bus pulled in, men stepped through its door one by one to be greeted by family members. Children greeted fathers. Mothers greeted husbands. Siblings greeted brothers. The men had returned. Regina's eyes scanned every piece of luggage and each face in the crowd, seeking some reflection of her husband, Winfred. But she saw nothing, only the familiar faces of community members returning to their families. Winfred was nowhere. When she saw their friend Xivura descend from the bus, she quickly went to him and questioned her husband's whereabouts. Xivura was a close friend of her husband, and he knew where Winfred worked and lived in the city. The two had come and gone together on numerous occasions.

"Xivura, where is my husband?" she asked, feeling shame. He explained that Winfred was still in Jo'burg. There was no reason he could give as to Winfred's lack of travels, but Regina went ahead and inquired. "Didn't he give you any money so I could buy something for my children to celebrate Good Friday?"

"No," he replied, his eyes wandering through the crowds that surrounded them. "He gave me nothing."

Having heard so little from Winfred in many months, receiving nearly nothing in more, she pardoned herself once again to explain. "I want to go with you to Jo'burg so you can show me where it is my husband lives. So he can tell me why he didn't give me any money for my children."

Xivura promised Regina that they could leave together on Monday morning and quickly ran off to find his family.

Regina arrived at the bus station for the first time in her life as a long-distance traveler. She walked the distance from her home into the center of Acornhoek with a small suitcase balancing atop her head, through the dongas, along the impala flats, and down to the main road following the tar to her destination. She was unsure how long she would be gone, but with the minimal number of dresses she owned, it mattered little when packing for more than a few days. She boarded the bus and settled in her seat for the six-hour ride.

Regina had never passed through the mountains that paint the skyline she wakes to each morning. She had never seen the grassy plains of the highveld and the fields of the maize belt. Regina's eyes were balancing the new and the old, filing away her visions for memories to last a lifetime. Her eyes peered over people sleeping through the trip and those moving about to stretch their legs. When Regina moved, it was for a better view and a perspective free from obstacles.

As they pulled into the Jo'burg bus station, she stood with Xivura and shuffled to exit the bus and collect their luggage. Buses were coming and buses were going. People were rushing from one location to the next, and even Xivura picked up his pace. He collected his luggage and helped Regina fetch hers. The two quickly followed the crowd toward the taxi rank where they boarded and drove away. They were headed to find Winfred.

It was Monday afternoon when Regina was dropped off in front of a strange house with her luggage in hand. She wasn't sure where to go, but Xivura had said this was where Winfred could be found. Having left a three-room cement block home behind, she looked at the wealthy residence before her and examined everything closely.

Behind the home, she could see seven shacks lined side by side like sardines in a roll-up can. The shacks were constructed with slapdash materials of cardboard, tin, rusted sheet metal, plastic bags, and any form of refuse that could be recycled to cover a hole, close a door, or form a wall.

Regina knocked on the door of the large home and inquired if the owner knew of her husband, Winfred. The owner confirmed that Winfred did rent a room from them and welcomed her inside to wait for his return. Regina entered the home and was welcomed like a friend into their dining room. She sat on the edge of her chair as if not to dirty the colorful upholstery, soaking in the room and its many things. Surprised to hear that Winfred was married, they inquired further about her home and offered her tea after her long travels. She could see a portion of the kitchen door from where she sat beside the long dining table. The sun's rays shone brightly through the windows, illuminating an electric stove where a kettle boiled. Regina waited there for two hours before Winfred came home.

Winfred rented one of the shacks for twenty rand each month. When he returned to his shack at the end of the day, the owner of the big house sent someone to call on him. Winfred, entering the dining room where Regina waited patiently, failed to recognize his wife's presence. After the owner inquired if he knew this woman waiting, he brusquely replied, "*Yes. This is my wife.*"

As the two left the owner's home and approached the shacks behind, Winfred turned to Regina and asked with anger in his voice, "*Who did you come with here?*"

"*With Xivura,*" she replied.

"*Why did you come?*" he questioned.

"*Because you didn't send any money,*" she explained. "*What do you think my children eat?*"

"*You mean this?*" he asked, pulling out the rand from his pocket. "*You have to go home tomorrow, because I didn't invite you here,*" he curtly instructed.

Regina, with her feet planted firmly in the ground, made it very clear that she was not going home without money for her children. She couldn't go home. She had used every last cent she had to board the bus in Acornhoek.

Regina stayed with Winfred that night and the following fourteen. The city frightened her. The differences frightened her. The cars were too fast and too many. The airplanes never stopped flying this way and that above her, stopping for neither light nor dark. She was frightened of the gunshots she could hear throughout the night and the noises she couldn't name. She was frightened when she woke each morning to be told of this one and that one who was killed in the night.

Regina spent her days within and around the shack of her husband. Considering it was large enough for only one person to lie down—slightly curled up—it was too small to do anything other than sleep. The six other shacks behind the big house were all rented. Despite their size, some were shared by two or three so they could collectively pay the rent.

On Sunday, Regina found refuge in the local Catholic church. She craved the familiarity of mass and sought a quiet place to say her prayers. Having made friends, she was invited to join them throughout town the following Sunday afternoon. She accepted.

It was the only outing of her two-week stay.

When the end of the month came, Winfred's job in construction paid his salary through which Regina's money came. He handed her one hundred rand and said, "*This is for transport, and when you return home, the rest is for what you need.*" It wasn't enough for more than a month or so, but Regina took it and boarded the first bus she could, leaving her husband, the father of her children, behind.

*   *   *

Simphiwe watched the reenactment from the edge of the pew with stress in her eyes. The boys acting as Jesus's guards and persecutors whipped him with long, fresh-leafed mango branches. Jesus, whose crown of thorns was a twisted branch of yellow and green snapdragons, was shorter than the others. His voice, though, despite the painful crack of each branch, exuded confidence and power.

He was barefoot, and his purple-and-white vestments were pulled from his body as the cross was laid on his back. The heavy gum pole leaned against his thin, nearly naked frame, pushing him closer to the ground as the mango branches continued to whip him.

He was forced to carry the burden across the chapel's front, out the side door, to the front stoop, and down the aisle toward the altar once again. The sound of the mango branches cracking and the yelling of his persecutors could be heard the entire time. Nearly reaching the altar, just to the side of Simphiwe and Emerencia, Jesus fell to his knees, sending a boom through the small yellow church. Simphiwe flinched. The sound echoed and could be heard across the mission grounds. He lay in the aisle, stood up, and landed again on the altar.

The tallest of his persecutors, wearing vestments resembling opulent curtains, pulled Jesus from the ground and held him against the cross, propped up by the others. His wrists and ankles were wrapped to the gum poles with rope. Nails were then pounded into the cross through the space between his fingers and into the platform on which his feet were propped. His body appeared to hang, the live Christ suspended from the cross mirroring the crucifix hanging above the bishop's head, stripped to a loincloth, with his head fallen to the side.

Eventually, at the motion of Father Anton, he was removed from the cross and carried out the door. Girls with hand brooms made of summer-cut grass swept the mango leaves and wood splinters from the altar.

An elderly Woman of Saint Anne with Tsonga tattoos covering her legs carried a crucifix the size of a small child to the front of the altar. The two priests and the bishop kneeled. The bishop kissed the body of Jesus on the cross. One by one, from child to elder, each took a turn. The Woman of Saint Anne was there with a white cloth to wipe Jesus's body each time someone kissed him. Toward the end, Emerencia slipped out of the second pew on the children's side with Gertrude's granddaughter, Simphiwe, and the daughter of Walter, to kiss the crucifix. Regina's youngest granddaughter stood in front of the crucifix alongside Emerencia and kissed Jesus.

Toward the end of mass, Regina left her cooking and slipped into the chapel, with a jacket draped over her shoulders, in time to be the last in line to kiss the cross and receive communion. When she quietly entered the chapel, she saw Anna Mdluli, who had just returned from the funeral of a family member. She was wearing the same brown patterned dress she had worn while hosting the stations of the cross at her house, with her rosary and a pink jacket over her shoulders.

Regina snuck in and out without most people realizing it, and she was already at the outdoor kitchen scrubbing a three-legged iron pot by the time Anna Mbetse returned to her cooking. As mass ended, the mission came alive. They were milling about greeting one another and talking with friends, or standing in line to greet the bishop, thanking him for saying mass on such an important day. When the parishioners piled out of the church doors, the mountains had a line of bright silver, a halo, around them, a silhouette in the sky of purple, blue, grey. The days were getting shorter.

DANKIE

Dankie had started selling cigarettes and boxers in Elandshoogte. Beneath his bed sat a crate of cigarette packs for eight rand, singles for one rand, and boxers for ten rand. He didn't care to smoke himself, but he'd watched everyone spend their spare change on something to smoke, their heavy change on alcohol, and their paper bills on prostitutes who make their way into the staff village. The men with less money took the lorry to the shacks just past the security gate at the base of the mountain. Dankie'd been there once. And would return again.

He'd saved just five hundred rand shy of what was needed to pay for his driver's license, and he'd convinced his former supervisor to "borrow him time" in his truck for practice. Once a week at least. Despite the long days with little to do and less pay in his new position, Dankie's spirits were up. On some days.

He still saw Maduzu now and again. But no one knew.

A few days before the weather started to turn and Dankie needed gloves during the day, a preacher moved into the long hall in the village. His teacher friend introduced Dankie to the tall Zulu man who traveled from staff village to staff village, and, soon enough, the preacher came around with a small Bible for him to keep. Dankie was thankful for the gift and hid the word inside his cigarette crate so he could keep an eye on what was most important.

What Dankie didn't know was that his savings, the numbers he saw on the ATM receipts, wouldn't be there for long. And it wouldn't be because he gave it to his mother to finish her partially complete home. It wouldn't be because he paid for driver's school. And it wouldn't be because he found a way to go to university.

When Dankie returns home at month-end, he'll wake up to a shake in his bed. It will be his mother. She'll tell him a story. And she'll ask for his help.

REGINA

As the sun set over the escarpment, the harvest moon climbed out of the bushveld, setting the tops of the acacia trees, the tips of maize stalks, the summits of thatch roofs, and each corrugated tin roof alight with a fiery glow. The usual silvery moon was painted, for that one night of the year, a flaming burnt orange and bright enough for a midnight stroll in the veldt or for a late night harvest. Regina was almost ready to harvest her plots of maize and groundnuts, to reap her fields for the year.

Over the mountains and in the nation's maize belt, farm workers harvested through the night in the fields by hand and by tractor, pulling maize for mealie factories, cereal manufacturers, roadside stalls. Even in the lowveld, a few small family plots were worked through the night, but Regina sat back a while longer to wait. She wasn't enamored by her crop's performance throughout the rainy season, but one out of three plantings had managed to grow without the help of fertilizer, something she, and most of her neighbors, could not afford. "I am tired," said Regina whenever someone questioned when she planned to begin harvest. But Regina wasn't tired from a long day of work or the weeks and months she'd been in the field. Regina said she was tired because she was old. Her body was tired from years of long days and long weeks of planting, weeding, and harvesting. She was tired of worry, years of working, and decades of mothering. The maize stalks in her fields were starting to wilt and wither, and the corn stalks were starting to fall from tall and erect to hunchback.

For weeks, Regina walked past her fields at home and near the mission. She would stop, examine, and continue walking. They just weren't ready, or more likely she wasn't ready. The roads had started to plume with dust again, and the fields were starting to turn hard. The stalks and grass had turned blond, and Regina's corn, still wrapped inside the husk, had lost its moisture, turning stony.

Regina and Gertrude harvested together. A late autumn breeze swept across Rooibok, and the strength of the sun's rays was bearable. After weeks of looking things over from the edges of her fields, Regina knew her crop would be small. As she walked through the gates and onto her quarter of the field, the stalks, long past due, looked already harvested: dry husks, crooked stalks, and withering weeds, dying in the cold and without water. With a PVC bucket and grass basket, Regina started on the western border, where her quarter met Gertrude's, and worked her way east, toward the fence line, toward and counterclockwise around the old tuck shop. Since the building occupied nearly one-third of her plot, she knew she would finish much faster than Gertrude.

Regina started to pull husks, peeling each side until a starburst of papery dry leaves and red-brown silks stood erect. She cracked the stem from each ear and tossed the flowerlike husk on the ground. Each stalk had at least one ear. A few had up to three. The more she shucked, the faster she moved, although she was in no hurry. The brittle, rocky ground produced small, misshapen maize. And the fine white dust tracing the borders of each kernel meant that maize worms had found their way into the husks.

Each ear was tossed in her basket or bucket, and when the two were full, she walked inside the old tuck shop and emptied her pickings.

After two rounds of emptying, she started alongside the southern part of the building. The stalks seemed heavier, and the husks felt solid. As Regina started to peel away the first husk, red earth crumbled from inside. Pulling close to a dozen layers, she discovered an ear of maize made of soil. It looked like maize, was shaped like maize, but was solid red earth. Regina looked at it, dropped it on the ground, and carried on. The second and the third and the fourth were all the same. Some worse than others, a few were part soil and part maize, but Regina dropped those just the same. One by one, a large section of her crops were ruined. She didn't know why. She just knew something didn't go right. If she had cracked the heavy stalk in half, she would have seen a solid pole of red soil encased by a stalk frame. Termites.

Termites live underground, and what people see above ground is like the tip of an iceberg; it's only a thumbnail of what exists, out of sight. Their kingdom of worker and soldier ants actively take over anything in their way. And, in this case, Regina's crops were invading their space. What they took over was replaced with rock, sand, and soil, creating a solid tunnel system, like highways through an overpopulated city. They had followed the roots and climbed up the stalk and into the husks, building an extension to their home in the shape of a maize field.

Regina wasn't discouraged. She tossed each crumbly rendition of her crop and moved on. She couldn't do anything about it, so why get upset. Her pace resumed once she passed through the termite-ridden patch; eventually she reached the northern side of the building, where she had planted a few rows of peanuts and groundnuts beside her maize.

Reaching down, she pulled up the peanut plants, and saw roots. She pulled up the second and saw roots. The third and fourth were the same. "Rats," she said. "If I had money for rat poison, this would be fine." The peanut yield was minimal, enough to bag up and use for planting next summer. Her groundnuts pulled up intact, row by row, filling two bags, one for eating, and one for next year's planting.

Sifting through the rows of peanuts and groundnuts, Regina noticed something growing beneath a few of the fallen maize stalks. She pushed them aside with her foot and discovered pumpkin leaves growing. She bent down and pulled the bitter tasting leaves, usually used for marojo, and started laughing. "Pumpkin," she cried to Gertrude, who was halfway through her harvest. "I planted this two years ago," she said, shaking her head.

Back inside the building, Regina examined her maize piled in the corner. It was about the size of a week's worth of laundry—nothing to sing about, but enough to feed her family for a short time. Regina didn't plant maize to sell on the side of the road or cook cobs over an open fire. She planted, nurtured, loved, and sowed each stalk to pull kernels, fill bags, and make mealie. Her mealie would then be used to make pap and xigugu. Regina had grown maize, pumpkin, peanuts, beans, and groundnuts since her first year of marriage. She used to harvest her maize and lay each cob to dry on top of metal roofs and tin sheets, waiting until the kernels were ready to be pulled and ground.

Behind her house sat an old pestle and mortar, the same one she's used for decades. She would spend days grinding until the hard white kernels were fine dust. But this year was different. Regina was retiring her grinding arms. She planned to visit the gristle mill, where the job that took her hours and days would be finished in minutes.

A week later, Regina and Gertrude were stuffed inside a small truck with five bags of maize kernels. Gertrude was running late that morning, and when Regina arrived with the truck, her old friend was shuffling around her homestead filled with goats, chickens, children, and grandchildren; yelling at the boys to load her maize; and searching for a scarf. When Regina saw that Gertrude had yet even to cover her hair, she turned around to shield her eyes, offering Gertrude a moment to tie her scarf and tidy herself.

They had convinced a few others to send their crop to the gristle mill, so Gertrude, who rode in back with the maize, crammed herself between half a dozen stiff bags and the roof. Regina sat up front with a few empty plastic bags, her purse, and a view.

They arrived at the mill located along the first road to Tintswalo Hospital and stood in a line of three cars waiting to offload. Gertrude peeled herself from the back of the car, dusted herself, and went to the open garage door where the gristle mill was working overtime. The owner of the shop was moving around in a panic, while the three sisters who worked the mill were weighing, carting, emptying, grinding, and collecting. It was a Friday, and everyone wanted his or her maize ground before the weekend. A few angry customers were waiting for the owner to respond to the stolen bags of mealie left out in the night for people to pick up. The electricity had been cut the previous afternoon, and, with bags waiting to grind, the mill workers started back up when the electricity returned, working through the night.

Regina and Gertrude had no plan as to how they were going to offload the bags. They were too heavy for either of them to pick up, and young men near their homes had loaded them. When it was their turn to offload the maize, they stood there with the back door wide open, looking around and at one another. More than a dozen young men just stared at them. A woman in her twenties chirped up, causing the owner to look disapprovingly at the young men. Four quickly started offloading for them.

The two smiled.

The bags were weighed, one by one. The weight was written on each bag before it was carted to the line in waiting. Regina's bag wasn't the heaviest, but it wasn't the lightest. Anna Mbetse's bags were, in fact, the heaviest, and Anna Ndzukula's bags were the lightest. Regina and Gertrude found a comfortable place in the middle. After each was weighed, the gristle mill fees were calculated, and Gertrude pulled out their collection of money to pay on everyone's behalf.

With a line quickly forming behind them, with cars waiting to offload, and with the angry customers still barking at the owner, who listened while weighing bags and collecting money, the two walked away from the loud rumble of the mill and stood under an old thatch roof.

Crossing her arms over her chest, Regina leaned back. She cracked a smile laced with pride and excitement and whispered, "This is my first time."

THOKO

Hopping out the front door, bobbing back and forth from her left bare foot to her right, Thoko slipped on a pair of orange-sherbet Converse All Stars while juggling a long braided hair piece just pulled from its plastic. With feet in, Thoko stopped and bent like a closed book to lace each pristine, fresh-from-the-box high-top. She had purchased the shoes and the hair the previous day from the Indian shop in town.

Earlier that morning, Thoko had walked to the street bordering the back of her property and down a block toward Gertrude Mbetse's house, where there were enough young girls living that, she figured, she could find one of them to cornrow her hair. She arrived with the sun to convince Gertrude's youngest daughter to help, with enough time to return home, get washed, and dress for tribal court.

Just a few days after Patrick paid lobola, a representative of the chief visited Thoko, explaining accusations made by neighbors within close proximity of Thoko's four plots. They said that the jukebox inside the shebeen had been played during funeral days. As a result, her presence was required at tribal court, held each Thursday in the nduna's homestead.

Several Thursdays later, Thoko, who was thinner than usual, was wearing her red lace T-shirt and her long red skirt that morning. This was going to be her second visit to tribal court. On the previous Thursday, she arrived at the chief's house only to be turned away for arriving on her own and not dressing traditionally. She'd arrived in pants.

When he started to tell her that her presence in such dress was not acceptable, Thoko's mouth opened like a trap door in a windy storm. She was turned around with a fine for both her dress and her rapidly moving lips, and instructed to return the following week with witnesses.

Two women, both neighbors of Thoko, arrived at her gate dressed in skirts, blouses, and jackets or sweaters and holding plastic bags within which traditional cloths were folded neatly. The three women climbed into a car waiting to take them from Rooibok A to section B, where the chief lived. On the way, they stopped beside Patrick and Lizzy's house. Lizzy was outside collecting water in her pajamas with her hair up and wrapped in a sleeping cloth when Thoko called for her. Lizzy crossed out of her dry, barren yard and through the gate. Thoko pushed her hand outward and, without a word, passed the long mane of coarse synthetic braids to her future daughter-in-law. As she turned around, Lizzy rolled her eyes and pulled on Thoko's shoulders, motioning for her to bend down closer to eye level.

As Lizzy began to fasten portions of the extension to her future mother-in-law's cornrows, Thoko yelled in the opposite direction at a little girl in a yard several neighbors away for a dollop of petroleum jelly. The little girl ran and handed it to Thoko, who was awkwardly crouched toward the ground while Thoko's neighbor, sitting in the back of the car, slowly started to unbutton her shirt. Her fingers moved carefully and gently unfastened each button on her loose dress shirt, from top to bottom, until she could pull each side outward. Her open blouse revealed her braless breasts with three painful lesions. Thoko held her hand outward for the woman to scoop small bits of the jelly and spread them along the edges of the open egg-shaped sores, making the least possible amount of skin-to-skin contact.

Once Thoko's hair was attached, she shook each leg like a runner preparing for a big race. She looked at Lizzy and said, "*You need to come along.*" Lizzy, still not dressed for the day, looked at her, looked at herself, and looked at Thoko once more, before running inside her one-room unelectrified house with irritation written all over her face. When she returned, Lizzy had a colorful scarf wrapped around her hair, a skirt reaching her ankles, a T-shirt, and a small shawl wrapped around her shoulders. The day was cold, and the wind cut through everything. She shuffled her black-beaded, pointy dress shoes along the dusty yard, through the gate, and into the front seat of the vehicle while Thoko piled into the backseat with her friends. Together the women traveled out of Rooibok A, along the road toward Dingleydale, through Farm Champagne, and into Rooibok B—turning left at the giant Castle beer can— toward Chief Nxumalo's house.

When the women arrived, they piled out of the car along the front fence line of the chief's homestead with their plastic bags in hand. They gathered in a circle facing one another and pulled folded pieces of traditional fabric from their bags, each turning to the right and handing her things to the person behind her. Everyone helped fasten shawls around shoulders, tied cloth around skirts, and wrapped scarves around the hair of those who hadn't already done so at home.

When they were finished, they all took a step back to examine one another. "*You look beautiful,*" one of the women said, admiring the traditional make-over of those around her. Thoko stood tall, towering above all. Her recently fastened braids had been wrapped in a white cloth in such a way that the only visible braiding was an inch or two peeking through the base in protest. Her red pleated skirt was covered with a bright yellow flowered cloth, and she was the only one without a shawl, opting to cover her arms with a Western-cut suit jacket. On top of it all, Thoko put on a pair of dark aviator sunglasses that looked as if they had been purchased on the side of the road and bent to fit flush against her face.

The women walked in a single-file line along the fence and into the gate, past the chief's grey cement-plastered house, stopping to lean against a two-room building behind. There was a group of men congregating and quickly talking just a few meters away, along the side of the large cattle kraal filling one-quarter of the chief's homestead. The women leaned quietly against the wall, waiting for the chief to arrive.

Within minutes, a dark-grey Isuzu lowrider bakkie drove through the wide homestead gate, parking between the women and two elaborate tombstones fenced with chicken wire. Two men jumped out of the bakkie's flatbed, and the chief, tall and round, stepped from the passenger's seat. The chief and his men approached the women like a receiving line, moving one by one down the line, greeting each formally, shaking hands traditionally. After each, they slid to the next, then the next, then the next, until they moved on to the mingling men and then led the group toward the northeast corner of the homestead and the tribal court location, beneath the giant fig tree.

Two red velvety chairs were placed at the base of the fig tree, where Chief Nxumalo and his assistant sat. To the chief's right, two long wooden benches helped form the northern half of the tribal court circle. Twelve middle-aged and elderly men, wearing rubber boots, sweaters with holes, work pants, and winter jackets, filled the benches like members of a jury. To the chief's left, a single bench formed the southern half of the circle, where the secretary sat alone. Several sangus had been laid out for the women to sit on the western side of the circle, directly across from the chief. After the men took their positions in order of seniority, the women sat. Each took their seat, beside one another with their legs swept to the right, using their traditional cloths to make sure that ankles and arms were covered.

Behind Chief Nxumalo, dozens of thick gum poles leaned against the tall, aged fig tree. From where Thoko and the women were sitting, the poles formed a sanctum-like frame around the chief, who was sitting tall in his ostentatious chair. As a sign of progress, construction, expansion, they leaned against the tree like bricks stacked in a yard.

The secretary began to speak, followed by the assistant and the chief, but their voices could hardly be heard. Chief Nxumalo's cattle were mooing like skinnering women in a taxi. They were ambling around the kraal, bells ringing. The women leaned in as far as they could, tilting their heads in effort to hear.

Thoko was called to the center of the circle. She took her place in court, positioned significantly lower than the chief. With her long legs extending beyond the sangu and her orange high-tops playfully bobbing back and forth, she waited for her trial to begin.

EPILOGUE

Months after I finished reporting, I returned to Thoko's ndumba, as a client. She'd said to me once that she'd never thrown the bones for a malungu and told the malungu the truth, the whole truth—only the shiny parts. She'd said that she'd be honest if I wanted, that I could count on her reading each bone as the ancestors placed them. At the time, I nodded and smiled. She knew little of my life, but after spending so many months, years even, so intimately at her side, inside her ndumba and shebeen, through obstacles and successes, I wanted to sit there and experience this with her.

I picked up Emerencia at Regina's home, where bricks had become their winter crop, multiplying with each passing month: *Khotavuxika*, start of the cold season; *Mawuwani*, light breeze; *Mhawuri*, wind speed strengthens. June, July, and August. It was a Sunday, and Regina was at church or in the mission. Simphiwe was in the yard with her chickens, the ones she had named and to which she would say goodnight. She was tall and lanky, and growing fast. She missed her grandmother and her mother as she lived with her aunt Theresa, but soon enough, she would permanently return home to Rooibok, and Regina would once again be happy to grow old with three generations inside her fence line.

Regina's new house would remain under construction for five years, but her hope for running water never materialized. She, Emerencia, and Simphiwe moved into their new home the same year Mapusha moved off the mission and into a building of their own, a beautifully designed open studio, paid for through donations collected by Judy Miller. It was built between the community crèche and the old tuck shop. Anna Mdluli continued to spin wool.

Together, Emerencia and I made our way to Thoko's. The tavern still stood incomplete. She had more goats, all of which were jammed inside a tiny ramshackle pen made with scrap-yard discards, and, on the tin roof of her small tuck shop, she still had maize drying in the sun, leftovers in need of her mortar and pestle. Either her harvest was strong or she was simply behind, but she had plenty of maize meal for the coming year—enough to last her through both tavern delays and, eventually, its grand opening.

In two years or so, Thoko would watch her son Patrick mirror his father's path, divorcing Lizzy and marrying another woman. Angry with Patrick, Thoko would refuse to attend his second wedding. He left Rooibok and became a preacher.

As MaSociatie, Thoko would continue to find herself embattled with the nduna. Although most frequently on her own, she would one day represent Rooibok in a real fight with the nduna over their right to decide community policies. After that, women in the community called her brave.

She would get her driver's license, build a three-car garage, and fill it with cars. Two would never work. They sat and spoke for themselves. And she drove the third.

Inside Thoko's homestead, Emerencia and I passed a few lingering Saturday night shebeen customers and two Sunday morning snooker players. Although no music was playing, remnants of month-end spending could be seen in the dusty yard—a stack of yellow cups on the stoop and a crate of empty beer bottles.

Dankie had come home for the weekend and visited Thoko's shebeen the previous night, but he was already on the minibus taxi toward Nelspruit and then Elandshoogte, where he would work for several more months, not much more. His savings had been depleted bailing out his brother, Jack, and helping him through troubles with work and the law.

Dankie would eventually return home and sit unemployed. He'd thin out, start looking less like a boy and more like a man, and find himself a job several miles outside of town on the road heading to Kruger National Park. He'd be a security guard.

Years later, just as Regina was moving into her own home, and the community exploded with new construction, he would secure himself a plot next door to Regina and build himself a home for his wife and two children. He'd work away from Rooibok and return on month-end.

Inside Thoko's ndumba, Emerencia and I sat, legs swept to the side. And I watched Thoko begin something I'd seen her do a dozen times over the previous year. Her necklace and bracelets. The wooden spear. My blue buffalo. And her burlap bag filled with the bones. She spoke to the ancestors, and her voice ran through my spine. She grew raspier with each call.

xa vuma,

    tap,

        xa vuma,

         tap,

            xa vuma,

                tap.

She lifted and released.

She pointed to the constellation of bones and told me my present. Her wooden spear pointed to specific pairings and single items. Some were shiny. Some were dark. A few secrets, things I'd recently discovered, were on her ndumba floor, for the three of us to see. She'd promised to tell me the truth, so—despite a moment of hesitation—she continued. Much of this felt surprisingly intimate. And true. Some things, if I thought hard enough, could always be morphed into truth.

Pulling my present together, tucking it inside her burlap bag, and shaking its contents again, she called to the ancestors to tell of my future.

xa vuma,

    tap,

        xa vuma,

         tap,

            xa vuma,

                tap.

She lifted and released.

And on the floor, the ancestors turned the bones and revealed what was to come. The story of my life had been plot-lined through futsu seeds and coins and the bones of animals that roamed nearby.

IN THE FIELD

To write *The Rainy Season*, I spent ten months of my life partially immersed (let's say 70 percent of my time) in Rooibok. My goal initially was to open a window, even if it could only be a crack, to life in a rural South African village—to paint a portrait of reality, of life filled with its happiness and sorrows, joys and burdens, successes and failures, births and deaths. I wanted to wipe away the ten-second B-roll shown across most American televisions and offer a chance to see life as it is: beautifully complicated.

Immersion journalists like Ted Conover, William Finnegan, Thomas French, and Jonathon Kozol were my teachers at a young age. And their books—*Rolling Nowhere: Riding the Rails with America's Hoboes*; *Dateline Soweto*; *South of Heaven*; and *Rachel and Her Children: Homeless Families in America*—were my textbooks in a journey of questioning. I read and reread their works and tried to pare away the story and find a process underneath, find a way to understand how each author was able to observe, record, and choose particular words, narrative movements, sections of dialogue, thoughts, etc. . . .

During and after my university years, I created scenarios in order to test out in-depth reporting skills and experiment on my own. I spent a week with a man from the Whitman-Walker Clinic in Washington, DC, during his last months reflecting on the past (his career as a model and his Studio 54 days) while managing the present (seventeen years HIV positive and a closer understanding of death). I spent a month partially immersed inside DC's public housing system to tell the story of a woman fighting the cycle of multiple generations within the same system. I experimented. I threw myself out there and put both feet in the water. And this, I knew, was the only way to truly learn the craft: read, question, and undertake.

In September 2005, I started my first month of intense immersion inside Rooibok with the intention of writing this book. The concept of immersion journalism was one in which, at that point, I had some experience and *basic* confidence, but never had I fully immersed myself (with the intention of long-term and long-form reportage) in a community with three languages—one of which I did not know, one of which I knew only basics, and one of which I could somewhat read, somewhat understand audibly, but verbally only greet and sprinkle a few token words in my sentences—and three distinct cultures bound together by the history of apartheid physically, emotionally, and psychologically. I knew, immediately, that I would need to keep myself in check: asking myself questions, examining each day, and learning from each successful and not-so-successful moment of reporting. I needed to be willing to ask for advice, and, as my acknowledgments show, I did this often.

STICKING AROUND

Tom Wolfe's The New Journalism emphasizes "sticking around" as the make or break in any immersion or narrative journalism. You need to stick around long enough to see the scenes happen in front of you. In many ways, just as a documentary film crew needs to keep their camera rolling and return to the editing room with two hundred hours of footage for their sixty-minute story, I knew I needed to stick around to witness the scenes I would bring to the page. And in order to do this, I needed access.

Access comes with trust, and trust comes in time.

When I first reported in Rooibok—nine months prior to starting the immersion for this book—I was doing a terrible job, or, rather, I was acting like a parachute journalist. I was writing a series of profiles about six women, the original members of Mapusha. The women were guarded and seemed distracted by my mere presence. Now, bear in mind that I was a twenty-something, white, educated, female American trying to tell the stories of a group of Shangaan and Sotho women in their fifties and sixties who had lived the large majority of their life in a country ruled by the minority with whom I share the same skin color.

Acornhoek, and therefore Rooibok, lies just inside the northern border of South Africa's apartheid-era Shangaan homeland called Gazankulu. The homelands were used to separate white from black and each tribe from one another. Up until 1994, the village—despite its location within Gazankulu (recognized by the apartheid government as a separate country)—had stores with white entrances and black entrances, white aisles and black aisles, white products and black products. The bank had separate queues. Public toilets were separated. Schools were forcibly segregated, and many people had been removed from their homes and placed within communities in and around the village, within the boundaries of the homeland. Although many in Rooibok would say (over and over) that they never had too many problems, and it wasn't until the 1980s when things were stirred the wrong way, the restrictions were there. The history is there, and history ingrains certain cautions, biases, and instincts in us all.

After a few days of interviews, I realized that I was going about things all the wrong way. The next day, I returned to their studio and just sat on the bench near one of the women weaving. I had a notebook and pen—a reminder, I guess—but I opened it only when I had a really great detail I couldn't bear to lose. I just watched and joined in when I could. If someone started to roll balls of wool from larger piles, I helped her. If someone went out to fetch water, I joined her and carried an additional bucket. If the younger women of the project walked to the tuck shop for cool drinks, I joined them. I drank what they drank.

Eventually, the women would ask me questions and, in turn, tell me about them. I was honest (although brief) about who I was, where I came from, and the type of writing that I love to do and was actively doing—stories about people, ordinary people, just like them.

And so, I continued to do that. I showed up, several times a week, for months. I practiced my xiTsonga. I learned more about their particular community and how it differed from other communities in Acornhoek, and I laid the groundwork for real immersion. I also started hanging out with more and more people, stretching beyond the mission where Mapusha was based and into the nooks of Rooibok A.

While I think there is always risk of becoming too close, you must build relationships—even if only surface—in order to build trust in rural South Africa. And I knew at the time that if I was to continue writing stories within Acornhoek, where I also ran a newspaper and writing school, it was imperative that I developed relationships of trust that broke down the historical barriers and resonated as a reputation for being honest and fair—a person worthy of telling your story, a person who wants others to learn from the real lives that make up the changing country of South Africa. This pre-immersion period (a few days of each week, a few hours each day) served as a way to make my presence within the community nonthreatening and less interesting.

CHARACTERS

While wandering Rooibok—sitting in shebeens, hanging out on the mission, sitting in school yards, and having tea with elderly ladies in the afternoon—I was searching for potential "characters." I sought individuals who would not only collectively represent the community well but also offer their own uniqueness, their own story, and their own voice. I certainly had an idea of what qualities I was looking for and what stereotypes I hoped to avoid, but whom exactly I would choose was something I knew could come only through sitting face-to-face with as many people as possible. I knew, eventually, that I would have an "aha" moment.

Eventually, story won out over any barriers I foresaw, and I chose to follow one Sotho boy and two Shangaan women: Dankie, a young man taking his matriculation exams and standing at a daunting fork in life that's associated with coming of age; Thoko, a middle-aged sangoma taking the steps to turn her shebeen into a fully licensed tavern; and Regina, a talented weaver in her sixties standing at the crossroads where her Catholic faith and the AIDS pandemic crash.

LANGUAGE

As luck would have it, Dankie and Regina spoke English very well, in addition to several other languages. Thoko spoke only xiTsonga and seSotho; therefore, I knew from the start that a full-time interpreter was required to start and that my learning xiTsonga would have to continue.

I knew that I couldn't learn xiTsonga overnight (I'd already been on a slow-but-steady path), but I did have several potential interpreters to work with from inside the community. However, with that convenience came more challenges. Issues of accuracy and bias concerned me. Locating interpreters for this particular project was not terribly taxing, since I'd started hanging out in Rooibok months before; but in order to assure that accuracy was being maintained, I had to build a system for myself of checks and balances that in the end, I hoped, would collectively reveal the accuracy that I was looking for and needed in documenting Regina, Thoko, and Dankie's true voices. My three tools to overcome language were the use of an interpreter in formal interviews, a meticulous note-taking system, and digital recordings. I chose to use a interpreter with Regina (in addition to Thoko) when conducting formal interviews so as to free her from the burden of any vocabulary limitations. I designed a note-taking system that divided observations, personal reactions, and reminders as to when I must refer back to language in the recordings. I recorded my days in digital form with an old iPod. At the end of each day, I downloaded the recordings and burned them onto CDs for future reference, and I wrote what I call "note drafts": a free write of the day, often referencing my notes and photographs, and sometimes adding up to twenty pages. The day's recordings not only allowed me to check on the verbal interpreter's accuracy but also served as a great tool from which I gained new language skills.

Months into my reporting (at which point I could listen to Thoko answer questions and understand the basics of her answers), I realized that different interpreters brought different challenges to the table, challenges that could both positively or negatively affect the narrative and story on the whole. I was listening to a recording from my first weeks of immersion and realized that Patrick, Thoko's eldest son and my backup interpreter, was adding commentary to his mother's answers. He wasn't altering her words or leaving anything out; he was simply adding commentary after he interpreted her words. At the time, I didn't know xiTsonga well enough to notice his addition of a sentence or two, but later, I could clearly tell the difference. He wasn't trying to hide the comments; in fact, he often spliced his mother's words and his own by adding the word "but" before his commentary. I just didn't catch it at the time.

From then on, it became more and more obvious that Patrick was giving me his take on things. Once he provided his mother's words, he saw it as a chance to provide his own two cents. In most cases, this could get quite frustrating, but in this case, it provided the method I was looking for to illustrate Patrick and Thoko's unique relationship and his feelings about his mother's life as MaSociatie.

The simple task of gaining basic language skills that improved with each passing month offered me the ability to understand the conversations that occurred with and without an interpreter. Without my efforts to learn the language, I would never have discovered that Patrick's interpretations were another part of the story rather than just his mother's words. I wouldn't have been able to drive along in the car and hear Thoko make a socially damning comment and refer back to it later. I wouldn't have been able to sit with Thoko in a room alone to observe with some basic understanding of what she was

CHARACTERS

THOKO MAKWAKWA

Mr. Makwakwa, a milk pint filler, ex-husband
eldest son **Patrick Makwakwa**, the only son of Mr. Makwakwa
future daughter-in-law and Patrick's girlfriend **Lizzy Sithole**
Patrick's ex-girlfriend **Suzette (Susan) Makhuvele**, mother of Evidence
granddaughter **Evidence**, the only daughter of Patrick and Suzette
boyfriend **David Mondlovu**, the father of four of her children (numbers two through
    five), an agricultural worker living away from home
eldest daughter **Shelly Mondlovu**, the mother of Thoko's second grandchild
Louis Hugo, the lawyer handling her legalization paperwork
Elizabeth, a close friend and neighbor in Rooibok
clients **Xisiwana*** and **Lindiwe***

DANKIE MATHEBULA

mother **Maggie Mathebula**
father **Lyson Mdunwazi Mathebula**
brother **Jack Mathebula**, living in Nelspruit
cousin **Mbangu Maduzu Mathebula**, the son of his father's elder brother
cousin **Maduzu's wife**, the cousin of his neighbor Gertrude
another cousin's daughter **Mabel**
niece **Busisiwe**, living with her daughter at his mother Maggie's
elder sister **Sizele**
elder sister living in the boulders and **brother-in-law** working in the trees

REGINA HLABANE

ex-husband **Winfred**
eldest son **Walter**

* The names of all Thoko's clients have been changed.

eldest daughter **Theresa**, a teacher
son **Aubrey**, lives in separate building in her homestead
daughter **Emerencia Mohlolo**, a new generation member of Mapusha Weavers
granddaughter **Simphiwe**, the daughter of Emerencia
youngest son **Koosh**
Mapusha elder and spinner **Anna Mdluli**, lives across the way
Mapusha elder and spinner **Anna Ndzukula**
Mapusha elder and weaver **Anna Mbetse**, lives down the road
Mapusha elder and weaver **Gertrude Mbetse**, cousin by marriage
Mapusha elder (first member) and weaver **Lindy Molemi**
Lindy's younger sister **Lizbeth**, a second-generation weaver
Lindy's daughter **Ambrocia**, a second-generation weaver
Gertrude's daughter **Wonder Mbetse**, a second-generation weaver
daughter of a deceased member **Angie Dibarwano**, a second-generation weaver
Anna Ndzukula's daughter **Emma Maile**, a second-generation weaver
Judy Miller, an American woman assisting Mapusha

GLOSSARY AND PRONUNCIATION

(xiTsonga, seSotho sa Leboa, Afrikaans, isiZulu, South African English)

ahee (eye-hee), v. to respond hello; a mirrored response to the greeting "hello" ("kunjani" or "avuxeni") or to someone announcing their presence ("tama") when entering a homestead or new place.

amandlozi (a-ma-n-dlo-zee), n. ancestral spirits.

bakkie (ba-kee), n. a pickup truck.

biamuthi (be-a-moo-tee), v. to de-witch; to actively remove a witch (or the effects of being witched, black muthi, vuloyi) from a specific location or person.

black muthi, n. *see* vuloyi.

bones, the, n. a collection of objects through which the ancestors speak to a sangoma. These objects are wide ranging and often unique to a particular sangoma (or the trainer of that sangoma). Thoko's bones include dominoes and currency; bones from the lion, elephant, zebra, bush pig, steenbok, and baboon; one small water level; marula and futsu seeds; an odd collection of shells including one large blotched cowrie; and several other objects with origins in the bush. The bones are used by a sangoma to communicate with his or her ancestors so as to diagnose illnesses, domestic problems, and ancestral conflict. They are also a way to paint a picture of the past or look into the future. It is believed that the bones hold the truth. A sangoma also uses the bones to determine the correct muthi for a client. *See* muthi.

boxers, n. tobacco rolled in newspaper.

Chochocho (cho-cho-cho), n. a small community in Acornhoek, just west of Thulamahashe and south of Rooibok A and the Nwandlamare River. Translated directly, "cho cho cho" represents the sound of movement, especially the sound made when someone sweeps or walks through dried leaves or branches, likely assigned to this area because of its origins in agriculture.

Coloured, n. an ethnic designation, propagated during apartheid, for people of mixed ethnicity including European, Asian, and black African. During this time, the distinct population of Cape Coloureds were considered a subset of this larger group.

dagga (da-*guttural g*-aa), n. cannabis. This word originates from the Khoi word "dacha," meaning lion's head, a southern African plant species with mild psychoactive properties smoked by the Khoikhoi. It can be found in literature as early as the seventeenth century. Eventually, it became the term of choice for all narcotics, smoked or chewed. In the 1940s, however, the word was modified and "ga!" (with a guttural g), an Afrikaans expression of disgust, was added.

doeks (de-u-ks), n. headscarves or cloth to cover hair. Short for "kopdoeks."

Elandshoogte (ee-land-shoo-*guttural g*-te), n. a ten-thousand-hectare forestry plantation owned by Sappi, and a worker village in the lower Northern Drakensberg escarpment; once an area of gold mining, part of the gold rush of South Africa; home to Stone Age tribes.

famba (fahm-ba), v. to walk.

Gazankulu (ga-zon-KOO-loo), n. an apartheid-era homeland designated for Shangaan people during apartheid (1969–1994). Acornhoek resides in one of four separate parts located throughout Limpopo and Mpumalanga Provinces (then considered the Northern Transvaal region). This area is named after the Gaza Kingdom, the original home for the Shangaan people under King Ngungunyane (grandson and successor of the original Soshangane) in southern Mozambique prior to being defeated by the Portuguese. The royal family then fled with many Shangaan people to Thulamahashe in 1895, just south of the first Tsonga settlement in northeastern South Africa established in the early 1800s. Gazankulu was one of the four (out of ten) homelands granted "independence" by South Africa. *See* homeland.

homeland, n. a territory set aside for each black African population, stemming from the Native Lands Act of 1913 and the Group Areas Act of 1950, originally termed Bantustans (ban-too-stans), by the apartheid government. Homelands accounted for 7.3 percent of the nation's land and 80 percent of the nation's population. Although the apartheid government considered most homelands to be separate nations functioning on their own (that is, their own parliaments, services, and budgets), requiring pass books to travel beyond their borders, this was never internationally recognized. *See* pass books.

inkomu (in-ko-moo), phrase. thank you.

inyongwa (in-yo-n-gwa), n. gall bladder.

jomela (yo-mell-a), n. the exterior of a dried gourd used for drinking.

knobkerrie (nob-care-ee), n. a short wooden stick, or club, with a knob on one end; a Zulu warrior weapon used in hand-fighting or at a distance like a missile.
kudzaha (kood-ZA-ha), v. to sniff.
ku hleva (koo-HLEY-va), n. secrets, gossip.
kunjani (koon-JON-ee), v. to say hello; to greet someone. *See* ahee.
Kwaito (k-wait-o), n. a South African fusion of hip-hop, house music, and jazz.

Lebowa (le-BO-wa), n. an apartheid-era homeland designated for the northern Sotho people during apartheid (1972–1994). Acornhoek resides in one of eleven separate parts located throughout Limpopo and Mpumalanga Provinces (then considered the Northern Transvaal region). Directly translated as "North" for its Northern Sotho residents, the least compact and smallest portion of Lebowa shared a border with Gazankulu, the Shangaan/Tsonga homeland. Lebowa was one of the four (out of ten) homelands granted "independence" by South Africa. *See* homeland.
lobola (lo-bo-la), n. a bride price paid by the groom to the bride's father, customary in Bantu-speaking tribes.

magwunya (ma-GWOON-ya), n. homemade sweet breads, often also called "biscuits" or "scones."
malungu (ma-LOON-goo), n. a white person.
Mapusha (ma-POO-sha), n. a weaving cooperative on the Roman Catholic mission, started in 1972, bringing together both Shangaan and Mapulaneng Sotho women. The name is a hybrid of the two ("Mapu" + "Sha") symbolizing a peaceful union between two cultures at a time when they were (supposed to be) geographically divided via homelands.
marojo (ma-RO-ho), n. peanuts and pumpkin leaves.
MaSociatie (ma-so-sci-a-tee), n. this is the name by which many locals referred to Thoko Makwakwa. Local slang for "business woman, the busiest entrepreneur." Directly translated, this means, "many societies or many businesses."
masotho (ma-SUIT-too), n. ancestral spirit of the Sotho people.
maveriveri (ma-very-very), n. rumor.
mazenge (ma-zang-gee), n. a shack made of corrugated tin sheets.
milawu (me-la-woo), n. the ancestors' rules of sexual behavior.
Moholoholo (mo-holo-holo), n. also known as Mariepskop, the highest peak in the Northern Drakensberg escarpment. Directly translated as "the very great one,"

Moholoholo is 1,947 meters above sea level, and, on a clear day, one can see as far as Mozambique and the Indian Ocean. Immediately to the west of Moholoholo sits Blyde River Canyon, the world's third-largest canyon and the largest green canyon.

Muchongolo (moo-CHON-go-lo), n. a traditional wedding battle dance; a modern-day competitive dance and lyrical storytelling competition; a traditional group steeped in dance and custom, often considered closely tied with spirituality and belief in the ancestors.

mundawu (moon-daa-woo), n. ancestral spirit of the Shangaan people.

mungoni (moon-go-nee), n. ancestral spirit of the Shangaan people.

muthi (moo-tee), n. traditional medicine treatment; a compound created—from flora and fauna that are typical in and around the region—by a traditional healer with the intention of alleviating or healing a medical ailment or a personal problem, or identifying and addressing a need. *See* sangoma.

ndumba (n-DOOM-ba), n. a round, thatch-roofed hut, traditionally a single room with mud-packed walls and dung flooring.

nduna (n-DOON-a), n. chief.

ngena (n-GEY-na), v. to come in; to enter.

Ngungunyane (n-goon-goon-ya-nee), n. ruler of the Gaza State, and the Tsonga people, of southern and central Mozambique between 1884–1895. His great grandfather was Soshangane, the head of the army that moved north from Zululand to found the Gaza Kingdom. *See* Gazankulu.

nkombe (n-COMB-bay), n. a long wooden handle with two crescent-shaped metal wires; a cooking utensil specifically used to cook pap. *See* pap.

pap (paap), n. white maize-meal porridge with multiple variations differing in water quantity and preparation only, including vuswa and crimmel pap.

pass books, n. identity document used throughout apartheid, often considered part of an internal pass system, designed to keep black Africans outside of urban areas and inside homelands, townships, or their place of employment, and to control worker movement. From 1923 (the Native Urban Areas Act) to 1986 (a partial repeal of the pass laws), all non-Europeans were required to carry pass books and could be asked to present them at any time. Failure to do so meant fine or arrest. Pass books were eliminated along with apartheid, but South African identity documents continued to be books until the transition to cards started in 2014.

poto (po-to), n. a three-legged, cast-iron pot.

robot, n. traffic light.

Rooiboklaagte (ro-ee-bok-laa-*guttural g*-te), n. a small community in Acornhoek split in two (A and B) by the Nwandlamare River, just southeast of main town and northeast of Thulamahashe; the community directly south of the Roman Catholic mission; directly translated as "impala flats," referred to locally as Rooibok.

sangoma (sang-go-ma), n. a traditional healer.

sangu (sa-n-goo), n. a grass mat.

Shangaan bag (sha-ng-gän), n. local slang for a rectangular bag (the size and shape of the bags in which comforters are packaged/sold) made of thin, plastic, burlap-looking material. They are inexpensive, readily available, and usually plaid in pattern. Most households have several and use them for everything from carrying groceries to serving as luggage.

shebeen (sha-bean), n. a backdoor illegal pub.

skinnering (skin-er-ing), v. to tell stories about or discuss the business of other people; to gossip.

takkies (tech-ees), n. sneakers.

tama (ta-ma), v. to say hello; greeting before entering a new place or homestead.

thandaza (than-DA-zee), v. to pray.

Thulamahashe (too-la-ma-hashe), n. a small village, distinctly separate from Acornhoek and its many small communities, located southeast of Acornhoek main town and tucked between two rivers, the Nwandlamare and Sandspruit. Thulamahashe is where many municipal or government buildings are located, like the courthouse, and is where King Soshangane Nxumalo settled with the Shangaan people he brought east from Gazankulu in 1895.

Tokoloshe (tow-ko-lo-sh), n. a small, hairy creature (often compared to a baboon) that pulls people from their beds at night to kill them.

uBhejane (oo-BAY-zhan), n. the name of Zeblon Gwala's muthi, specifically a treatment for HIV/AIDS, sold in his clinics throughout the province of KwaZulu-Natal.

uKhahlamba (oo-ka-HLAAM-ba), the Drakensberg mountains, directly translated as "the barrier of spears."

vuloyi (voo-loy-ee), n. muthi created with the intention for bad.

vuswa (voo-swa), n. *see* pap.

xa vuma (she-voom-a), v. to speak.

xifolane (she-fo-lan-ee), n. a specific type of black muthi placed on the ground so that an unsuspecting passerby steps on it, sometimes (but not always) intended for a specific person.

xigiso (she-GEE-so), n. a specific type of black muthi, sometimes put inside someone's food, created to cause a slow, painful death.

xigugu (she-goo-goo), n. a snack made of ground peanuts and fine, white corn maize meal.

xikhapaka (she-cop-a-ka), n. traditional beer; a fermented brew based on fruit and/or maize meal, usually homemade and grainy.

xilungu (she-LOON-goo), n. the present.

xintu (SHEEN-too), n. the past.

xiTsonga (she-TSONG-ga), n. the language of the Shangaan and Mozambican Tsonga people, descendants of Kings Ngungunyane and Soshangane.

yebo (yea-bo), adv. yes.

ACKNOWLEDGMENTS

From my first day of reporting inside Rooibok to publication day, this has been a ten-year journey (2005–2015). Thank you to everyone who helped make this happen.

To Thoko Makwakwa, Dankie Mathebula, and Regina Hlabane, for your willingness to share your story and have me by your side for a very long time. You welcomed me into your homes and your lives and let me document (photographically, via audio, and in writing) the beautifully complicated sides of daily life.

To Emerencia Mohlolo, for years of translation, long conversations, and friendship, for being my cultural broker and teacher of language. To Heidi Smith, for introducing me to Mapusha Weavers and taking a young American journalist with you to a meeting of taxi drivers in Thulamahashe. Both led me to write this book. To Judy Miller, for your desire to do good, and your genuine commitment to and love for the women of Mapusha. To Sarah Morgan, for your commitment to bettering and bridging divided worlds, and your friendship in my best and worst of times.

To my Goucher College mentors: Tom French, for guiding me through your own work, supporting me through some of the hardest reporting of this book, and teaching me to know when I'm ready to start writing and to know definitely when I'm not. Joe Mackall, for long discussions around our shared challenges and experiences, as you were immersed in Amish country, eighty-five hundred miles away from Rooibok, and for always believing in me when I often don't believe in myself. Laura Wexler, for pushing me to be a better critic of my own work (and for helping me see light at the end of the tunnel). Diana Hume George, for wearing a watch with two faces, being a hard-ass editor, and having high expectations. While I am so thankful for your mentorships, I am also lucky to consider you friends.

To Patsy Sims, for overseeing the program that changed my life.

To Anne Fadiman, Paul Salopek, and Davan Maharaj, for speaking to me on the phone or back-and-forthing via e-mail (as I sat in rural South Africa with patchy cell service and even worse satellite internet) about the challenges of reporting inside a foreign country, community, or culture. Without knowing, you (and those conversations) were a huge influence on this work and continue to touch my writing, reportage, and thought process. Thank you for responding. You could have just as easily said, Sorry. Too busy.

To my writing family at Ohio University, specifically Dinty W. Moore and Eric LeMay, for opening a door when I needed one most. You've given me a home and the gift of time to make my way through a doctorate, write books, and live a life that is both cushy and not. (And, again, to DHG, for knowing this was the right choice and being my supreme cheerleader.)

While writing can be lonely, I make it through every day and every page with the love and support of the writers in my life. They are family. I am forever grateful to be surrounded by generous, creative people who genuinely believe, Your success is not my failure. In fact, your success is our success.

I worry to name anyone since I know the list is too long to write and I'll inevitably (unintentionally) leave off some names. Despite this, I will name a few. Jeanine Boulay, for nearly fifteen years of friendship and adventures, first steeped in writing, and for knowing me possibly better than I know myself at times; Carrie Kilman, for instantly being my writing sister and showing me that I'm not alone in wanting to sit and listen and tell important stories; Sarah Green, for being my Emily Dickinson on Sundays and the best person I have ever met in line for coffee; Erin Celello, for being real about the business and daily life of writing and being someone I call when strange things happen; Aaron Olver, for giving me shit, and showing persistence with a five-hundred-page manuscript; Ann Garvin, for taking life by the horns and showing me genuine heart; Susan Gloss, for illustrating both dedication and determination to get what you want; Marysa LeRowe, for having more talent in your pinkie than I've seen in a long time and giving me someone to watch; Sheri Booker, the little sister I never had, for the privilege of watching you grow as a writer and a person; Traci Macnamara, for your life as a literary adventurer and strong woman, showing me how to get through the darkest parts; Towles Kintz, for a kindness that is unparalleled and the best literary momma I know; and Jacob Wheeler, for a shared love of what we do and determination to do it.

To every other writer in my life, thank you (over and over again).

To all the places that welcomed me to write, thank you for your quiet and inspiration: the old farm house near Mariepskop; the top house on Frog Pond; my little cottage on Lerato; inside Sleepers Railway Station Restaurant, early in the morning, before it opened to the public (thanks, Craig Williamson!); Monyela Mountain Lodge, high in the clouds, overlooking the lowveld (with Sheri Booker); in the lake house on Monona; and at The Porches in the Blue Ridge Mountains (with Bronwen Dickey and Gelarah Asayesh).

To a few important people who had no idea they were leading me here: My junior high English teacher Mrs. Phyllis Piazza, for two years of diagramming sentences and writing poetry (every time I cross a bridge and teach grammar, I think of you). My high school English teacher Mrs. Peg Olson, for noticing that the quiet freshman beside her in the discussion circle had a page full of annotations and color-coded ideas on her copy of Maya Angelou's inaugural poem, and saying, "It looks like you have a lot to say." I did. My high school principal, Dr. Charles Baker, for handing me a copy of Thomas French's *South of Heaven* and saying, "You need to read this. This journalist in Florida is doing exactly what you want to do." My Boston College professor and friend John Boyd Turner, for weekly coffees during which we discussed social justice, philosophy, and the world, and for pulling me into the computer lab one day to show me the website for Visionaries. And Bill Mosher, for letting me inside your doors and opening up a world of new possibilities in true storytelling.

To Mr. and Mrs. Jacques, childhood neighbors who I always wished were my grandparents, thank you for telling me long stories on hot summer days as you sat on your folding chairs in the driveway. And thank you for making me look both ways before crossing the street. You have been with me every day, in the heaviest thesaurus and dictionary I might ever own. They have followed me from Chicago to Boston to DC and San Francisco. They made it through years in South Africa (with some minor termite damage) and back to the United States, only to be dragged to Madison and now southeast Ohio. They are well travelled and well used, but, most impactful, they represent your steadfast support and confidence in my writing.

To my brother, Jack (whom I still call Johnnie), for showing me early on that the world is full of story and that making movies and writing books are things we can do with our lives. Thank you for making me someone who wants to bungee off bridges, travel down rivers with crocodile and hippo, and eat mopani worms. Because of you, I am afraid of very little, and I understand that a creative life is often about staying the course. *It will all work out, and, sometimes, it's a game of last man standing.* Because of you, I just put my head down and keep going.

To my eldest sister, Kathy, thank you for being my second mother and a best friend. Thank you for believing in me and telling me this out loud. I will always treasure our time as Little Women.

To the entire Messitt clan (Kathy, Patty, Jenny, John, Annette, Mom, and Dad), for showing me what it means to want something and work for it. It's a blessing and a curse.

To my parents, thank you for letting me believe I can do anything. While this isn't true, it was a great foundation from which to springboard into the world. Thank you for loving me despite being your child who bought a one-way ticket to Africa. I know I haven't been easy, but I like to think of my life choices as a reflection of what I've learned from you. While that list is too long for this space, I will say, because of you, I have the bad habits of all-encompassing focus and doing things like giving the coat off my back to strangers in the middle of winter without a backup. Thank you for these. They define me.

To the editors of *River Teeth*, Dan Lehman and Joe Mackall, who read excerpts of my dusty manuscript (out loud, to one another) in the car between Iowa City and Ashland, for giving Thoko's story ("MaSociatie") its first printed page. To Duke University's Center for Documentary Studies and writer-in-residence Duncan Murrell, for honoring an excerpt of *The Rainy Season* in their first Documentary Essay Prize.

To Bambi Edlund, for your lovely illustrations, obsession with maps, and care for detail.

To Jim McCarthy, my agent, for believing in this book and me. There is more to come. And to my editor Elisabeth Chretien, for your genuine excitement and faith in *The Rainy Season*, and helping it find its way to readers and bookshelves.